My Cup Runneth Over

Collected Stories of a Lifetime

Mary Binkley Williams

To Nan, my precious friend, Bennie's daughter—
Love, Mary

Perfect Memoirs ❦ *Nashville, Tennessee*

Cover photos by Dennis Carney, Photographer
Cover design by Abe Goolsby

Project Management,
Editor and Interior Design:
Deborah E. Wilbrink
www.Perfect Memoirs.com

My Cup Runneth Over

Collected Stories of a Lifetime

Mary Binkley Williams

Dedication

My book of memories I dedicate to my lovely children: Charlie, Mike, Marilyn, Sam and Doree and their daddy, Thurman, whom I loved. This will give you some insight into my life as a person and as a mother. A perfect mother? Of course not, are any of us? Ever relying on the truth that God loves me and forgives my imperfections, and in turn my children have as well.

I have lived life with a passion…full of love, laughter, tears and heartbreaks, yes, and even tragedy, seeking the joy in each day. Learning to step over obstacles that can't be resolved, however difficult, continuing to move on with life, a cherished gift which I hope not to waste.

These words I've written at random with thoughts flowing freely from my heart. I may have written a paragraph or two on a given day, put it aside for weeks, months, even years, before getting back to it.

I hope you will enjoy putting it all together and find some joy in the reading of it.

Fill your pages with the breathing of your heart.

—William Wordsworth

Contents

Introduction to My Memoir

Once upon a time, I decided to jot down a few stories of my life as a child, a teenager, a wife and a mother, thinking maybe at the end I'd call it *My Memoir*. It has become over a twenty-year process, and the writing of my story has helped me conclude that *My Cup Runneth Over* with blessings. How did I ever get started? Let's go back more than twenty years ago…

A thought kept me from sleep, needling my brain. This had never happened before, so a bit disgruntled, I climbed out of bed and left Thurman asleep. I picked up my *Victoria* magazine and headed for the couch to read. But once settled, it was time to deal with my recurring thought or there would be no relaxation. A few weeks earlier, Charlie, my oldest child, and I had discussed that I should jot down a few stories about my own life and what I remembered about my parents (his grandparents Mae and 'Granddaddy'), and what I'd been told about my grandparents. It was an appealing thought. Was it time to start?

I pulled a legal pad and pen from the secretary and began my journey into the unknown – that of the literary world. Realizing my lack of training and knowledge, I wrote anyway, deciding to keep my effort a secret. When I grew sleepy, I slipped the loose pages inside the *Victoria* magazine and hid it away.

So it began, and more stories were written. If I found myself inspired and unable to sleep, I would then rise and write, and again file my legal pad pages inside the latest issue of *Victoria*. And so my memoir grew.

In later years, with Thurman's grave illness, we decided to move closer to our daughters and their families. Our home filled with friends and family to help with the move. I heard my son Mike's wife, Vickie, call out from another room, "Grandmamma, what do you want me to do with all these magazines I'm finding?"

Without a second's thought I hollered back, "Just pitch them all!" Of course, she followed my direction and they went into the accumulating trash. It was a few days later that it dawned on me what I had done! After we settled into our new place, I knew there would come a time when the mood to write would again overtake me. And it did, several years later.

It's a known fact that my first born son Charlie could influence me "to do" or "not do" all his life. This side of his personality was a major factor in his becoming a successful attorney. When Charlie learned of my first writing efforts, he was certain I needed to continue and finish what I had begun. Writers need encouragement, and with that I was able to continue to record my many blessings, and the lessons I learned along the way from my family and friends, the beautiful people I have known.

As they learned of my project, all my children have encouraged it, another blessing in my cup. I began to share with friends the fact that I was writing, and they too encouraged me to finish and publish. It's my deep wish that family, friends, and any readers enjoy my memoir, *My Cup Runneth Over,* and find not only stories of the past, but encouragement for the present.

I am seeking, I am striving. I am in it with all my heart.

—Vincent Van Gogh

Those Who Know Don't Debate With Charlie

By HERMAN CARLTON and CRAVEN CROWELL

What kind of guy is Charles Williams?

He's a friendly chap, adept at the art of persuasion, smart, and always on the ball. That's the way his speech classmates size him up.

Charles Williams
"On the ball"

He's such a logical debater he can hold his own with the best—

Despite the fact debaters don't make it a point to match wits with him more than once, Charles has a number of friends as is evidenced by those who surround him in the student center or wherever he happens to be.

Charles came to Lipscomb from Litton high school where he was student council president his freshman and senior years, and class president during sophomore and junior years.

He was elected Mr. Litton his senior year and received the Balfour Award, a four-point award emphasizing both leadership and scholarship.

At Lipscomb, he is on the debate team, having participated in the Southern Speech Tournament at Houston, Tex., last year, and the Tennessee State forensic meet.

"Lipscomb offers a solid and high class education where the environment encourages you to keep your feet planted firmly on the ground," Charles said as he gave his views on Lipscomb.

As if school work wasn't enough to keep him busy, Charles works part-time as employment director of Junior Achievement, a national organization to teach the fundamentals of free enterprise.

He formerly served as president of the area Junior Achievement which includes seven southern states.

A seventh quarter speech major, he finds time for hobbies which include tennis and boat racing.

For the future, Charles hopes to attend Vanderbilt University law school, thus following in the footsteps of his uncle, Joe Binkley, a prominent Nashville attorney.

Charles is a clean-cut guy with plenty of determination, and, having leadership qualities himself, he is interested in putting the right people in leadership roles.

MY CHILDHOOD

Stories from the Sisters of Mother's Old Neighborhood

Eudora "Dora" Burt Anderson, my mother, was born in October 1887, a city girl on Berry Street in East Nashville in a two-story, white, colonial, clapboard house. It was a typical southern neighborhood of families enjoying their homes, gardens, rambling porches, school, church, and each other. The many stories I'll share were learned at the feet of my mother and her "sisters." After one of Mother's "Little Luncheons", down through the years they would gather in our East Nashville Russell Street living room and talk, reminiscing for hours on end. I was not fortunate enough to know Mother's parents because they died before I was born, but because of their stories these persons came to life and I grew, I felt, to know them well.

Her Papa was a successful businessman owning the Frank Anderson Produce company, located in one of the Victorian warehouses on the Square behind the old courthouse. It actually was the last of these buildings to be torn down, 204 Public Square, so I remember it well. As he served in the cavalry under General Nathan Bedford Forrest during the Civil War, "Papa" was referred to often as "Captain Frank Anderson." Mother said, "He was a true Confederate and proud of his dedication and service to the South." The people in Nashville referred to him as a "Southern Gentleman." He was known to take care of the needy families in the city and was generous in his business almost to a fault. Mother recalled the many times when she was older and kept the business for him when he was called away. His last words before leaving her would be "Now, if these customers," whose names he would repeat, "come in and cannot pay, just put it on their tab." These tabs, she said, more often than not, were never paid. This spoke of his true Christianity and desire to help the less fortunate. During these times I was not just listening to Mother recall these stories out of the past. Also telling stories at these luncheons were Mother's three older sisters as well as her best friend who moved into the neighborhood when they were third graders, Annie Gary Bentley. Annie Gary was like a second mother to me all of her life.

When my mother's sister, my Aunt Mary, who lived in Arlington, Virginia, was in town, I was beyond excited! Not only am I her namesake, we always had a special bond between us. Aunt Mary had only one child, her son David. She had longed for a daughter and as she often said, "Mary is the daughter I never had." And so it was, for her lifetime. These five women gave me great insight into their past, while at the same time revealing wonderful tales about my Grandfather and "the Wives."

My maternal grandfather, Papa, married three times, not unusual in this era. He and his first wife had a son and three daughters and they lived in his house on Berry Street. Papa's first wife died, leaving him to finish bringing up their teenagers: a son Lovell, daughters Ruth, Elizabeth, and Frances. These were known to me then as Aunt Ruth, Aunt Elizabeth, whom we called simply "Beebee," and Aunt Fannie. The oldest, whom I never knew, died as a young father.

Papa's second marriage was to my grandmother, Mary Ralston Anderson, who of course, I never got to know other than through the stories told during these delightful sessions in our living room. There were three children born to this couple: Mary, my mother Dora, and Baby Frank, as they always referred to him. I want so much for you to know the story of how close the older sisters were to their little sisters Mary and Dora, and of course, Baby Frank. They became indignant when some person mentioned they were half-sisters. I wouldn't want to cross them, even today, on that subject!

Gran, Papa's mother, lived with the family after losing her husband, my great-grandfather. Mother adored Gran and often said, "All her children and grandchildren loved her and enjoyed her company all of her life." Mother spoke of Gran's lovely clothes and that she always smelled of a special cologne. In the photograph of the four generations, Gran looks serious. However, Mother described her as quite jovial.

I heard many stories as a child. Oh, the stories the older sisters shared about their new stepmother, with not only me, but with Aunt Mary and Mother as well! Aunt Mary and Mother remembered their mother with great fondness and the pictures I have of them as children show the perfect motherly care given them. The story goes: My grandmother was from a Nashville family of some means, and after marrying Papa, was not too happy with the life he provided her. Actually the result of his extreme generosity, a picture shows a pretty woman who evidently spent a great deal of time styling her beautiful hair and paying attention to every detail, lovely clothing, and the jewelry she was wearing. I must have been very young, listening at the feet of these sisters, when I heard Aunt Ruth say to my mother, "Your mother was considered haughty by some of the congregation of Foster Street Church of Christ," where the family attended. I was pondering over what the term "haughty" implied, so Mother gave me the definition. I felt sad that my grandmother was considered haughty, so foreign to my mother's personality and disposition. A photograph helps me picture my mother and Aunt Mary, ages two and four. Their mother died when they were quite young. How sad for the children! However, they would have been much sadder without their older sisters to lean on.

Later Papa was courting a widow, Mrs. Mack Hennessey. The sisters learned she had a daughter, Kitty, whose age was between that of Mother and Aunt Mary. They felt he should not be thinking of marrying because of this fact. Their little sisters would not be receiving undivided love and attention! The older sister, Ruth, was known as an adorable woman—petite, beautiful, and quick to speak her mind. She took it upon herself to speak to Papa about what she considered to be a real problem brewing. When she spoke to him, hoping to convince him what inappropriate behavior it would be to place this woman's own daughter in age between Mary and Dora, his answer was, "Daughter, I appreciate your concern, but when I want your advice I'll ask for it." And so, the wedding was held.

Papa's third wedding was a quiet one with close relatives attending, at the home of his bride's sister, Mrs. A. A. Gosnell, on September 20, 1897. A reception followed at 223 Berry Street, Papa's home, where the new wife moved in, along with her daughter Kitty.

At this point in their story, I loved hearing the three sisters talking almost at the same time about when they told Mary, Dora, and Baby Frank not to worry about the new stepmother and daughter: "There are three of us and three of you. Each of you will have one of us caring for you as your own mother would, had she lived." Aunt Ruth claimed Baby Frank, naming her own son "Frank" a few years later. Aunt Mary's guardian angel was Fannie, the artist in the family, and my mother's was Beebee, the delightful, funny one. The three oldest all worked together to see that the younger ones had beautiful clothes and parties held in their honor. Their new stepsister Kitty Hennessey was taking piano lessons, so right along with her, Mother and Aunt Mary were offered lessons as well. Aunt Mary told me that the three of them wanted for nothing. The bond of love that grew out of this between two sets of sisters was a thing of beauty and existed throughout a lifetime. I'm sure there was never a little girl who loved her mother's sisters more than I loved these three special women, whose children were so much older that I called them "Aunt" as well. Although I didn't have the love of grandparents as a child I had love on all sides from an older generation. Mother's own sister Aunt Mary and I were extremely close as well, along with Annie Gary, my "second mother." When I look back on my life I feel great gratitude for all the people who made life special.

The sisters actually grew to love Kitty, their stepsister, early on and as they grew older. "She was just lovely," I heard repeatedly, and I knew she was never the threat the sisters had anticipated all those many years ago!

Papa was a dyed-in-the-wool believer and devout follower of the rules and regulations of the Church of Christ. Mother and her sisters told of his application of these to his children. They loved him, but hated that he was so terribly strict in rearing them. At Captain Frank Anderson's home in the old neighborhood on Berry Street, entertainment was confined to music, games and good food. Not all the neighbors were Church of Christ. The three older sisters loved to dance and when a party was held in a neighbor's home, the highlight was music and dancing. When dancing was going on they would cover for each other, being on the lookout for Papa to come walking down the street. Later they covered for Mother and Aunt Mary so they too would have the joy of innocent dancing while growing up. If Papa was present when music was playing, Mother said, "Under my long skirts where Papa couldn't view them, my feet were moving to the beat of the music. I tried to keep my body from swaying, because he would have called me down immediately!"

Mother was sociable in so many ways. She told of one day when she and Aunt Mary were walking home from church, Mother lagging behind. She talked with many people, speaking to everyone on the street whom she knew, and some whom she didn't know. Aunt Mary turned upon her and said, "I am going home and tell our mother about you speaking to all these people!"

My mother replied, "Now you just hurry up and be sure and tell it as quickly as you can. Just because you're a 'high hat' doesn't mean that I am!"

I would have thought that Aunt Mary would be embarrassed at this story being told with her present there in our living room on Russell Street, but she just laughed heartily, saying, "I was so silly at that age!"

The Anderson family attended the Tennessee Centennial in 1897, and they often told about how absolutely phenomenal the whole exhibition was! After listening to their stories I felt as though I'd been there and taken in all the beauty and excitement of that grand occasion! When I visit Centennial Park today, I envision my mother and Aunt Mary, ten and twelve years old, holding hands while walking through the exhibits.

After my parents died, Annie Gary and I were spending the day together. Conversation got around to the "old neighborhood", and she expressed a desire to go back. She and I would knock on the door of her old home. Then, I would do the same at Mother's place, that is, if the houses were still standing. We would ask, after explaining our desire, "May we come inside just for a moment?" I was absolutely thrilled over the prospect of seeing 223 Berry Street, where Mother grew up. Even though I had gone with Mother and Daddy to visit the old neighbors when I was a child, I had only seen the outside of the house. All I remember is that the neighbors I met were a brother and sister, and much older than my parents. Perhaps today I would see the inside of Mother's birthplace, and where she lived until she married.

We knocked on the door of Annie Gary's former house first. The person who came to the door was not at all cordial, so there was nothing for us to do but leave without even a glimpse inside. I felt so sorry that Annie Gary, now in her late eighties, was denied a small favor that would have made her so happy. We walked down the shaded sidewalk in the direction of Mother's house, but without much hope. I bravely gave a loud knock and the sweetest little lady came to the door! When I explained why I was there she opened the screen door, inviting us in. She talked a blue streak about how she loved the house and said "Take all the time you need. Enjoy going over every inch of it!" Annie Gary was quite as animated as she shared memories of those childhood days where she spent hours in this house with her best friend, Dora.

It was almost an out-of-body experience as I walked through, seeing two little girls playing in these rooms long, long ago. In every room I found a fireplace, even in the bathrooms. I thought that amazing! Annie Gary could not climb the stairs to those bedrooms and bathroom, so my thoughts were all my own there, unhampered by the sound of anyone's voice. I felt so close to Mother as I moved from room to room. She had told me stories about the beautiful furniture, portraits and art. I have a mirror that once hung in the entrance hall, a Nippon vase and a few pieces of silver from Mother's heritage. When the house was sold most things went to the older sisters and were eventually handed down to their children. Mother said at the time, "It is a fair decision. It was their mother, who with Papa moved into this house when they married. It was their mother who selected the furnishings." Many of those objects remained in the house when Papa married again, having more children, including my Mother. I suddenly wanted to cry for my precious mother as a child, her sisters, Papa, and her mother, who died too young.

Papa, Captain Frank Anderson, is buried in the Confederate Circle in the historic Mount Olivet Cemetery. His funeral was held at the Foster Street Church of Christ, and his burial service, at his request, was performed by the Troop A, Forrest Veterans Cavalry in full uniform, with the ritual of the United Confederate Veterans. Clearly his service and that of other veterans of the Civil War was of such importance to him that he wanted it to have prominence even unto death. I've visited his grave several times and stood there loving this man I never met, but felt I knew so well.

Years later, we found several 1916 newspaper reports of Frank Anderson's critical illness, followed by a surgery, and then his death at home. I learned more about Papa from his obituary. Captain Frank Anderson was a considered a "moving spirit" in forming the Confederate veterans' organizations and remained very active. He organized the Frank Chatham bivouac, was a charter member of Troop A, Forrest's cavalry. My grandfather served the Confederacy in a cavalry company, Capt. James Briton's "Cedar Snags," of the "Paul's People," a regiment commanded by Col. Paul Anderson of Lebanon, Tennessee, a relative. The regiment was attached to General Wheeler's brigade. More about Caption Frank Anderson, and many others of my forebears, is documented in our family genealogy records.

The Nashville newspaper stated Papa was very active in a leadership role in many local, state and civic organizations. He was lauded as fearless and fair-minded, and noted as a consistent and active churchman. His obituary in the *Nashville Tennessean* and the *Nashville American* of July 7, 1916 concluded, "He did a man's part in the world's work."

Mother attended the very first public high school in Nashville, Hume Fogg. Mother, Aunt Mary, and Annie Gary all graduated from this historic school around the same time. This beautiful gray stone building, home to Hume Fogg since 1912, is still a high school, a Magnet School for the Performing Arts. Almost 100% of the students who graduate from here today go on to college and graduate with honors. This is a select group of students who apply from over the entire city.

The Anderson girls enjoyed school. Mother's sisters were all attractive, fun-loving, and using the expression I heard for a lifetime, "married extremely well." This included Aunt Mary's marriage to Uncle Mack, a socialite from New York City (David McClelland). How I wish there was someone left to ask how those two met!

Aunt Mary and Uncle Mack married simply but beautifully. My mother, her sister, was her only attendant. Their brother,

Frank Hardee Anderson, was the best man. Fashionable in their day and forever stylish, the girls shone.

According to the newspaper of the time, the bride wore a "beautiful gown of white messaline, fashioned Directoire, and trimmed with Irish pointe lace and net. Her bouquet was of bride's roses. Miss Dora Anderson wore a becoming gown of pink messaline, made Directoire, and her bouquet was of pink sweet peas." Messaline was a thin, soft, satin-weave silk. Directoire was a revival of a French style in the late 1790s and probably had a high waist with fabric softly draped to the floor or even trailing. Mary and David McClelland moved to Birmingham after their wedding on February 17, 1909. When I was born, I was named Mary McClelland, for my aunt Mary.

Mother lived in the Berry Street home where she was born, in the old neighborhood of East Nashville, until she married in 1915. I suspect when the sisters told this story, they might have just said, "Dora married a good, attractive man who was well educated." That would have been an apt, though understated, description of the man who married my mother.

Beauty and Grace command the world.

—Park Benjamin

Mother's Entertaining

My lovely, Southern mother entertained more than anybody I've ever known. It seemed every week she would have another "little luncheon" for her friends with fresh flowers always on the table set with her Haviland china. The thing I admired so much about Mother's entertaining was how she accomplished it all with such ease, never seeming to get flustered over any part of it. Her entertaining skills were honed early, for she appeared several times as a hostess in the society columns of the local newspapers long before her marriage. The descriptions below are based on these columns and include some direct quotes.

December 30, 1900, found the Misses Kittie Hennessy (remember the stepsister?) and Mary and Dora Anderson giving a Christmas entertainment on Berry Street. Miss Annie Gary Gosnell and David McClelland were among those present. David was known to me as Uncle Mack, Aunt Mary's husband, and Annie Gary, again, was Mother's best friend.

Sept. 14, 1907, Mrs. William Bennett, "Beebee," introduced her sister Dora to society with a party at her home, inviting fifty people. Decorations included a lavish display of fresh flowers throughout the home. Entertainment included a game called "Poetry" and the newspaper article stated: "Ice was served" at Mother's coming out party.

The newspaper later reported that on March 30, 1909, Dora Anderson hosted a "charming meeting" of the Sophronian Club in her home on Berry Street for club members. I have yet to find out what the Sophronian club was! Here it was, seven years before my mother would marry, and she was already acting as hostess in her home on Berry Street.

July 24, 1909, the Misses Dora Anderson and her friend Vera Payne hosted a picnic for fifty guests in Centennial Park, around Watuga Lake, to honor their friends and visitors, Misses Adcock and Parker. Afterwards the crowd of young people enjoyed the rides available in the park, and together watched the sun set over the lake. I wonder if those were carnival or carriage rides? At that time the park had a new swimming pool and athletic facilities, and still had buildings, including, of course, the Parthenon, left from the Tennessee Exposition in 1897. I'm sure Mother enjoyed hosting that party too!

Those who bring sunshine into the living of others
cannot keep it from themselves.

—James M. Barrie

A favorite postcard of Lake Watauga, Centennial Park, was issued around the time of Dora Anderson's parties in the early1900s.

My Parents' Wedding

Daddy was born September 29, 1883. He was a boy from the farm who had earned his teaching degree at Peabody College after graduating from Nashville University. Two of his three sisters were teachers in the Davidson County Schools.

My mother was a city girl, a graduate of Hume Fogg High School. Afterwards, Mother went to Goodlettsville School, which housed students from first to twelfth grade, and taught third grade there, where Daddy was principal.

Daddy told the story of meeting Mother many times. It was his favorite story. As he told it, Daddy looked up from his desk and saw a beautiful young woman, with whom he fell in love on the spot. Never mind that at that time in the Davidson County Schools, a strict rule was enforced that there were not to be any relationships between male and female teachers. Never mind that Mother was already being courted by a Nashville doctor. I don't know how Daddy got around the ruling, nor do I know what happened to the doctor. But I know what came next.

By all accounts from family and friends, the wedding of my mother and daddy, Dora Anderson and Samuel Herman Binkley, in 1915 at the Foster Street Church of Christ was rather lavish for an upper middle class family. I'll just bet my mother's three older sisters were responsible for achieving this for their baby sister, whom they adored. Again, I would never want to be guilty of mentioning or even whispering that they were half-sisters, because those three would have my head for that statement. After all these years maybe my guardian angel will obtain forgiveness for me, who sat at their feet as a child and teenager, eagerly hanging on to their words, loving their stories and loving each one of them.

I learned about Mother's parents, whose role in my lifetime was never to be, as they departed this world before I had made my entrance in 1924. The stories I heard are told elsewhere. Both Mother and Daddy's parents died before I was born. I loved being a grandmother and great-grandmother, and know that I would have loved this special relationship.

Daddy had a brother and sisters. Daddy wasn't a city boy, but rather lived on a farm in Hermitage, Tennessee. He had several half-brothers and sisters as well, however, unlike Mother's they didn't sit around laughing and talking about their parents. So, I don't have as many stories about his family to share. His parents, Joseph Pitts Binkley and Alice Eliza (Moss) Binkley, were well known in educational circles. The Binkley family had lived in Davidson County in the Hermitage area since before 1810 and traced their ancestry to Switzerland. There's a picture of my Daddy's mother and dad on my wall. Want to know the genealogy of both the Andersons and the Binkleys? I'll spare you the tedious details found in other documents. This is not a genealogy, but is story-telling time. I must say, however, that revealed in Daddy's genealogy is the exciting fact that many of his ancestors were educators at the highest level.

Mother and Daddy married in May of 1915 at Foster Street Church of Christ where she attended as a child. Reverend J. C. McQuiddy officiated; he had also performed Mother's father's wedding. I do know from the newspaper accounts that Henry Binkley of Louisville, Kentucky, one of Daddy's brothers, was in Daddy's wedding, and that his parents were there, along with Mother's family. This was the neighborhood where her mother and daddy still lived, along with Annie Gary, her best friend, and her family. And also her friends, the Draper girls.

When I was a child, Annie Gary told me it was a beautiful wedding. Much later it was thrilling to read the newspaper account that confirmed this. Plants played a major part in the decorations, as usual: ferns, palms, hydrangeas and stands of lilies. The music had multiple vocalists and was played on the organ, accompanied by violins.

One thing done differently from today's weddings is that the bride entered with the groom. The newspaper stated that Dora Anderson "was lovely in a white embroidered organdy and crepe gown." She wore a Neapolitan hat, and carried a bouquet of bride's roses and lilies of the valley.

Dora and Samuel honeymooned in Richmond, Virginia, and Washington, D.C., staying with Mary and David McClelland at their home. Since Dora and her sister Mary were very close, I imagine this was a fun time for all. They returned to a home on Ordway Place in the Lockeland Springs neighborhood of East Nashville.

Isn't it odd? I have the picture of the children: Dora's niece, Margaret Ransom Horton (the flower girl), and William Blankenship, the son of one of the Draper girls. I have the framed, engraved wedding invitation. I don't have Mother's wedding picture! I do have however, the lovely picture made just a few years earlier in an exquisite batiste gown she wore in her graduation. She's holding two dozen red roses, and I'm sure she couldn't have looked lovelier in her wedding gown.

Life itself is the most wonderful fairytale.

—Hans Christian Andersen

Childhood
1509 Russell Street

In a neighborhood on the east side of the Cumberland River, where there were well-tended, fifty-foot lots, with alleyways behind where men who collected the trash traveled, and children loved to play, where adults cut through to make their walk a little shorter *en route* to the streetcar, and later to the bus stop, stood a spacious clapboard house. It was painted barn red with stark white trim. Its ceilings were high and its rooms were ample in size. The large porches, front and back, ran the length of the house. In the summer, the front porch would be beautiful with hanging baskets of ferns and blooming flower boxes. This attractive house stood at 1509 Russell Street in East Nashville, a dead-end street, today referred to as a *cul-de-sac*.

On one side of the sidewalk leading to the front was a very large water maple tree, and on the other side, the most beautiful, huge sugar maple. These lovely trees spread their branches, providing shade for almost the entire front yard. There were no subdivisions as we know today, just the wonderful neighborhoods with each house totally apart in design and color. In this neighborhood, in this house, lived our family.

My daddy was called "the Professor," as for all his life he taught children as a teacher in the classroom and as a principal in both elementary and high schools. Later, Samuel Herman Binkley was Supervisor of Davidson County Schools. After retirement he was a math tutor for college students. I always thought him, because he was my daddy, to be the most brilliant of men.

Miss "Dora" Burt Anderson taught third grade at Goodlettsville School, after graduating from Hume-Fogg High School in 1910. There, Dora met Principal Sam Binkley, and the couple who would become my mother and daddy fell in love. Daddy had attended Nashville University, which became George Peabody College for Teachers, where he continued his studies for several years and graduated. Mother entered the classroom having only a high school education, but she also continued classes off and on at Peabody. Later in life after my brother and I married, she finished her education and returned to teaching. It was during this time, in the forties, that the superintendent of the city schools sought me out to tell me how much Mother was admired and the fact that they found that if the problem children were placed in her class, her gift of love and understanding, along with the fact that she was a gifted teacher, these children were happy and so progressed much faster. This bit of news did not surprise me at all.

In this house in 1916, a son was born. Anderson, their first child, was welcomed with great love and adoration. I never knew anybody who loved children quite like my Mother. Anderson was seven years older than Joe and eight years older than I, so of course was the only child for seven years. I recall hearing her speak about that long wait between Anderson and Joe, and how she became distraught at the thought that they would have only one child.

Mother was thrilled beyond words when Joe was born. Evidently he was a beautiful baby as all the family commented on his unusual good looks, not only as a baby but even as a young child. I can testify that as a teenager and adult he was thoroughly handsome. When we were older, even men referred to his good looks, which I found unusual. He had beautiful manners and great charisma.

Sixteen months after Joe was born, I came along. I learned later that although my parents were delighted with their baby girl, the fact was that I was not planned. This became something for me to ponder. When I was older I questioned

Mother concerning this. She lifted me onto her lap, a big smile on her face. She hugged me tightly as she answered, "Of all the gifts you remember receiving, I'll bet the most exciting ones were those you didn't expect. Well, Daddy and I have cherished our 'special gift' and thank God for her every day!" My spirits soared at that revelation. Mother always knew how to make everybody feel good about themselves. She loved everybody and everybody loved her.

Let me open the screen door of the front porch for you, and then the big glass door with long narrow windows on each side, all covered with a thin marquisette fabric, light and airy. Then step with me directly into the living room of my family home. In this comfortable, high-ceilinged, old house, with no formal floor plan, I lived a storybook childhood.

The largest room would have been called the master bedroom, or even the "gathering room" today. I loved the Birdseye Maple bedroom furniture in this room all of my life. Mother's father Frank Anderson, or "Papa," presented her with this gift of furniture along with a beautiful diamond ring, which I wear today, when she graduated from Hume-Fogg High School. I was born on that bed, as were my two brothers, Anderson and Joe, before me. There was a coal fireplace and mantle in the bedroom, which of all things, had a blue and pink tile hearth which extended around the grate. Probably this complemented the Cabbage Rose wallpaper! I can't imagine a designer's reaction to that today!

A small room, entered from Mother and Daddy's room, was Joe's and mine as babies. It had colorful Mother Goose linoleum on the floor, first a baby crib, then a pretty youth bed, and a large dresser. Between my little room and another bedroom was the bathroom. Its big window gave a view of the back porch and yard from the claw-foot tub. When I was about eight years old, I moved upstairs where my space was private, and the little room's drawers and added wardrobe became storage space for out-of-season clothes. It kept its unique flooring, though I tried to convince Mother that "Mother Goose" needed to go. I think she couldn't let go for sentimental reasons, and the linoleum stayed.

Upstairs, I loved my new Jenny Lind furniture, my own little sitting room and a big closet. What I didn't love was the attic room, closed off with no windows, and frankly, scary! Old trunks of "stuff" which I now realize were priceless items of Mother's when she was young, small pieces of furniture from her childhood home, and Papa's Civil War sword and uniform were some of things stored there. I kept that door locked, and many years later, through ignorance, let many of those things go. If I had only realized the sentiment attached, not to mention the monetary value of the objects in those old trunks! I never thought to ask Mother about them.

While in Winter my parents read to Joe and me in front of the fireplace with its coal inset, in the summer our nightly reading took place in the overstuffed chair in the living room by the library table, or on the porch. The living room had a window seat which was filled with books, serving as the children's library of classics. The windows had a view of the Mosbys' house. Both the table and the side-chair, along with the wonderful antique, signed Tiffany lamp that we read by were later used in my son Charlie's law office. Another piece of that group, a rocking chair, I can still enjoy, as it is in my daughter Marilyn's living room. Each time I sit in it, which is often, I love remembering the days when I was rocked, later memories of spending hours rocking myself, and later still rocking my own babies when I was at Mother and Daddy's house. I spent much time there. I kept the love seat from our old home for myself and today I think it's the most beautiful piece of furniture I own. It was in front of this fireplace that Joe and I would sit with our mother around Christmastime and help her with the many steps it took for her unbelievable fruit cakes.

Mother gave family members a very special gift for Christmas: her fruitcake, made with loving hands. By word of mouth she was contacted by several people who offered a nice little sum to make not only theirs, but more to give to their friends at Christmas as well. This little business grew beyond what she ever expected. Because she was too busy to supply the demand, she returned to baking only what she herself needed and for her gifts to her friends. Mother used a lard stand, the large metal container used to contain lard sold in bulk, to make her fruitcakes. She placed her fruitcakes in the lard stand, on a rack, steaming them for the desired length of time. Later, she covered them with cheesecloth, placed them again in the lard stand, and poured wine or Jack Daniel's over them. By the time they were to be served—I can tell you they were not like any other fruitcake ever! Today when someone will comment that they are not fond of fruitcake, I know it's because they never tasted Mother's.

In December, Mother, Joe and I gathered around the fireplace. The children's job was to crack the walnuts and take out the pieces, keeping them as large as possible. We cut the dried fruit into small chunks, dipping the scissors in hot water many times while cutting. The most fun, however, was skinning the almonds, which were first blanched in boiling water—of course, that was Mother's job. We could skin the almonds quickly by taking them between thumb and forefinger and pushing them gently while we held them. It never took us long to engage in an almond-skinning fight! If we pushed hard, the almond would flip out and we could aim it, hitting each other in the face. Initially mother laughed, but when it got really crazy she quickly gained control.

The big kitchen was inviting with a large, round, oak dining table and six sturdy oak chairs. Big windows gave a view of the Davis house next door, and if you sat at one end of the table you could view Mamie Lou's garden with its blooms all summer long. A large "built-in" cabinet held Daddy's tools, and the gas stove looked dinky in comparison, on its tall, skinny legs. An old-fashioned kitchen cabinet with an enamel pullout was where Mother would place her homemade hot taffy. As it cooled we pulled it into shapes we wanted. Mother colored batches of it in various colors, so as usual, her creation was not only delicious but also beautiful.

The dining room was large and airy, with windows dropping to the floor and looking out on the front porch. Another outside wall had high, diamond-shaped windows providing light. The furniture here was by far the newest in the downstairs. I was probably in my early teens when Mother declared she was going to town that very day and buy some new dining room furniture because she was "sick and tired" of what she had! The new set was pretty, but I loved the old, perhaps because it *was* old! Mother explained her choice this way: "I didn't want to spend the day shopping so I only went to Castner Knott and to Beesley's Furniture Store." Actually, she found what she liked at Castner Knott, Nashville's second oldest department store. Even at an early age, I was not fond of "matching" furniture, or for that matter, "matching" just about anything. I would rather enjoy coordinating—in furniture, jewelry, clothing ensembles, etc.

The sidewalk which led to the street continued around to the back of the house. It was our playground on a summer evening. The neighborhood children would drop over for Hopscotch, Hide and Seek, Rock School, I Spy, and various other games. Kick the Can, a favorite, had to be moved to the street where we were allowed to play safely, as it was a dead-end street with a high stone wall across the end. When we became hot and tired, Mother would serve lemonade and cookies, often homemade.

On the other side of the stone wall was the "hollow." Now that I look back on this setting for our picnics it was rather amazing. In the middle of the hollow was a huge rock, level enough to spread our food on a large, checkered tablecloth. Mother loved to fix a picnic hamper for us to take down and share with the neighborhood children. It could be fried chicken, stuffed eggs, pimento cheese sandwiches, and cantaloupe balls, always delicious. Whoever heard of frying chicken for a bunch of kids in the middle of the day?

During the summer months, the heaviest meal was served

during the middle of the day and a light supper in the evening. This was because Daddy was on summer vacation from school when I was a child. His favorite contribution to the preparation of dinner was his fried chicken. Daddy was extremely meticulous while getting the chicken parts ready. He lined them up by size, dipped them in buttermilk, rolled them in flour, to which he had added lots of salt and pepper. Then they were ready to drop into the sizzling Crisco in the big iron skillet on the stove. Mother refused to let him use lard. This is still my recipe today, or at least it was before I retired that big iron skillet! I used it for many years. Now I slip over to Publix. However, my children make me aware that the fried chicken from the grocery story is inferior to that from the old iron skillet.

Another cast iron skillet was used by Mother to fry corn, and I carried on her scrumptious tradition for many years, remembering how others had raved about her recipe.

Dora Anderson Binkley's Fried Corn

(as remembered by her daughter, Mary)

Use Silver Queen, not yellow corn. With a very sharp knife, slice through the top layer of kernels, then cut in through the next layer. Most of each kernel will now be in your bowl.

Then use the knife to scrape the rest from the cob into the bowl.

If the corn didn't produce enough moisture, add pure cream.

Place butter and bacon drippings into the iron skillet and heat. Add the corn and cook at low heat, stirring frequently. Add salt and pepper to taste, and a rather large pinch of sugar.

Your fried corn should be soft and fluffy. If you try this recipe, you will be glad you did!

How well I remember shucking corn with Daddy on the back porch! He let me help shuck and silk the ears. He inspected every ear as I finished, hunting for embedded silk between the kernels. He was quick to praise and quick to point out ways to improve a job. Many were the times the ear of corn was handed back to me to be redone. Removing corn silk has always been so tedious! I can almost hear Daddy chuckling when I asked, "Can I go get my rabbit's foot?" He quickly made it very clear my good luck charm would be of no help in this case, saying, "Sugar, you have to try a little harder and slow down." I never liked that job, then or today, even if I almost became a professional "silker."

Mother's cooking was famous. As I've mentioned, Mother entertained family and friends more than anyone else I knew. Not only with big dinners, the heaviest meal of the day, but what she called her "little luncheons" as well. She did it all with such ease. She never owned a measuring cup or spoons. It was a pinch of this and a dash of that. She prepared the most mouth-watering food! She balked completely when other people began to use margarine and continued to use real butter on her yeast bread and rolls and to flavor her vegetables. There are still times I yearn to sit and eat my fill of fresh bread from the oven with a glass of freshly brewed iced tea. It always had a wedge of lemon or lime in it along with a sprig of mint, which grew around the water hydrant in the back yard.

I can tell you about the preparation of the yeast rolls, so you would think I might be able to make them myself. No way! I tried. As an adult after Mother passed away, I finally located the recipe for Mother's Cloverleaf Rolls. Her method was to put three little balls of the risen dough together, placing them in a muffin tin and letting them rise again, then baking them. The roll top looked like a three-leafed clover. She then brushed them with lots of melted butter and served them, piping hot!

I wanted Joe to be surprised, so I invited him over and served Mother's rolls thinking he would notice, because he, many times, had mentioned how delicious they were! He thought the rolls I had made were good, saying, "These are a little like the rolls Mother used to make."

"What?" I said, "They *are* Mother's recipe, the very same rolls!"

He laughed and only replied, "Well, if you say so!"

Mother's little luncheons began to be famous among her friends and family. I would run next door and meet Mamie Lou, the matriarch of the Davis family, in her garden, where she and I would gather flowers for the table. While Mother had the beautiful swinging baskets and flowerboxes, we did not have cut flowers to use. On the other hand, Mamie Lou had a perennial garden filled with old fashioned calla lilies, flowers which bloomed profusely all summer long: roses, multi-colored snapdragons, narcissus—which were yellow and orange in color. In the spring, tulips and buttercups. With the wealth of these beautiful flowers, even as a child I could create a table arrangement of beauty. I loved the compliments for this effort from Mother's guests.

Her sister, my Aunt Fanny, was an artist. She had ordered china from France and hand-painted the dishes in beautiful pale blue and pink forget-me-nots, outlined with 14-carat gold paint. This set of china was Aunt Fanny's and Uncle Malcom's wedding gift to Mother and Daddy. So Mother's little luncheons were not only delicious, but enjoyed while seated at a beautifully appointed table. Some of these luncheons were held for "Baby Frank," Mother and Aunt Mary's baby brother. During his adult life, he lived in Chicago. When he visited, Mother and his older half-sisters, Beebee, Aunt Fanny and Aunt Ruth would roll out the red carpet! Mother was the one chosen to prepare her fabulous meal for the family. As always, I enjoyed setting the table and running over to Mamie Lou's garden, gathering those flowers for the table arrangement.

Daddy put up a basketball goal and a sandbox in our shady

backyard. Mother hated the sandbox! She must have wearied with cleaning up the sand from our shoes and clothes. Like the other houses in the neighborhood, our garage backed up to the alley. It was painted barn red to match the house. I longed for some beautification: white trim and added windows. I discussed this plan with Daddy, but it was not to be. He often seemed to get a kick out of my young "suggestions" on many topics. However, he didn't take my advice very often! He once said, "Sugar, you have to learn that everything doesn't have to be beautiful." The alley stayed busy with walkers, children, and the garbage trucks. In my early years the ice-man traveled through the alley, leaving his ice in the icebox on the porch. As a little girl, I knew all the people making deliveries to our house: the iceman, the postman, the milk man, the delivery boy from the drug store, the paper boy, and the trash man. They all became my friends.

Did I mention the back porch at the old house where I grew up? Just as the front porch did, it ran the length of the house. It was screened above the paneled lower half. It was not pretty. I always thought it was neglected and not as beautiful as the front porch, by any means. As a child I wanted to make it pretty but never got around to doing so. However, it certainly offered a safe alternative for sleeping on a hot and humid summer night. An unattractive wood table served as a catch-all. Among other things, this was where Daddy kept his Rocky Ford cantaloupes which he bought at the Farmer's Market on the square. They were hand-picked by him according to ripeness and sorted accordingly. The ripest were eaten immediately and so on until the last ones were eaten at the end of the week. Then back to market. We had cantaloupe for breakfast, lunch and supper. When in season, all of us found this to be our favorite melon with its sweet, juicy flesh.

I always loved to go to market with Daddy on Saturdays. "Come on sugar, let's go!" he called and off we went. The farmers came with their horse-drawn wagons filled with a colorful array of fresh vegetables and produce from their farms.

I also remember cured meat being sold. (I thought it looked nasty!) In time came the picturesque old trucks from the farm, loaded and overflowing. This was the scene around the old courthouse the remainder of my childhood. It is etched in my memory as a favorite time to be with Daddy, helping him select the finest fruit and vegetables for our table.

Daddy more than once shared the story of Mother's daddy, Frank Anderson, who owned the building behind and to the left of the courthouse which still bore the sign, Frank Anderson Produce, in gold lettering. It was the last of the old warehouses on the square to be torn down. Today, an image of the warehouse can be viewed at the Opryland Hotel, in the Tennessee Ballroom's mural where the entire wall depicts early Nashville. When later in life I gave tours in Nashville, I loved pointing this out, for I found all visitors from Canada, Europe and all over the United States, enjoyed most the personal stories I shared.

Ordinary riches can be stolen. Real riches cannot.
In your soul are infinitely precious things
that cannot be taken from you.

—Oscar Wilde

No Happiness in My Heart

My life under that roof in "the old neighborhood" on East Nashville's Russell Street was filled with laughter, love, and a wonderful sense of peace. All would change abruptly when my big brother Anderson became quite ill. I was five years old, Joe was six and Anderson was thirteen. I quickly felt the pain, even seeing the heartache of pain in my parents' faces. I just wanted to go hide somewhere I would not be touched by all of this. I couldn't understand when the doctors at Vanderbilt Hospital suggested Daddy take Anderson to Mayo Clinic in Rochester, Minnesota for evaluation as they were unable to make a diagnosis. Daddy called home twice every day. Mother, Joe and I sort of hovered around the phone, not really in the mood to get on with our lives in a normal way. It was late in the afternoon, much later than Daddy usually called. The phone finally rang and in those moments that followed I saw all my life change, as I had known it. Anderson had leukemia. Leukemia was a new word in the medical world. "No cure for it," the doctors explained and so, Daddy brought his son home to die.

The weeks and months that followed until his death were nightmarish. I was just a little child, but that horrible ache in my heart became bigger than I was. I wanted to feel the warmth of Mother's arms around me and for my world to be right again. How heart-wrenching for a child to see her mother so sad and so lost and not know how to help her. I wanted my days to get better so badly. Today I have a name for what I felt so many years ago—my heart was broken into pieces. I had to have been a pitiful little thing, but you know, I never cried. After seeing my mother cry all the time, did I not want to hurt her further by shedding my own tears? I have to wonder. I've no idea—I vaguely remember having this thought.

Mother and Daddy were so distracted; my only relief was when I was with Joe. How could I tell Mother's friends and sisters, "Please don't take me home with you without taking Joe too?" But we were separated. Joe got to stay with Beebee, Mother's sister whose house was on Dickerson Road. Her daughter Margaret lived across the road with her husband, Herbert Harrison. Uncle Herbert was one of the four brothers who owned fashionable Harrison Brothers Florist on Sixth Avenue in downtown Nashville. They had three children: Francis, Herbert, and Hilda. Herbert and Joe were great pals, which was a huge help to divert his thoughts. The florist greenhouses were on the large property and there was a pool, not only for watering the flowers, but also for the children to swim. Joe was content.

On the other hand, I was miserable. I stayed across town with Aunt Ruth's daughter, whom Joe and I called Aunt Lillian. She lived in a lovely stone home on Fairfax Avenue in Hillsboro Village. Aunt Lillian and Uncle Edgar had one son, William, who was a few years older than I. I thought, "So good-looking!" He, along with his parents, did everything possible to make my visit there as happy as possible. William noticed one day I was having trouble reaching the tall sink in the bathroom, so he asked his mother to get me a little stool to use. They were all very kind to me, but Joe was not with me. I just wanted to stay home with Mother, who was really not able to cope with anything other than caring for Anderson. I loved Aunt Lillian, and she was wonderful to me during this time. But there was no happiness in my heart and soul and I just wanted to go home and have everything be like it always was.

On the day of Anderson's funeral, Aunt Lillian took me home. Certainly, I had no idea what to expect. When I walked into our house it was filled with people and flowers were everywhere. I wanted to find Joe, along with my mother and daddy. I found Daddy first. It was a picture I wish I could erase from my mind still, after all these years. My daddy was seated at the library table in his comfortable chair, wearing what I thought to be a new black suit. Just seeing him caused my heart to soar! This relief was short-lived, however, when I became aware of tears in his beautiful blue eyes. Daddy never cried. He lifted me onto his lap and hugged me tightly. Daddy didn't get up out of his chair, but told me to go find Mother, who was waiting for me. On my way to find Mother, I had to pass through the dining room.

Anderson's funeral was held at our home. The casket was placed in front of the big windows which went down to the floor in the dining room. I adored my older brother who called me "Sweetheart." He was lying in his casket, a sight I was too young to fathom, but it's never been erased from my mind. My heart was pounding by now. I was looking for my mother, where I knew her warm embrace would "make me feel all better."

She was seated in the chair in the little walkway between the dining room and the kitchen, looking like a stone statue. She was dressed for the funeral of her first-born, thirteen-year-old, adored son. The contrast of seeing Daddy all in black, and now Mother in all white left a lasting impression. So many things did on that sad, sad day. Mother's batiste dress was soft and flowing. Her hat and shoes and pocketbook were all white. Tears were dripping down her face onto her lap, but she never bothered to check them with the white lace handkerchief she was holding in her hand. She just sat there, crying at times terrible sobs which frightened me. She did not take me in her arms, as I expected she would. I'm not even sure she was aware of me standing in front of her, waiting for some show of emotion such as simply being glad to see me. I don't recall a funeral procession or Spring Hill Cemetery, but I do remember I couldn't go home with Mother and Daddy. My heart ached. I was witness to how deep the hurt—losing a child.

❦

After Anderson's death my mother went into a terrible state of depression. Returning home later didn't relieve my sadness at all. I found Mother crying, still unable to function, wearing a blue chenille bathrobe. My aunts were there to cheer her up to no avail. Among the faces were Mother's best friend Annie Gary. As always she had brought Joe and me a little gift. I was not cheered by any gesture, nor did I find any happiness for a long while. Mother didn't respond to any attempts, and it only got worse. I know she tried, for she continued to cook our meals. Most of the time she wore that blue chenille bathrobe, which I grew to dread seeing. She would knead the dough for biscuits or rolls, tears falling into the bowl as she kept on kneading, folding them in. Letting us make thimble biscuits with leftover dough was always such fun, but there was no fun anymore, even in that.

Poor Daddy tried so hard to turn things around, but Mother couldn't seem to divert her attention from her tragic loss. Sitting around the big oak table one evening while eating supper, Daddy looked over at Mother and bless her heart, the tears were flowing. I don't know what he said, but she broke down and cried again. Daddy said something to the effect that she had two cherished children living for her to love. She whispered that she wanted her son. Daddy's answer to that was, "Dora, you have a son. And that would be Joe." But she said she wanted her big boy.

Joe stood up in his chair, putting his hand on top of his head and said, "I am a big boy." With those words spoken, Mother left the table, sobbing. She headed to her bedroom, where she stayed the rest of the night.

Joe and I continued to feel the terrible loneliness. Guilt that Mother felt in not being able to cope, even losing her faith in God for a time, caused her to have what doctors referred to at that time as a nervous breakdown. As I remember Annie Gary would stay with us day after day. All of Mother's sisters were doing everything they could to help. Daddy showed complete love and consideration; as I look back, he was my rock. I never saw my Daddy cry. On several occasions I saw tears welling in his eyes but I never saw him cry. It could not be as devastating as the time the sounds came from the basement one evening where he had gone to tend the furnace. I suppose all the emotion pent up was finally released. His sobs racked the house. All of us were very quiet as we waited upstairs. I can't remember whether Mother went downstairs to console him, but I remember kissing him on the cheek when finally, he came upstairs to join us.

Every day that summer after playing in the mornings, Joe and I came in and bathed and went to bed for our naps. In the afternoons I always looked forward to being dressed in something feminine and pretty. As soon as Daddy got home we piled into the car and visited the cemetery. There Mother and Daddy tended the flowers they had planted on Anderson's grave. In sight of our parents, Joe and I played games around the fishpond, with many goldfish hiding beneath the beautiful lily pads. Mr. Owens, overseer of the cemetery, had a water hydrant placed near the grave to make it easier for them to water the buttercups and other flowers they had planted for that season. Afterward, Daddy felt so sorry for Joe and me and did little things for us. Late in the evenings, after leaving the grave, he always stopped at Baxter's Ice Cream Shop and bought us their biggest cone, served cut on a slant, rather than in a rounded scoop. Mine was always the rainbow ice cream.

Mother was becoming a recluse. Not wanting to see or speak to anybody, even to people who loved her so much. Daddy worked hard, doing his best to make up for our loss. He'd read to us, taking Mother's place, reading Bible stories, *Mother Goose*, and *Grimm's Fairy Tales*. Before Anderson's death, Mother's laugh was infectious as she read. Daddy was much more serious. Nothing was right in my world.

A while later, life had begun to take on a more normal sense to me, and I was beginning to be a little bit happy again. That was short-lived as Mother agreed that she would leave Joe and me with Mrs. Childress, our neighbor across the street. Mother went to stay with Daddy all day at DuPont School where Daddy was principal. Here she would do little jobs around the office. The doctor advised that Mother must get out of the house to help with the ongoing depression. Did anybody know or care how sad I was? With each day coming and going, I saw no hope for a change in my own sad little world.

Another turning point in my childhood came when Mother was planting flowers on Anderson's grave. She turned to observe Joe and me playing around the fishpond, across the road in the distance, and she realized she must take advantage of the blessings she was left. Realizing how much we needed her, the trips to the cemetery gradually leveled off. Mother's smile began to thrill me once again. Annie Gary told me more than once that Mother's smile was never quite the same after Anderson's death; it was sufficient for me. I loved her so much and again felt her love for Joe and me shown in every possible way. As the years went by we became closer than most mothers and daughters I know. We always enjoyed each other's company to the fullest.

When she looked up on that particular day while she was tending the grave, she said, "The Holy Spirit touched me." Daddy had kept telling her, over and over, "You have two children to love." She said at that moment it came to her, that yes, she did have two children to love. She ran across the road. We were so surprised when Joe and I felt her arms pulling us close. Later she told us that it felt like an angel had touched her, to remind her of her two children across the road, waiting for her to wake up.

And I think she spent the rest of her days making up for those two lost years. My mother was one of the most wonderful people. Everybody said it, not just me! And years later, after my son Charlie died, I too felt the Holy Spirit touch me, reminding me that I had other family who needed me. I looked back on my days as a child and remembered how Mother's tears saddened me. I prayed for strength to not add to my family's pressing sadness.

Angels—perhaps they are not stars,
but rather openings in heaven
where the love of our lost ones pours through,
and shines down upon us to let us know they are happy.

—Eskimo Proverb

Anderson Binkley

In the Care of Mrs. Childress

Mother went to work with Daddy to DuPont School to help out in his office with filing. This was part of her treatment for the grieving, which she could not seem to overcome after the death of Anderson. While at work, Mother left Joe and me across the street with Mrs. Childress.

None of the children in the neighborhood liked Mrs. Childress. We well knew her dislike of dogs coming into her yard. She had even stooped to pitching hot water on Blackie, the Davis' dog, at which time we agreed we couldn't stand this neighbor.

The house of Mrs. Childress was dark and ugly and always smelled of leftover food. I hated being there! I was much happier when I could go outside and play on the sidewalk. At least I could look across the street and see our house, which made me feel a little better.

There were other ways the house was different from ours. The first time I entered the kitchen I noticed a washing machine, making a swishing sound before it came to a halt. The wringer above the big tub had a handle on the side. This Mrs. Childress turned as she fed the clothes between two round bars, wringing out the water. I found this old contraption fascinating! When Mrs. Childress asked me if I wanted to turn the handle one round, I was thrilled. I became her laundry helper, handing her clothespins as she hung the clothes on a line in the back yard. At our home, a laundry truck took the dirty clothing and the responsibility, returning our linens and everyday clothing ready to wear. Maggie washed my good dresses and a few other items by hand.

Although her home was dark and smelly, Mrs. Childress did have pretty flowers growing front and back. I especially loved the lavender sweet peas. My heart began to warm a bit in their glow. The day she handed me some scissors, asking, "Would you like to cut some flowers for your mother?" my heart melted. Did she have a little vase for these? Together we went into the dark kitchen. There we found no vase, but a small Ball jar. It was a lesson in improvising, and I could hardly wait until Mother got home to give her my beautiful sweet pea bouquet! This was the first time I detected a bit of animation in Mother when she actually "oohed and aahed" a bit over my gift. I was beyond happy! A part of my happiness was mending my feelings toward Mrs. Childress. And it was the first time I came to know what forgiveness feels like. It felt good! It still feels good.

Mr. Andrew lived with Mrs. Childress and I hate to say it, but he was known as the neighborhood freak. He was her only child. He was absolutely huge, had very heavy black eyebrows, had no job and was at home all day. I was a little afraid of him. His eyebrows were so thick!

It turned out some years later that the fear became real to all the neighbors. I was a teenager by this time. Mr. Andrew married a woman who was very strange herself, and the two of them lived together a short time in his mother's house. One Saturday morning, a loud shot rang through the neighborhood. He had killed his new wife. This quiet, genteel neighborhood would have liked to have kept this our secret, but the radio was blaring with the news. We were all completely stunned. Of course, Mother and Daddy tried to help Mrs. Childress any way they could and cautioned us to be kind to her.

Mr. Andrew was sent to prison. When released he stated he experienced more happiness and freedom there than he had experienced his whole life. Mother said Mrs. Childress was an extremely domineering mother, which didn't come as a shock to me. Earlier, when Joe and I were in her care for a while, I could never find any warmth in her attitude toward the poor man. At some age I felt a great sorrow for him. This was before the terrible happening. I found myself joining him in a game of checkers when he asked me. I despised the dark, smelly parlor where it was setup, so it was a great relief when it was moved to the front porch. I know now that Mother and Daddy found excuses for my not being available when he asked. With the exception of Mrs. Childress and Mr. Andrew I dearly loved all of our neighbors and felt enriched for having lived there all of my life before I was married.

As the years passed, the neighborhood went through great changes and finally was not all that desirable. Mother and Daddy were the last to move out. I'm not sure they were aware of the changes, but Joe and I really were concerned that they needed to move. That story is told later...

I can have peace of mind only when I forgive
rather than judge.

—Gerald Jampolsky

My Daddy, The Professor

Daddy was called "The Professor," or by those who knew him best, "The Absent-Minded Professor." With his beautiful piercing blue eyes, thick black eyebrows and lashes, he appeared stern and unapproachable to those who didn't get to know him. If they only knew!

I remember him as a good neighbor who was always there and first to help if there was a need, the only one actually who insisted that Shep, the African-American neighborhood handyman, use the front door, not the back door. Shep was treated with the same respect as if he were coming into our home as a guest.

Daddy was a man who studied and loved the Bible, teaching for many years every Sunday morning the Men's Bible Study Class at his church, East End Methodist, located on the high hill of Holly Street in East Nashville. Certainly, he didn't seek accolades for himself. However, Mother saved newspaper clippings and articles written about him. I have read about my father in books written by Nashville authors about Nashville.

But in my eyes, he was my big, cuddly Teddy Bear, my soft Easter Bunny, my generous and jolly Santa Claus, my best Valentine, my Teacher, and my Protector. This was the daddy I knew and loved.

Whoever wants to be great must become a servant.

Mark 10:43

Holiday Memories

Mother's Big Heart

During the holidays, Mother would make sure I paid a visit to Chapel Avenue Church of Christ Home for the Aged on Eastland Avenue, leaving gifts of sweets that she had made. I also visited the girls' school for the blind. The Blind Girls' Home was founded in 1903 by the Episcopal Fear Not Circle of The King's Daughters and Sons. I visited many times during the year as it was located in the East Nashville neighborhood, at 1309 Forrest Avenue. I walked by on my way home from school. I loved styling the girls' hair and painting their nails.

When they were older, my daughters believed I did a poor job of fixing their hair, so you may imagine how those blind girls appeared when I was finished fixing theirs! However, it brought them and me great satisfaction, along with my mother.

Thanksgiving

As soon as summer was waning and that first nip of cold air was felt, I began to think about the next big family holiday: THANKSGIVING! This was an especially meaningful celebration. Daddy told us the story of the founding of Nashville, which really occurred at Christmas time. He chose Thanksgiving for the telling of it. The French Haviland hand-painted china along with Mother's best crystal and silver were used on this day. Mamie Lou's garden couldn't produce flowers this time of year for a table centerpiece, so Daddy bought a bunch from the florist. This was given to me to arrange as I saw fit, even when I was a young child. I felt so very important and really thought I was quite "The Floral Designer."

Our family was just Mother and Daddy, Joe and myself. I was so glad we often had guests for Thanksgiving dinner, including Annie Gary after her husband died, and her two cousins who lived with her. I'm afraid I compared our dinner table to our next door neighbors, with the Davis family's nine children. Several of the older ones were married with little ones. That's the excitement I loved as a child. I always planned to have a big family around my table if I ever married.

Our dinner was the traditional turkey and dressing, scalloped oysters, cranberry sauce, sweet potatoes, and a few other side dishes. Best of all were mother's homemade Cloverleaf Rolls. The butter would be soft and spreadable. Oh my, how I miss my mother's cooking.

After dinner, Mother would retire to the living room with her guests, while Daddy, Joe and I did the dishes. I didn't really enjoy this part of the day. I'd much rather have been at the feet of the grownups listening to their conversations. I loved it whenever Maggie, Mother's African-American "help" was available to come late in the evening and relieve us of the job. If I was lucky, most holidays after dinner or sometime later I ambled over to the Davis house to be part of that celebration. I loved Thanksgiving get-togethers.

The holiday spirit is in the air. It's November in 2011, and after eighty-seven years I'm still excited to be a part. I'll have to admit that as Thanksgiving approaches, I'm remembering the heavy iron skillets I use to cook and the necessary lifting of the large turkey. (This was after several shoulder surgeries for rotator cuff tears.) Well, actually Marilyn's husband Ken ran over, placed the turkey in the oven, and ran back later to remove it! That way I could get the turkey stock and continue assembling the dressing.

There's no way I can complain about what I can't do, when there're so much I can. However, after the surgeries on one shoulder without 100% success, and a rotator cuff tear on the other shoulder, I'm finding increasing difficulty in reaching and lifting. I do want all who might be reading this to know I'm not expected to load myself down with cooking the turkey and other "stuff." This is purely my desire. The girls in the family are all standing by, willing and ready to take over when I decide to bow out. At this moment I'm not really sure that's needed, but I'll have to make that call soon. I love the fact that they leave decisions to me until I ask for advice. Do you understand what a gift this is?

Thanksgiving today is as meaningful as it was when I was a child. I loved the years I hosted all of the holidays at my home, when Mother was getting older and was perfectly happy to relinquish her job. Today, Marilyn does such an outstanding Thanksgiving dinner for the family, all seated at a long table extending from one end of the dining room through the living room to the entry hall. All thirty of us devouring the delicious food each person has contributed! This, my ninetieth year, I reluctantly bowed out and actually simply was a guest at the table. I missed cooking the turkey and dressing.

Marilyn was concerned. She said that the food might not taste like mine, which of course was what the family was accustomed to and loved. Only to find out that Marilyn's was better! This child is my mother made over in so many ways. "How my cup runneth over!" with this wonderful family: children, grandchildren, great-grandchildren, and this Thanksgiving, my great-great-grandchild will be with us too.

The Magic of Christmas

I loved going to the woods with my brother Joe and Daddy to the farm where Daddy grew up, to find a beautifully shaped cedar tree. They did all the work while I stood by with hands in my pockets.

Why didn't we hang stockings on the fireplace, I have often wondered, *as other families did?* Rather, we placed on either side of the hearth big paper maché Santas with bags on their backs, which were filled with small gifts and candies–always peppermint candy canes. I would love to know the origin of those Santas, as well as the fate of them, with their beautiful happy faces, red cheeks, black boots and trademark wide black belts. They were truly works of art! Perhaps Uncle Henry purchased them while vacationing in Europe.

Our tree was decorated several nights before Christmas Eve, and taken down on New Year's Eve. There were no electric lights, but big stained glass ornaments, and loads of icicles. A star topped the tree, which stood in a bucket of water, secured with who-knows-what. A white sheet covering the bucket was an attempt at snow. Today, it would not be considered special; but to me it was simply glorious and magical. So magical that I found myself in my rocking chair for hours on end, staring at the bulbs. They became a scene for no one's eyes but my very own. The reflection from the lamps that shone in the thin glass bulbs were, for all the world, like those of a magnificent mansion. As I continued looking, I was the child living there. I was living up to my nickname, "Pollyanna."

When I was probably eight or so I could play "Silent Night" and a few Christmas pieces on the piano. So again, magically, I found myself in a great concert hall with the Christmas tree a focal point on the stage. These are only a couple of the times my imagination ran rampant. I could transform myself into a rich girl, a little poor girl, whoever I chose to be on a given day. My imagination was sparked from the reading of many children's books.

Mother and Daddy were forever seeking little ways to help those in need. But Christmas was an all-out effort and Joe and I were included in learning the happiness of sharing. There were always many gifts under the tree, but always one big one along with many smaller ones.

The house was filled with smells of Christmas. This was before the days of artificial greenery, and while Joe and Daddy were finding the live cedar tree, they were looking for other trees that offered a smell and loveliness for touches around the home. This brought the feel of the Holiday Spirit into most rooms. Mother's kitchen also added to the magic of Christmas with smells and tastes, anticipation, creativity and special dishes.

Sad to say my church refused to acknowledge the birth of Jesus on any given day, and therefore church was not a part of our celebration, except for the fact the beautifully decorated East End Methodist Church was Daddy's church home. Without that, I wouldn't have had the opportunity to join in the Christmas music or to stop to reflect on the story of Jesus' birth. I was whisked back in time to that manger in Bethlehem and my heart was once again touched by that old, old story and knowing of God's hand in the plan. Because I was a little child named Mary, I loved the name of the mother of Jesus. Because I had a big brother whom I adored, named Joseph, I thought we had a bond with the family. I had yet to realize that all of God's children had the same bond.

One of my fairytale Christmases was actually conceived in the mind of my Daddy. We were all feeling the depression of losing Anderson. I was five years old and Joe was six. Mother, in her terrible state of mind, could not bear to take part in the holiday on this first Christmas after her son's death. I knew there would be no Christmas parties given for Mother and Daddy's friends this year. I did wonder whether Mother would buy me a red dress to wear and whether we would attend Daddy's church for the musical program. But there would be no tree, not anything to remind Mother, not even placing the Santas on the hearth.

Daddy had a plan. He brought the tree in on late Christmas Eve and joined Joe and me in decorating. The next day he took it down, all done without Mother taking part. My heart ached, not only for my older brother who was not with us, but I felt my mother's pain, and actually she was not with us either, confined to her bedroom.

Christmas morning arrived. Santa had surely come and with more gifts than I could ever anticipate! The highlight being the adorable pink bassinet with pink skirt and pillow, and inside, an adorable baby doll covered with a pink blanket. *How did Santa know?* We hadn't even made him a visit or mailed our letter to him at the North Pole, as we were accustomed to doing.

The secret was that Daddy had taken us downtown to Phillips & Burtoff on Second Avenue, the store that carried fine silver, china and crystal. In the rear of the store at Christmastime, and alluringly in the store window, were Santa's best toys displayed.

Jim Davis, our next door neighbor, went with us. He was selected by Daddy to stick close to me and take a mental note of everything that inspired me to *ooh* and *aah*. Before even walking into the big doors, I spied the pink bassinet in the window. Jim picked up on my desire for it. I don't remember any of the other toys I found interesting, but I do remember there were several more under the tree as well.

Daddy was a strong man. How else could he carry on our traditional Christmas while he was feeling his own loss and the great pain of having lost his son. I'm sure he had to be devastated seeing my mother grieve, as he so adored her. So what might have been a sad Christmas for Joe and me instead seemed one taken right out of a happy story book.

❦

Another Christmas, when I was six or seven, Santa brought me a huge tricycle, bright red. Joe got his first bicycle. Nobody had a tricycle as large as mine. So I had to share it with all the neighborhood kids on Christmas day. Not that I wanted to; Daddy insisted.

Christmas when I was a teenager was always exciting because of get-togethers with friends exchanging gifts, having lunch downtown where everything was filled with the Christmas spirit. I recall the sound of silver as it fell on coins deep in the black, heavy pot hanging from a chain. Everyone dressed up to go to town and most everyone would be wearing red on some part of their clothing. Music would be playing from the store's loudspeakers, both inside the stores and on the street. We all loved Christmas for the gift-giving and socializing, which still mean much more than any gift received.

I'm married, with children of my own, and Mother's cooking for Christmas Eve and Christmas Day, as well as taking care of my little ones. Why would she be doing this? Well you see, I always saved two gifts to buy on Christmas Eve so I could go downtown and mix with all the late buyers and feel the excitement of the city. The music of Church Street, decorated to the hilt. Castner Knott, Cain-Sloan, Harveys...and all the small shops glowing with color, each one competing for the most beautiful window display. I loved watching the shoppers, arms filled with packages, some already wrapped lovingly in colorful paper and ribbon. The expression on shopper's faces was always interesting. Some were drawn with the last minute rush and desire to finish. Some were jovial and light, having already finished the bulk of their shopping. Some walked briskly, arm in arm and others sauntered alone. All were getting ready for

Santa. Commercial? Yes. But exciting and great fun. This little Christmas story wasn't from my childhood, but was written in 1969, when I was forty-five years old.

Again it's Christmas Eve and I'm hosting at my home on 1920 Moran Drive where we lived for forty-two years. The time came when I felt Mother need no longer be responsible for all the cooking and planning for a big dinner so I took responsibility. She didn't really seem to mind at all and loved coming to my house. After every meal I can hear her now: she would follow me to the kitchen as I cleared the dining room table and whisper, "Are there any leftovers I can take home for Daddy and me?" How I loved getting it all together, wrapped and ready to go. I'll bet she and Daddy ate for several days on this food. I would do the same thing later when Marilyn took over. On the other hand, I still prepare a portion of the meal, as well as Doree and Vickie, at those special occasions when extended family and friends attend.

Marilyn hosts Thanksgiving and we all go to Doree's on Christmas Eve, and these are the times I look around at this beautiful family, children, grandchildren, great-grandchildren, and once again say, *My Cup Runneth Over*. I've learned that nothing's perfect in this life, but I don't allow that knowledge to take away my heart and thought—those things would ruin the moment of joy and Thanksgiving.

I always loved the holidays and as my children know: I still do. No tabletop tree for me! How could I ever begin to get all these sentimental ornaments on a small tree? How could I miss having children and grandchildren here on the day after Thanksgiving, serving leftovers along with a bowl of soup, sharing stories together about some of the old ornaments as they bring them to me, before placing them on the tree. The youngest one here this Christmas is ten years old. This means you will find the ornaments well-distributed, not clustered on the lower branches where little hands could only reach a short time ago.

New Year's Eve

On New Year's Eve when I was a child, a party was held at our house for both children and adults. After dinner, the tree was stripped of its ornaments, taken onto the hill in back of us and burned. While the flames were leaping, everyone had their sticks prepared by Daddy in advance and we had a marshmallow roast. As the magic hour for the turning of the year approached, church bells chimed all over the area. Fireworks filled the sky and our little group ushered in the New Year. The boys lit small firecrackers and the girls danced with sparklers glowing in the crisp air.

Valentine Cards

On Valentine's Day, when Joe and I were preschoolers, and I'm sure first and second graders as well, we would sit at that big round kitchen table making valentines. Not much has changed today in the style of handmade valentines. All that was needed was red construction paper, white paper doilies, glue and ribbon to create works of art, that is, if one had the knack for it. As always mine were not quite as well done as I would have liked, even though I could at least say mine were more creative than Joe's, but we were both pretty happy with our creations.

When we graduated to buying our cards at the drug store, we took bunches to school for our classmates and special friends in other classes. After school we delivered to every house in the neighborhood. Whether children were living there or not, we knocked at the door, dropped a Valentine on the porch and ran off as quickly as possible.

I loved getting little gifts from the boys: candy, sometimes a little piece of fake jewelry and maybe, as I remember, a pretty little handkerchief inside of the card. The most cherished though, were from my Daddy, his daughter's sweetheart.

Easter Parade

When I was a child, our church did not celebrate a Sunday as the exact date of the resurrection of Jesus. We were, I suppose, celebrating the resurrection of Spring after the long, dead winter. Children in all churches burst forth in their colorful Easter dresses and bonnets. Even the very young boys wore white suits of linen. Some were ruffled. Adults joined in this tradition as well, and were seen in their newest and finest on this Sunday at our church. I loved the music of Irving Berlin's "Easter Parade" and its lyrics "…in your Easter bonnet, with all the frills upon it," still thrill me. I'm sure it will always come to me on the way to church on Easter Sunday. Even though I wouldn't be caught dead today in a new dress and hat!

My very first black patent leather Mary Jane shoes were sported on Easter when I was five years old. I remember them probably because they were so cute. But oh, how they pinched my toes! I wouldn't forget that, either. But these would not be the last darling shoes that killed my feet. The shoes I'm wearing in one early picture were very soft white leather that buttoned down the side with a button hook. My teeth are visible on my bottom lip in that picture. Mother explained this was not an overbite, but a bashful habit. I did this in almost every picture. I'm sure Mother was happy when I became less shy.

Joe and I jumped out of bed very early Easter morning, scrambling over the front and back yards looking for hidden eggs from the Easter Bunny. We always tried to outdo each other: *Who would find the most eggs?* Joe was always the winner. One year, Daddy slipped eggs into my basket and declared me the winner. Two golden eggs, each with our names attached, were chocolate. Those hard, colored eggs with sticky marshmallow centers were not that tasty. The fun was in the hunt.

❦

I wish I could remember how old I was when as usual, I rushed out of bed, waited for Joe to follow, flew out the front door and hit the yard with great impatience. *Oh my gosh, where were the eggs?* Of course I knew the Easter Bunny was not real by now, but he should have warned me. He knew I had outgrown this fairytale. I cried. Off I went to church with a heavy heart.

Not to worry. When we returned home all the excitement of Easter and the Easter Bunny was out in full force. Bright colored eggs were scattered everywhere. There had to be at least a hundred of them where we would have normally stepped! We had to inch our way around them.

The sweetest Easter Bunny in the world never made it to his church after dropping us off. He went home and called the man who owned the grocery store where we traded. No stores were open on Sunday back then. He explained his predicament and the owner unlocked the door. Daddy evidently bought all the eggs left on the shelf. Daddy, with his heavy black eyebrows and piercing blue eyes could to other people appear to be stern, whereas I knew him to be a big teddy bear.

Mother's Day Gifts

I can't remember my gifts to Mother as a child nearly as vividly as I remember her animated *thank yous,* said every time she received one of our hand-made gifts. We made these surprises for her special Mother's Day at school. She loved them all and saved them all, after displaying them on the wall in some fashion for a time.

Daddy took us shopping for our gifts to be given before church at the breakfast table. Although I can't remember my gifts to Mother, other than the *Toujours Moi* cologne from Cain-Sloan's Deparment Store, year after year, how well I remember Daddy's annual gift to her. For as long as I can remember, on the Saturday before Mother's Day, Daddy drove to the flower shop and brought in tons of plants. By Mother's Day, our long front porch with its white lattice work on each end and in the middle the flower boxes in between and hanging moss baskets above would have all been filled with petunias, geraniums, and baskets overflowing with lush Boston ferns. A long white wicker fernery with three pots of the same ferns on one side of the steps; and on the narrow side of the steps, another white wrought iron fernery would be filled with the Boston ferns as well. By the end of summer, the ferns would have received such loving care that they would almost reach the grey wooden floor. The floor and all porch furniture: rocking chairs, swing, bench, flower boxes, would have already been freshly painted for summer. Mother had cushions made in a fabric which picked up the colors of the flowers, so that comfort and beauty were enjoyed in each relaxing seat. We lived on this porch in the summer, as there was no air conditioning. The happy hours I spent there will forever be a part of my being, and its beauty was renewed every Mother's Day.

Daddy hummed a lot when he was working, often "Heart to Heart." For as long as I can remember I enjoyed this musical picture, as each year he repeated this same task for the perfect Mother's Day gift. Daddy always included in his gift a loving card and his promise to tend the flowers all summer long.

Mother's across-the-street neighbor grew beautiful roses, and she offered each of us roses to be worn to church on Mother's Day. Mother and Daddy wore a white rose in memory of their mothers who were no longer living. Joe and I wore a red rose in honor of our Mother. Somewhere down through the years this tradition seems to have been lost. As I reflect on it, I think this was a beautiful, very touching tribute to mothers everywhere.

After I married and had children, I was totally shocked when Mother's Day came and went without any observance. I learned that not every family observed holidays in the same manner to which I was accustomed! This included virtually every holiday, a

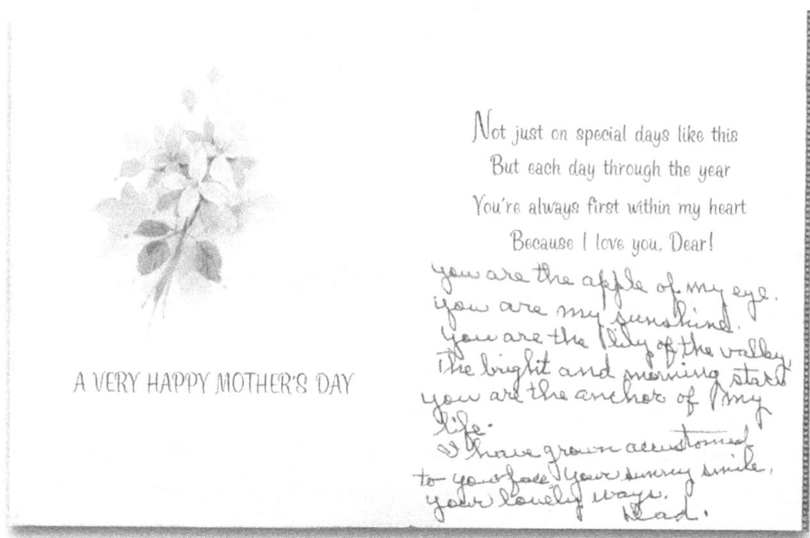

Daddy wrote this loving card to Mother.

fact I never willingly accepted completely. Perhaps this accounts for the fact that I tended to go overboard on these occasions. At least my husband was sure of that fact! Holidays were not his family's traditions except for Thanksgiving and Christmas. Both occasions were a source of great joy, being with the large Williams family, whom I loved dearly—traditional "Commercial Holidays," as Thurman referred to them. His most welcomed gifts came at any time he saw fit, or perhaps later on, at his girls' insistence when they thought it was important to act on tradition like everybody else! Bless his heart, he wouldn't want his girls to be upset!

Therefore I was the recipient of some cherished items I had previously pointed out to the girls while we were exploring little shops. These gifts were never pieces of fine jewelry. For many years I loved wearing only my mother's jewelry, or a simple gold bracelet given to me by Joe, along with a gold dolphin necklace. The necklace disappeared while I was swimming in the ocean, and Joe replaced it with a cross. I wear this cross all the time, seldom removing it.

My selfless husband had a big heart. However, he loved to

be just who he was, and that included being unconventional. Thurman's gifts to me were not prompted by our culture, but he gave instead every day of his life to me, to our children, and to anyone he learned had a need. He was much more at ease giving than receiving gifts.

Halloween

Another holiday to observe! Thurman declared that I made up holidays to celebrate. How I loved Halloween as a child. Joe and I helped Daddy carve the pumpkins and our Jack-o'-Lanterns outshone everybody's on our street. One with a smiley face, the other sad.

Daddy went with all the children trick-or-treating. It was helpful when we were little, but, *good night!* The time came when I felt I was old enough to go with the gang which had pulled out of Daddy's group, leaving me with the *babies*! He let Joe go, but not me!!? I wonder how many times I uttered this statement. I pled my case repeatedly: "He's only sixteen months older than me!" Well, forget it! When Daddy said *NO*, that was the end of it. Finally, I was allowed to join the more mature kids. I learned pretty quickly that Daddy had a point. I didn't enjoy these outings as much as I had expected.

When I began to make friends at school, Mother tried to solve the problem by having little parties at home. However, Joe and his buddies left after the party and had their own party! My brother had a curfew, but rarely made it in on time on Halloween, which caused problems under our roof. Joe was as hardheaded as Daddy. Our "precious" little family life was beginning to have some kinks in it, which would develop into some tangles as we became teenagers.

All the parties at our home were fun. Bobbing for apples was our favorite game. I wonder if children today ever include this activity in the Halloween party. Because all the neighborhood children of varying ages were invited, there was nothing actually frightening. Mother made ghosts out of large white dinner napkins to hang; they were not really very scary. I'm remembering one year she used a pillowcase to pull over my head with the eyes and nose cut out; it was not too intimidating!

I much preferred being a princess, which was one of the store-bought costumes. Sometimes I had store-bought costumes, and other times I could create a really awesome one from whatever we found in the attic, with Mother's help. When I was a little girl I wore costumes pulled together out of the attic, like the "little old woman" costume. The very best of the attic costumes was the year I was a Gypsy! Mother bought me a crystal ball and that night I was the hit of the party.

Today I still "dress up" for Halloween. My best costume is my witch costume. I still enjoy wearing it, even though I seem to have misplaced my broom and couldn't find my witch-nose this past year. Do you think it might be time to hang up the witch costume? Well, we'll see next Halloween, 2016, when I'll then be ninety-two. Just hope I'm invited to a party!

The best and most beautiful things in the world cannot be seen or even touched, they must be felt with the heart.

—Helen Keller

A Visit to Aunt Mary

We were on our way to Arlington, Virginia, where Aunt Mary lived with her husband, Uncle Mack (David McClelland) and their son David, who was several years older than Joe. Uncle Mack was a well-educated, attractive New Yorker, a civil engineer who worked in Washington, D.C. with the Federal Government.

It was an overnight journey by car. Mother fixed a large food basket with homemade cookies and fruit and a jug of iced tea. After a long day's drive, Daddy asked us to watch for the big, colorful neon signs announcing "Tourist Home." Once found, he arranged for us to stay the night. The four of us shared a pleasant upstairs room with two double beds. I thought I would sleep with Mother and Joe would sleep with Daddy. Not so!

Joe and I were tossing and turning in our bed as Daddy was snoring and we found it hard to sleep. Joe finally threw a shoe which landed as aimed, close to his head. This had the desired effect, as it did cause him to be so startled, he sat straight up in bed. When Daddy picked up Joe's shoe, I remember pulling the covers over my head, and thinking, *Poor Joe's in for it!* I expected one of Daddy's verbal reprimands, which could be scary. However, he simply pitched the shoe back at Joe, laughing at the whole ridiculous scene. The rest of the family awoke not terribly refreshed as the snoring didn't stop with the pitching of the shoe.

Mother, Joe and I reluctantly dressed and all went down to the dining room, where they enjoyed "a delicious breakfast." I was not feeling very well and declined to eat. Then we said our goodbyes to the nice lady and once again, settled ourselves in the new Ford to complete our journey. The remainder of the fruit and water was placed in the front of our car. There were two bananas in the basket, along with an orange and apple or two. This was where the aroma from the basket began to affect my stomach.

When we finally arrived at Aunt Mary and Uncle Mack's beautiful, two-story home I was so impressed! I could tell even at my young age that I was very special to Aunt Mary. Her home was more elegant than our home—there was a grand piano in the music room. I was to learn later how Aunt Mary had taken full advantage of the piano lessons she and my mother had received as children. She played beautifully and was in demand to play at different events in Arlington. (In contrast, our upright piano was used by Mother to play hymns and a few pieces of popular music, but she did not play publicly.)

Shortly after we arrived, Mother took my temperature, which was alarmingly high. As the evening wore on, I was dismayed to find that my nausea was getting worse. It was evident there was more concern than usual about my being sick. Uncle Mack suffered from diabetes and it was imperative that he not be exposed to any illness. Their family doctor came to the house and I was immediately diagnosed as having red measles—which developed into a severe case. I was immediately banished to a small room upstairs where I was to remain for what I thought to be a lifetime. I still remember how very sick I was feeling; I felt like an outcast as well. Of course Mother was with me constantly, giving me tiny little sips of ginger ale and nursing me back to good health. The drink was new to me, and when I was able to eat again, Aunt Mary's grilled cheese sandwiches and ginger ale made the very best lunch I've ever tasted. Aunt Mary made this for me each day until I left to come back home.

Eventually, the doctor's house call led to a pronouncement, "Little Mary was well and no longer a threat to Uncle Mack!"

I was elated to then spend some time with him and my cousin David, both of whom I enjoyed. I was singing "Springtime in the Rockies" and Uncle Mack thought I sang it so beautifully, or so he said! (I sang the song, recorded by Bud and Joe Billings in 1929 and again by Gene Autry in 1937, to my children later while rocking them to sleep. Many years later, I was singing it again, to my grandchildren.) I had the spotlight because brother Joe and Daddy drove back to Nashville earlier. Mother and I would travel home by train after a few more days.

How very special this mode of travel was! In the 1930s, the dining cars had tables set with fine linens, crystal and silver. As a child I was so impressed by the huge silver pitchers filled with water and poured by the stunningly dressed server who never spilled a drop, just as though he were in your dining room at home rather than being swayed and lightly bumped along on the tracks. To look out the windows, traveling daylight hours, seeing the landscape and little towns swishing by was exciting enough, but the one time I traveled after dark, the dining car was exquisite, with the sconces and little lamps providing subdued light.

I felt like a princess on this trip because I didn't have to share anything at all with Joe, and had Mother's undivided attention. Even then I missed him because we were so close and I loved him dearly. I'm sure he and Daddy were enjoying their time together as well.

This was the first of many visits to Aunt Mary. Sometimes we were also able to visit Mother and Aunt Mary's stepsister Kitty, in Roanoke, where she lived in a beautiful Southern Colonial home. I was thrilled whenever Daddy drove Mother, Joe, Aunt Mary, and me to see her family. The sisters were overjoyed and still very close. Kitty's daughter had been in Mother and Daddy's wedding.

After Uncle Mack's death, Aunt Mary came back to Nashville and we had time to bond, and did we ever! Aunt Mary always wanted a daughter badly and she lay claim to me. Before I was born she was so excited over the possibility of mother having a girl. Of course Mother's first child was Anderson and Aunt Mary was gambling on the second baby being little Mary. She spent hours making the beautiful little dresses for my layette, including baby pillows for the crib—all with tiny embroidery announcing "Mary McClelland." Joe must've been quite incensed later to learn that he wore all those clothes before I did! Mother said it was quite acceptable as baby boys wore more feminine clothing back then. How did she explain the name embroidered on all of them? The wonderful stories Mother told us as children included her "Good Luck Story" of how, when sixteen months later her baby girl could finally use the layette intended for her in the first place.

Mother always said that Aunt Mary had beautiful taste and wore her clothes with flair. I was thrilled to receive her hand-me-downs, because after dressing the children I could never have worn clothes as lovely and expensive. I had a seamstress who altered Aunt Mary's old clothes to fit me, and I was the best dressed young mother around. With my savings, I could splurge on a hat, which was a must in those days! Aunt Mary, for all her stylish living, didn't seem to remain "well fixed" as they once said, after Uncle Mack died. She always continued having lovely clothes, however. Mother and Aunt Mary were devoted to each other and the three of us had great times together, shopping, having lunch out on the town, or simply sitting for hours, talking.

A cherished friend and a personal cheerleader,
who will always see you through rose colored glasses.

—Unknown

Childhood Style

I look back on the beautiful clothes I had as a child. Shirley Temple dresses were popular for a while, and I think I had all of them from her movies! Aunt Mary continued to send lovely clothes that she made. Because I enjoyed wearing long dresses, Mother would ask Aunt Mary or her seamstress to make something just darling for special occasions. These might be going to plays held at the schools when Daddy would want me to attend with him, or even birthday parties, either for my little friends, or parties given for Mother and Daddy's friends. I also dressed in my finery for more professionally produced plays at the War Memorial Building. *Hansel and Gretel* was my favorite, although I attended many productions portraying well-known children's stories, like *Cinderella, Snow White,* and another of my favorites, *Rumpelstiltskin.*

Mother had a knack for making me feel special in every way. Making sure I was dressed stylishly as a child was only one of her ways to accomplish this. I'm quite sure my mother was not referred to as a "clothes horse." I do wonder that she saw to it that I, all my life, even after I married, had beautiful clothes! What a precious person she was! Her heart was big as all outdoors, and while attending to the needs of her little family, she extended that love to help families less fortunate. In so many ways, for so many reasons, I was blessed by this lovely person I was privileged to call "Mother."

Some pursue happiness, others create it.

—Unknown

Naptime

When I was a little girl, Mother was a firm believer in naptime. I hated taking naps. I don't think I ever closed my eyes and slept either! Joe and I played outside in all kinds of weather with the neighborhood children. We would be called in for lunch around noon or a little later, or sometimes, served lunch outside during the summer. After lunch, it was time to tell our playmates, "Goodbye!" We had to go inside for our baths and naptime—every day!

I recall feeling really sassy one day, when I blurted out, "When I get big, I'm not going to take naps." Mother just smiled and pulled up the sheet. The windows in our house came down almost to the floor in the bedrooms. Outside my windows, all along the side of the house were four o'clocks, which made a nice hedge along the walk that went to the back of the house. These flowers actually bloomed at four o'clock, which always amazed me. Mother had our clothes laid out to put on after naptime, which could be when the four o'clocks bloomed. I would look out the window and will those little red blossoms to open!

Do you suppose those "required" naptimes as a child has anything to do with the fact I've never taken naps, not to this day, when I'm in my late eighties! Mind you, if I happen to be home around three o'clock, which is seldom, I may pick up a book or flip on the TV, and a little short doze may overtake me. But you can't call that taking a nap! All my life I have felt napping to be a waste of time.

Dost thou love life?
Then do not squander time,
for that is the stuff life is made of.

—Benjamin Franklin

Piano Lessons

At age eight I began taking piano lessons from Miss Hattie Cartwright, who lived in the neighborhood of my school, Ross Middle School. She was a friend of Mother, a concert pianist, teaching me classical music, which I wasn't interested in learning. But the lessons were a must, so I labored on…

I asked Mother to talk to Miss Hattie and see, if along with the classical, she could teach me a popular piece of music. She did: "HOME ON THE RANGE"!!! I was ready to quit, but poor Mother just knew there was some talent hidden in there somewhere! I muddled through six and a half years of more lessons. The recitals were held at the Centennial Club and each year in the early spring, my dread began. It only increased as I prepared for a performance which I knew, even as a young child, would be at best, mediocre! Certainly Miss Hattie's reputation did not hinge on this pupil's performance.

Maybe Daddy finally determined it was a lost cause, and that money might as well be spent elsewhere. I always had a beautiful long dress for the recitals and that was thrilling—the only thing that was! Of course, the two of them always praised me for my efforts.

Bless parents' hearts! As hard as we try we can't often steer our children in the paths we happened to choose for them. Backing off can be a blessing for both parent and child in many cases. I will add this thought: "How stupid of me not to take advantage of the opportunity!" Today and for many years past, I'm so sorry for the choice I made.

Consult not your fears but your hopes and your dreams. Think not about your frustration, but about your unfulfilled potential. Concern yourself not with what you tried and failed in, but with what it is still possible for you to do.

—Pope John XXIII

By the Fireplace on Russell Street

My memories of living in my home on Russell Street are vivid, loving, and fun, yet a time of great heartache as well. Mother and Daddy's large bedroom had a fireplace that burned coal. This fireplace became in many ways the focal point in the home of my childhood and teenage years. It was in front of this fireplace, Mother and Daddy read to Joe and me, and to my older brother before his death, every night before bedtime. I can still see the very large *Mother Goose* book, so beautifully illustrated. Always, a story from *Hurlbut's Story of the Bible* was included and our prayers were said. This concluded our nighttime ritual. It was not far to go to my little bed in a room next to theirs, and for Joe to his bedroom in the back of the house.

Daddy and Mother, both educators, read with great expression. There were even times when Daddy acted out a role of one of the characters as he read. He scared us to death when he decided to be Goliath, the giant in the story of "David and Goliath." Joe was David and let me tell you, the picture of Daddy/Goliath being slain by Joe/David, was quite unnerving! Daddy had a knack of scaring the daylights out of me when some of the stories were reenacted, and mind you, just before he or Mother tucked me in bed. I'm wondering just now, could that have been the reason I wet the bed so often? I'll bet anything Mother later reprimanded him for those shenanigans when Joe and I weren't around to hear her.

There is a running joke in the family that even though these two were careful to not argue ever, perhaps that was only in front of us or their grandchildren. Marilyn, my third child and first daughter, was playing at Mae and Granddaddy's house with her cousins and brothers. She distinctly remembers my mother saying for some reason—she doesn't know why—loudly enough for her ears to pick up, "Shut up, Booby!" Marilyn was shocked and amazed. We laugh today about the fun the children had at Mae and Granddaddy's house. Had I been able to pattern myself after any person I've ever known, it would have most certainly, without a doubt, been my mother.

Daddy was "Booby" to Mother and all their friends and Mother's family. She nicknamed him on the spot when they were dating. They were at a party with friends, playing a game. It seems that Daddy won the *Booby Prize*. This is the prize given to the last-place finisher. Daddy's siblings and stepmother never, ever in a million years, would have ever referred to him as *Booby*. They all adored my mother, but I think not her nickname for him. Daddy's name was Samuel Herman. Now I love the name "Sam" and that is the name of my third son. But it is true: "You can't account for other people's tastes." Samuel Herman Binkley's family called him "Herman." As an adult and educator, he was S. H. Binkley. Maybe Daddy wasn't overly fond of either of his names—I never thought to ask.

In front of the fireplace, one Saturday evening, Daddy was teaching Joe and me the Bible verse on our little Sunday school card, so we could recite it Sunday morning in class. It was something extra of my daddy to take an interest in our learning our Bible story lesson and the verses we memorized. For you see, Daddy was not *Church of Christ*. Mother taught the Teenage Girls' class at Chapel Avenue Church of Christ. Daddy taught the Men's Bible Study Class at historic East End Methodist Church on Holly Street in East Nashville, all of my life until he retired. This was no problem with our family, even though as a child I became more than concerned. Our Church of Christ preacher expounded many times on the subject of being "unequally yoked," found in 2 Corinthians 6:14. This is a real taboo when choosing a mate for life! I can assure you there was a time I was convinced all attending East End

Methodist Church, including my daddy, were in trouble and should fear for their salvation. I breathed a sigh of relief when Daddy explained that verse didn't mean he and Mother were "unequally yoked" just because he was reared Methodist and she, Church of Christ! He explained how they both believed in God and loved God, placing Him first in their lives.

In front of the fireplace on Russell Street, which Mother began calling "The Gathering Room", Daddy was engaged in doing what he loved to do best: teaching young people of any age. For him, the greater the challenge, the greater the enjoyment! Every Saturday evening, Daddy would teach Joe and me our short Bible verses. I can still see the little cards with the verse and the colored picture pertaining to the verse. One evening, after Joe and I had mastered these for Sunday morning, Daddy decided to let Joe leave, but I was to stay a bit longer. The Professor bribed me! He knew even then my addiction for chocolate candy.

"How would you like to go to Parson's Little Grocery and get a big sack of chocolate?"

I vehemently approved. Parson's was on the corner, just a block up the street.

"Well, all you have to do is learn this special Bible verse."

Come on, I was five years old and some of those words caused me to be almost tongue-tied! When Mother became aware of what was going on she stepped in and in no uncertain terms with a firm reprimand. "Booby, what in the world are you doing? Let this child go play! Polly doesn't even know what the words mean." (Her nickname for me was "Polly" for Pollyanna, my nickname from the novel's character, known for her optimistic outlook.)

Daddy as usual didn't intend to be dissuaded. He simply explained, "Now Hon, I know what I'm doing. She's a smart girl. This will be a good lesson for life. She will master this, and I can say for certain she will never forget it."

Do you know I haven't?

Take heed and keep thyself from all covetousness for man's life consisteth not in the abundance of things which he possesseth.

Luke 12:15.

Daddy was truly a "Wise Old Owl," the nickname I gave him later in my teen years. Not only did I learn the verse, I never forgot that evening, nor have I forgotten the verse. At that time, the real bonus was when I took Daddy's hand and walked to Parson's Little Grocery store and, sure enough, I got a sizable sack of chocolate candy.

On the whole, I would describe this as a very profitable memory that took place by the fireplace on Russell Street. I reluctantly shared a little chocolate with Joe. I felt so in control handing him one piece at a time! Surely, that didn't make me happy, or did it? Today, I can only think how generous Joe was with me when we were older."How dare I?"

Happiness is a by-product of an effort to make someone else happy.

—Gretta Brooker Palmer

The Binkley Homeplace

As I've written, I was not fortunate enough to know grandparents on either side, with the exception of Daddy's stepmother, who still lived on the family farm in Hermitage, Tennessee, where he was born and grew up. Daddy came to Nashville to attend college at Nashville University, which later became George Peabody College for Teachers. Joe and I spent just about every childhood Sunday afternoon at the Binkley home where Daddy's stepmother and his sister, Aunt Lois, were living. Daddy's brothers lived in the surrounding areas on farms.

I loved playing with our cousins and eating dinner in the big old kitchen with a wood stove, then running across the street to the family cemetery or playing in the creek, jumping the big, smooth stones as water rippled over our feet. This was all I knew about the country. Oh yes, we had great fun in the hayloft in the barn! I hated walking through the cow pasture and smelling the pigs. The chickens that scratched round and round outside the kitchen door evoked only sadness, because I knew they were destined to end up on the dining room table. Joe, on the other hand, absolutely loved the country living and would drag me through the cow pasture, laughing his head off at my most careful steps.

The Binkley house was a modest frame house at the corner of Earhart and John Hager Roads in Hermitage, Tennessee. It was larger than the picture shows, for it went back farther than shown. A big bucket sat on the long side porch, collecting rain water. Even as a child I had heard it was beneficial to shampoo your hair in rainwater, so maybe that's how they used it.

I don't recall how the house was heated except by the one huge fireplace. In the winter we all gathered in front of the fire in the combined sitting-bedroom. There were two double beds with beautiful quilts spread on top and several on a blanket rail. All kinds of chairs sat around: some looked pretty and some had the hard, straight back.

The parlor remained stiff and cold. The sofa was mohair and the chairs were covered in some kind of heavy fabric. A most uninviting room! A closed staircase off to one side led you to a rather large room with two big beds under the eaves. There were heavy wool blankets with no pretty bedspread covering. I was frustrated when I climbed the narrow steep steps to the upstairs, which seemed more like an attic. Daddy and Uncle Henry slept here and Daddy declared there were mornings when he awakened to snow falling through the cracks, onto their beds! He said he was never cold, however, because of the thick wool blankets and quilts.

The kitchen with the big sideboard loaded with several cakes on Sundays when the family came was my favorite place. Standing in the middle of this room was the round table groaning under all of the many dishes of food and bread. In the winter we enjoyed big slices of homemade cake, with at least three choices. In the summer, there was homemade ice cream to be served along with the cake!

The long porch on the side of the house held rocking chairs and straight-back chairs. I can still hear the creaking of the ice cream freezer, when the men sat in those straight-back chairs on the porch and cranked, seemingly forever. The women and children gathered on the lawn, soon to benefit from their labor. I couldn't wait till they packed it, because I knew that a little later I would get to eat all I wanted! Mother wasn't watching and she was not going to see Aunt Mildred serving me much more than the other children. I was Aunt Mildred's favorite. I was close to Daddy's youngest sister all her life.

When we were teens, Joe loved to spend the night in the Binkley farmhouse, but I confess I really didn't. He would have lived there if it were possible. Joe talked me into staying with him one night and I was horrified when I had to go to the outhouse after dark. One more time, Joe laughed so hard that I became mad at him. I asked Aunt Lois to bring me with her the next morning when she went into town to work at Washington Manufacturing Company on the Square, and Daddy picked me up there. I truly loved the place on Sundays, but I never spent the night again. While later in life I would have been a good country girl, I found I fit in better with Mother's *city family* when I was young—even though I dearly loved the Binkley family all my life.

Like my mother's father, Daddy's father, Joseph Pitts Binkley, married more than once. His first wife, Alice Eliza Moss, was the mother of Samuel (my daddy), Uncle Henry, Aunt Mabel, Aunt Frances, and Aunt Margaret. Two of Daddy's sisters taught school and his brother Henry was a criminal attorney in Louisville. Their mother died and their father remarried.

The second set of children were Uncle Ben, Uncle Haynes, Aunt Lois and the youngest, Aunt Mildred. The younger children were Douglas, Carmack and Ruby. All the family loved the wife I knew, our loving stepgrandmother.

Daddy's family was close knit and his sisters' homes were open to family dinners where Joe and I enjoyed the company of our cousins. There were times on Sunday, after my grandmother died, that we went visiting to the homes of Aunt Frances (Binkley) Phillips and Aunt Margaret (Binkley) Carver. Aunt Frances and Aunt Margaret were Davidson County school teachers, and had come to Nashville to get a college education, rare for that time, good Christian women whom I loved. Again, the food was overwhelming. The children were fed last, which was a switch for me because mother always served the children first.

Aunt Lois married Mr. Barnett, a well-to-do bachelor. Later,

Aunt Lois lived in a rather large stone home on Lebanon Pike and often as a child I visited this aunt whom I loved.

Aunt Mildred was so cute and a great hostess. She had me over for lunch with her close friends many times when she lived in the Hillsboro Village as a young mother. She and her husband, John Burke, had two sons. When she divorced, Aunt Mildred managed to rear her children without returning to work full-time. I know this was with the help of Aunt Lois. So many people must be mentioned as I unravel the story of my life because of their influence on who I have become. Mildred was one of those people. As a teenager, I spent a lot of time at her home. She was a member of McKendree Methodist Church in downtown Nashville. Aunt Mildred did a lot of volunteer work there, as well as some paid work. McKendree Church was one of the many churches who opened their doors for the servicemen during World War II. Parties were held with good music and dancing. I loved to be there to entertain the servicemen, helping Aunt Mildred.

Aunt Mable never married. She moved to Washington, D.C. to work for the federal government. These aunts loved my mother and often remarked, "What a smart man Herman was to marry Dora. I doubt anybody else would have been able to live with the fact that he is more than a little absent-minded and is always right!" I didn't notice these traits until I was older, but it was true. While Joe was willing to lock horns with Daddy over a difference of opinion, Mother and I would simply let Daddy think he was right, whatever!

I think of the Binkley family reunions where all these people, their spouses and children attended, creating quite a gathering. For some years the reunion was held at Aunt Lois's house on Lebanon Road. I'm sure the move was made to her church in Donelson because the numbers were increasing.

When I was a teenager there were times on a Sunday afternoon, in the midst of the Binkley reunion, when I would have loved to have been elsewhere. Today I long for those reunions to happen again. I would be the first to arrive and the last to leave! What truly wonderful and intelligent people they were, coming together in a spirit of love and acceptance.

Kiss your life. Accept it just as it is. Today. Now. So that those moments of happiness you're waiting for don't pass you by.

—Unknown

Grandparent Stand-Ins

There were no grandmothers or granddaddies to spoil me. However, in looking back I can recall no void. That isn't to say I wouldn't have loved that special relationship, and occasionally I have wondered what it might have been like. Our extended family was great in number and showered their love on Joe and me. These were both family and friends, old and not so old.

The first grandmother figure I remember was "Aunt Lily," an older teacher who lived in Goodlettsville and took Mother under her wing when they first taught together in Goodlettsville School with Daddy as their principal. I wonder what advice she gave Mother concerning dating this cute man when it was strictly against the Davidson County Board of Education's rules.

Aunt Lily was a frequent visitor in our home. She loved books, filling Joe's and my library with many of the classics on birthdays and Christmas. Those of course were bound and illustrated so beautifully that in my mind's eye I can still see them, and have to wonder whatever happened to them. *Did I leave them in the window seat where Joe and I kept our books when we were children?* They would be priceless today.

"Aunt Randy" also lived in Goodlettsville and was another teacher from the school who added a substantial number of books to this collection. I enjoyed the love and attention of both of these older women.

These weren't the only older women in my life who played the role of grandmother. Mother's older sisters by her Papa's first marriage had actually been more like her mothers rather than sisters, after her own mother's death. I loved all three of these lovely ladies dearly. It was this close relationship that I enjoyed so many, many times in our home at Mother's famous "Little Luncheons" or in their homes when they would entertain.

You might think by now, "That's enough grandmas for any little girl," but it didn't end there. In Mother's old neighborhood where she was born and lived until she married, there was the Draper family. The two oldest sisters of the girls were Ollie and Bess, several years older than Mother. They never married. Once again, because they loved Mother so much, they too sought out her children to nurture and love. It was a blessing to have all of those Christian women enriching our lives.

Even though I grew up never calling any person by an endearing name like "Grandmamma" or "Granddaddy," you can see I wasn't denied having wonderful people as Grandparent Stand-Ins. Again, Thank you, God, for bringing all those precious women into my life. Memories of them bring such joy to my heart!

Beautiful young people are accidents of nature,
but beautiful old people are works of art.

Marjory Barslow-Greenbin

It's Fair Day!

How exciting! A school holiday! As usual for our annual trip to the fair, it was a beautiful fall day. Joe and I started getting dressed early for a whole day and night to be spent at the Tennessee State Fair. We knew Daddy had a pocket full of money to be spent on us and we could eat all we wanted and ride all the rides as many times as we could. I was practically jumping up and down in anticipation, wanting to get to the Midway as quickly as possible. As we got closer to the fairgrounds, we began to hear the sounds of the rides and the shrill laughter and squeals of the children. Floating in the air was the aroma of food as it was being prepared—it didn't take too much to whet my appetite! Mother was particular about where we ate our food, however, and she always chose a church booth where the ladies of the church prepared the food in their kitchens, as opposed to the hot dog and hamburger stands where the food might not look so savory on a hot day as it was being cooked and served by a person who might not pass Mother's hygiene inspection. The person cooking had to look scrubbed—with flies not an issue—before she was comfortable with us eating their food. That's quite alright, because we had all the cotton candy and candied apples we wanted, which was enough to make me sick when riding some of the rides afterward.

Every year I would jump out of the car wanting to make a beeline to the Midway where all the fun was taking place, only to be stopped by Daddy, who would say "Not so fast, Sugar. We're going to view the livestock first." How I would have loved to bypass that portion of the Fair, but no way! Joe loved it, and I do have some fond memories of seeing some of the sights even though I wasn't into the pigs, the cows, or learning what a sow was.

I embarrassed Daddy, I think, by asking questions about an animal's not so private parts. There on the spot he knelt down beside me and taught me a quiet lesson about female cows and male bulls. He explained it wonderfully well, in language suitable for a child, and I skipped off thinking how very smart I was that I had learned so much.

On another day during the week of the State Fair, Mother packed all her cakes, candies, and cookies. Joe and I, as well as Daddy, were on hand to help her in this project. This was an annual event for Mother when Joe and I were young, and we all got a kick out of it. We assisted her in placing all her baked goods in their particular categories in the large area where the competition would be held, in the Women's Building. Then we would find a bench close by and take our seats for the wait. It was uncanny how she continued to get a blue ribbon on EACH food item EVERY time she entered. She was always thrilled. However, Mother was always very modest about her accomplishments and in accepting compliments.

The blue ribbons were objective proof of the fact that her reputation as an unusually fine cook and superior baker of breads and desserts wasn't just confined to her family and friends. The yeast rolls and bread mother baked were works of art. So much so that many years later the pictures in color, by Henry Schofield, photographer, were used in magazines, and that story is told elsewhere. Why did I not save those magazines?

After the ribbon awards, we would saunter around the huge competitive area checking out all of the other booths. In 1965 the Women's Building burned; its charm was gone forever. But on our days at the fair, it was still standing, a wonderful place to wander. Invariably we would linger at the sewing booth where Mother would remark, "I should have learned to sew, but I never found a thimble to fit," followed by her little giggle.

When I was a teenager, a group of Joe's and my friends met and drove to the Fairgrounds. Daddy warned us over and over about the terrible state of the Big Dipper: the roller coaster's wooden underpinning was rotting and should have been torn down. He told us repeatedly, "Do NOT get on the Big Dipper." When we arrived, Joe being the daring, devil-may-care person that he was, and I, being so influenced by him, immediately took our seat on the Big Dipper. When we got to the first incline I was so petrified I began to pray. I don't know about Joe, but I prayed that if the Lord let me survive, I would never again disobey my Daddy and do something like this! I had to stay on through the end of the ride. When I got off, I thanked God. By the time the next State Fair rolled around, the Big Dipper had been torn down. So I was not bothered with that dilemma any longer!

I see nothing in space as promising as
the view from the Ferris Wheel.

—E.B. White

Mean Little Girls

Aunt Beebee's daughter, Margaret Harrison was a delight to young and old. Though she was my cousin, Joe and I called her Aunt Margaret. Then she was a young mother with three children, Frances, Herbert Jr. and Hilda. Herbert was Joe's age and they were as close as brothers. Hilda was a year younger, and we were best friends. I grew to love their wonderful home, as I was invited there many times for overnight and weekend visits. When I would visit Hilda, Herbert Jr. would visit Joe at Mother and Daddy's house. The next visit, Joe would go to Aunt Margaret's and Hilda would come to our house. It was such fun for us all!

There I learned to swim when Uncle Herbert threw me into their pool and hollered, "Swim, girl, swim!" I dog paddled all the way across the pool. That night to celebrate, after Hilda and I were in our pajamas, Uncle Herbert loaded us into his convertible. Off we went for ice cream! I was so happy in that home!

Remember Mother's nickname for me? Pollyanna, yours truly, must have dropped her halo while visiting her cousin Hilda Harrison for the weekend. I was about ten years old. Hilda, every bit the angel my mother and Daddy declared me to be, was a year younger. To this day, I can't imagine what on earth got into us on that beautiful summer day. The two of us devised a plan to create, evidently, what we thought would afford us a lot of fun at the expense of hurting another child. *What in the name of peace and common sense were we thinking?*

Hilda's little neighbor was invited many times to come over and play when I was visiting Hilda. I loved her! Hilda and I must have turned into two bored brats when we decided to call this child and have her come over—not to play, but to humiliate her! She was not told I was visiting nor would she know when she arrived. I would be hiding in the closet.

Our devious plan began to unfold when Hilda brought up my name, saying things she disliked about me. She cleverly drew our friend into agreement. As time went on, these opinions became uglier and uglier! I was all ears, listening to the two of them as "sweet" Hilda guided her into a loaded conversation. Eventually Hilda got our little friend on a roll, not just agreeing but expressing her own reasons for disliking me! Even today as I relive this childhood memory, I shudder to think what this child felt—when I abruptly slung open the closet door and appeared!

The look on her face I'll never forget. Nor how sorry I was that the two of us could ever have thought this would be at all funny. I wanted to cry, not laugh. This child flew out the house, sobbing on her way home to tell her mother. Hilda and I came to the conclusion that this little prank would prove to be disastrous for the two of us, when the phone rang. We were aware that this call had to be from our little friend's mother. My Aunt Margaret, Hilda's mother, minced no words while reprimanding us, taking us by the hand, practically pulling us into the neighbor's house to apologize to our friend and her Mother.

I had the urge to plead with Aunt Margaret not to tell my mother. Then I realized she was already on the phone with her! My weekend visit was cut short when Mother and Daddy came to get me. Mother saw the state I was in. She spoke softly as she explained her disappointment in me. All in all, it has been over eighty years ago, and while I can't seem to remember this child's name and all else who were involved, Hilda, Aunt Margaret and Mother are all gone. I have no one to ask. But I'll never forget that day nor the lesson I learned in how not to treat friends!

Occasionally down through the years this memory will again stir in my thoughts. How fortunate Hilda and I were. Our mothers didn't take our act lightly but took the stand of protecting the innocent one and being aware of the fact there are "Mean Little Girls" whether they be six or sixteen. You can rest assured their two little angels, who for the moment had lost their halos, never again mistreated a friend. The positive outcome is that we both were fortunate later to have many wonderful girlfriends we respected and loved. I think we have our wise and loving mothers to thank, don't you? Thank You, God, for lifelong lessons learned at the feet of Christian parents.

Be careful who you trust. The devil was first an angel.

—Ziad K. Abdelnour

My Best Ever Boy-Friend, Jim Davis

The Davis family who lived next door, Mama, Papa and nine children, were our family as well. The love that existed between the two families lives on today down to the youngest son, Jim, who was the last surviving sibling. We had bittersweet visits at Richland Home as he aged; that man loved me as I loved him.

We could still laugh at our memories of a lifetime. Of course my brother Joe was the funniest of the funny and those two, Jim and Joe, were like brothers. Martha, Jim's lovely wife, and I still today reminisce about those exciting evenings that Joe afforded us on the town. He filled our lives with fun and excitement as well as love. But let me share some stories of Jim Davis:

In October 1924, Mother, Daddy, Anderson and Joe laid out the welcome mat for their new baby, Mary McClelland, who would remain the baby in this family. Next door, four years before, in 1920, Mamie Lou, Papa and their eight children, the Davis Family, welcomed their last baby as well. His name was Jim. I suppose because our two families were so close it wasn't too unusual that baby Jim would be baby Mary's best boy-friend for a lifetime. With Joe, Jim and I being within two years in age of each other, for many years we were the Three Musketeers: Joe, Jim, and me bringing up the rear. The three of us stuck together through the years, through happy times and sad, playing all the games of childhood. At all times we looked out for each other.

As small children, the three of us would pile in Daddy's car, along with some of the neighborhood kids, for a morning of fun at Shelby Park. We walked to the park's playground, pausing at the big sandbox. That's when Mother would say, "Let's wait and play in your sandbox at home, where the sand is much cleaner." It looked clean to me but you can bet I didn't argue, but walked away, as did the neighborhood children she brought along. Besides, we might not have been able to come back on Saturday night for a free movie along with popcorn and candy sold at the small concession stand.

Jim and I spent many an hour at Shelby Park. Picnics in the summer, weenie roasts in the winter at Sycamore Lodge, demolished years ago. We were inseparable. Ten cent movies on Saturday night, after we outgrew the free ones in the park. We were found skating down the steep hill on nearby Holly Street in the summer and sledding down it in the winter. Or see us at the park, watching the baseball games, playing around the lake, walking across the bridge.

We were growing up. We were allowed to go to boy-girl parties with chaperones. (Mother and Daddy were among them.) Many of these were held at Sycamore Lodge or in our homes. We were beginning to dance and play more sophisticated games like Spin the Bottle! I didn't play, for fear it might be a boy whose spin landed in front of me who wasn't cute (or so I thought) and I would have to endure a kiss on the cheek. Horrors!

A teenager too, Jim knew all my boyfriends and I knew many of the girls he dated. My best boyfriend and I exchanged information about our prospects!

When I was dating there were times I'd ask Jim to be my escort. That way I'd get to go without Mother and Daddy having to know another's date's pedigree. Besides, I loved dancing with him. When I look back I wonder where Jim learned to dance so much better than Joe. He was a beautiful ballroom dancer. And oh, how he could jitterbug! There was always a stag line waiting to break in and whisk me away. It seems just *fun* was all we thought about. Maybe that is the way it's supposed to be, footloose and fancy free when you're young!

Joe got his driver's license, and our friend Jim and I were his first passengers. The two of them thought they could actually escape me, slipping into the car. Who were they kidding? I flew down the stairs and out the door, jumping between them in the front seat. It was the most reckless driving anyone could ever imagine! I can't account for Mother's trust in her teenager's ability and commitment to rules behind the steering wheel of an automobile! I feel lucky to be around to remember that ride and many other crazy, dangerous, breath-taking experiences as brother Joe's passenger.

I was angry at Jim twice. When I was a little girl, Daddy had built me a tree house in the back yard. Jim proceeded to furnish it one day. On his orders I lugged in and out of our house, lamps, small tables, rugs, a magazine rack and all kinds of stuff, until I got tired and refused to make another trip. This ended with both of us being angry. Jim stormed out of the tree house and ran home. Guess who had to bring all the stuff back into the house?

When we were in our seventies I told him, "I've never forgiven you for that day." I continued, "And I've never forgiven you for bringing me home at midnight intermission either, when our sorority dance began at 10:00 PM and ended at 2:00 AM, just because you were tired!"

Our friendship was lifelong, and there are more stories to come about Jim Davis…

And in the end, it's not the years in your life that count.
It's the life in your years.

—Abraham Lincoln

Four Generations of Andersons: my grandfather Frank, his son Lovell and his son Lovell II, and Frank's mother, Gran

"Gran"
My great-grandmother

Mary Ralston Anderson and
Capt. Frank Anderson, CSA
Parents of Dora Anderson
(My grandparents)

Capt. Frank Anderson and Troop A, Forrest Veterans Cavalry, CSA
Frank Anderson Produce, 204 Public Square, Nashville, 1897

Friends vacationing at Monteagle, Tennessee. Upper photo shows 2nd from left Annie Gary, Ruth and Dora, my mother. Lower shows from left, back row: Aunt Ruth, Dora (Mother), and Annie Gary.

Dora Burt Anderson (Mother)
High School Graduation, 1910

Dora holding wildflowers provided by her beau, Sam (Mother and Daddy)

David McClelland and Mary Anderson (Uncle Mack and Aunt Mary)

Eudora "Dora" Burt Anderson and Samuel Herman Binkley

Staff, Goodlettsville School, circa 1914, with Principal Sam Binkley, left, and Teacher Dora Anderson, 3rd from left.

Ringbearer and flower girl at the Binkley wedding

Mr. and Mrs. Frank Anderson
will give in marriage their daughter
Dora Burt
to
Mr. Samuel Herman Binkley
on the morning of Saturday, May twenty-ninth
nineteen hundred and fifteen
at ten o'clock
Foster Street Church of Christ
The honour of your presence is requested

Mother and Daddy's wedding invitation

Annette and Martha Binkley were the children of Samuel's half-brother Ben Binkley and his wife Pauline. The girls, my cousins, and I played together on many Sunday afternoons on visits to the Binkley Homeplace.

Mary Binkley, Age 4 (Me)

My brother Joe and me

The Anderson Girls: Dora, Fannie Flippen, and Mary McClelland, standing. BeeBee (Elizabeth) Bennett and Ruth Joy, seated.

The Draper Girls
Bess, Mamie, Ollie, Kate
circa 1950

TEEN YEARS

Teenage Dating

When I turned fifteen Mother and Daddy finally offered me the "freedom" of dating along with their unbelievable restrictions. I actually found there was not any "freedom" connected at all with this new beginning phase in my life! No car dates, only parties held in my home or close friends' homes, where either my date's family (if they knew them) or mine would be responsible for getting us there. This included school sports events, movies, home parties, or whatever. Several of my friends were granted much more freedom which made me feel somewhat awkward and unsophisticated.

Mother, I could tell, was happy when my "church" boyfriend, Harold Scott, came to call riding his bicycle! He always showed up around lunch or suppertime, of course always getting a heartfelt invitation to join us at the dinner table, which in turn was always heartily accepted. I wonder if anybody remembers the cute outfits I wore—the shorts, one piece with shirtwaist top and skirt matching? There would be times I might be on the porch swing wearing my shorts, when Harold would arrive on a hot summer day. It didn't matter HOW hot, before being seated at the table I knew to go fetch my skirt, have it on, and fully buttoned!

"Sweet Sixteen" brought me more freedom, but not as much as I thought it should have. After my date's first time interrogation, by either or both Mother and Daddy, at least I could ride in their cars now. Most of the time we would meet up with friends at various places. Would you believe Mother still felt relief if I double dated with Joe and his girlfriend? Little did she know! Why was I so loyal to my good-looking brother, whom all the girls adored, and not snitch on him? Could it have been because I thought he'd never let me ride with him again? Or was it because I simply adored my big brother? Much later in life we had some laughs together while remembering, and I learned he was aware and grateful for my keeping my mouth shut! So I was thanked—when we were in our seventies.

Mother and Daddy were strict. Of course, they were stricter than the parents of most of my friends! I was forbidden to go to night clubs and "honky-tonks," which didn't pose a problem after hearing from several friends concerning their dates taking them. This had no appeal to my friends, nor to me. Daddy took it on himself to scout out Burrus, a place that was once a small gas station on Gallatin Pike. Mr. Burrus was a grandfather with teenaged grandchildren. If I recall correctly, he was in Daddy's men's Bible class at East End Methodist Church. When he retired and closed his business, he enlarged the building, adding to the back a dance hall and a small grill where he served sandwiches and soft drinks. Absolutely no alcoholic beverages were allowed on the property with signs stating this fact, both inside and out. Daddy sat in the parking lot in his car one night to observe. He found this rule was strictly enforced. I could only hope my friends didn't recognize him!

You can believe, I was one happy teenager dancing to the tune of Guy Lombardo, Glenn Miller, and others while the music was blaring from the colorful, magical nickelodeon in the corner. Thank you Daddy, for making that possible! Mother, being Church of Christ, was never quite sure this should have been allowed even though I knew the stories about how badly she had wanted to dance when she was my age. It warms my heart seeing some of our elders dancing so beautifully with their wives during wedding receptions today. Even though I long to be on the dance floor, I sit and swing my foot to the beat of the music. I wish I didn't think eighty-seven-year-old women look sort of silly dancing the modern dances. There's not much waltz music or any ballroom dancing at these occasions, not as we knew it all those years ago. I certainly do enjoy watching all those young couples on the floor, however, and if possible am among the last to leave!

I really do think most of us have a real first love. While I dated several East High School boys, there was one I really thought I was in love with: Harold Cummins, who was the drummer in the East High School Band.

Then there was the new boy, Paul Ledbetter, who came from Monterey, Tennessee, and took the school by storm. The girls were falling over each other to get his attention. Was I ever shocked when I got the invitation to his fraternity dance, to be held at the Hermitage Hotel! (That story is included elsewhere.)

Teenage years brought varied emotions. It seems there were not too many ups and downs, though I remember being anxious about this and that, but what exact crises they were, I can't pinpoint today. I do remember one. I loved church, although I didn't always agree on the teachings of "the Church of Christ." This created unrest in my heart. This was a subject I didn't discuss, because I felt a disloyalty toward the church and my sweet mother, which killed me. It has taken me years to be comfortable in expressing my differences in opinion. Could it be because of the fact my fellow worshippers today are of the same opinions I've embraced from early teenaged years?

Before World War II was declared, Joe and I and our groups of friends were simply enjoying life. Martha Davis, Jim's sister next door was five years older than I, and dating the boy she eventually married, Walter Myers. One evening when the three of us were on the porch visiting, Walter mentioned it would be a great idea if I would meet his good friend, "Chip." Then we could double date which turned out to be a lot of fun. With a couple of school friends whom my parents had gotten to know, Chip in the picture, and double dating with Martha and Walter, Mother and Daddy were resting easy with my dating. Chip left Nashville when his family moved to another state. I can't remember that I ever was at all upset over his leaving, but Walter, Martha, and I were going to miss being together on our double dates.

Walter had a solution: "Hey, Mary," calling me over to the end of the front porch, "I've got a little cousin who you should meet soon. He's fun, and if all goes well we can continue going out together.

"Well, why not? What's his name?" I asked.

"Thurman Williams," replied Walter.

"Is he good looking?"

Walter remarked, "I think so."

"Is he tall?"

"Taller than I am, and I'm pretty tall. Will you go if I work it out with him?"

"Oh sure. Just let me know when."

Soon after that conversation I was at Old Jefferson Springs, a little summer resort on the Stones River, a place I had been going every summer with the Davis family next door, ever since I was a little child. On this visit, a group of friends and I were invited for the weekend by my friend Jean Woodring to her family's cottage, known as "Dr. Woodring's Place." Jean, his daughter, I learned was in love with none other than Brother Joe! She kept asking, "Do you think he might be here with his cousin Herbert this weekend?"

On Saturday night we all headed over to the Dance Hall. There was a group of nice-looking older boys standing together across the room who didn't seem to have dates. We observed them, making comments. I well remember my saying, "The tall guy with beautiful hair is my pick." None of them seemed to even notice us, so we danced together and had a ball.

This story I'm telling you is 100% true, believe it or not. My pick of the lot spoke to his cousin Walter, explaining about the girls in the Dance Hall at Old Jefferson Springs. He even mentioned seeing one in particular and asked if anybody knew her name. It was me! A friend from school was there with his date and knew me. *So here I was admiring Thurman from across the dance hall and he was getting my name at the same time.*

Walter was already planning how to get us together. It wasn't long until the "blind date" was arranged, and it turned out that neither was actually "blind" to the other's looks although never having met. Walter and Martha said, "It was meant to be," and so it was.

Life is a great big canvas,
and you should throw all the paint you can on it.

—Danny Kaye

Those Damn Bastards!

I continued going out with Thurman and with others whose company I enjoyed. Going steady was not done early on in a relationship then. I loved to dance. My dating was confined to the friends who enjoyed dancing as well. Most of the time we double-dated or triple-dated and met up with friends at various places. Mother and Daddy were strict and certainly I was never allowed in the honky-tonks. So, many parties were held in the homes where there was strict supervision. Certainly, there were times when the boys were drinking, undetected by the chaperoning adults.

The girls didn't drink, but most everybody smoked. Mother and Daddy frowned on that. I remember the day Martha Davis introduced me to smoking. There were many times I joined the crowd to smoke and found it kind of fun. We bought the cigarettes for penny-a-piece at Brown's Drug Store.

As I continued dating Thurman I began to appreciate his maturity. He didn't drink or smoke and certainly didn't approve of the girls smoking. When Charlie asked me at one point why I married his daddy, I flippantly answered "Because he was so good looking." And that he certainly was! However, my reasons went deeper than just his looks. Thurman was intelligent, kind, witty, loving, and very protective of me. He being almost five years older than my friends at the time, I was beginning to greatly appreciate and respect him, but was not ready to go steady.

Couples were dating in school and most of us had plans

to go on to college and finish our education. But our footloose and fancy-free life was soon to end. One Sunday afternoon in December, Jim and I were jitterbugging to some loud music on the Victrola in the big wide hall in his house. Suddenly, the front of the house became noticeably and completely void of any sound; the Davis family had quit their lively conversation. Jim and I abruptly stopped dancing and ran into the living room to see what was going on, just in time to hear the words of President Roosevelt announce that the Japanese had bombed Pearl Harbor. What a somber atmosphere engulfed the room on what had been an enjoyable Sunday afternoon.

I ran home to be with Mother and Daddy. There I waited to speak to those who would call. A couple of boyfriends from school did call; but I didn't hear from Thurman, whom I was dating. He had been out horseback riding with his brothers, but soon he came running up our porch steps.

Declarations were made. From Joe and the other boys came outbursts: "I'll be enlisting in any branch of the service where I can fight those damn bastards!" I felt like Scarlet in *Gone with the Wind* when she heard about those "damn Yankees" at the barbecue at Tara. I declare! My boyfriends had never cursed around the girls and their families before, so it was shocking to hear the words *those damn bastards* uttered time after time.

Life was changing quickly as the boys were enlisting in the Armed Forces left and right. I had witnessed a few rows before between Daddy and Joe, but this was decidedly the most serious. In the end, Daddy won, and Joe finished high school, but postponed further education until the war was over. He was a good soldier, I'm convinced. Another good soldier in the Army was my best friend Jim. I felt so sorry for Mamie Lou, his mother, after all, he was her baby boy. I don't know who was the saddest on the day he left: Mamie Lou, Mother, or me. The boy I was dating, Thurman Williams, enlisted in the Army Air Force. We did later marry.

Joe enlisted in the Army and it broke Mother's heart when he left. His best friends were Billy Berry and his cousin, Herbert

Harrison, whom he convinced to join him in enlisting in the Army. Billy and Herbert were the two he loved most. Neither serviceman came back from the war. My heart ached for my brother, seeing him grieve for so long.

There is a time for everything,
and a season for every activity under the heavens:
...a time to mourn and a time to dance...
a time for war and a time for peace.

Ecclesiastes 3: 1,4,8

The Servicemen

Parties held for the servicemen all over the city were chaperoned and well-organized. Many of my friends and I volunteered to help entertain. As mentioned before, I loved to dance, and while Mother wasn't too keen on my dancing, she didn't stop it as it was for the boys serving our country. Brother Joe was among the boys overseas. So Mother and Daddy generously opened our home as well, offering good meals, encouragement and a touch of home away from home.

We all fell in love with the young Frenchman from New York. Roland was handsome and personable. Mother was much relieved knowing he had no transportation other than the bus or cab. On one occasion he came with a friend who somehow had gotten a car for the evening. She panicked. Families were gracious many times offering the servicemen their cars for an evening out. I was absolutely forbidden to go in a car with anybody in uniform they didn't know. That covered them all. After I had teenage daughters, I well understood their reasoning.

The two young servicemen were anxious to take advantage of having transportation and explore something of the town. Daddy suggested that I take them to East End Methodist Church where the USO was hosting a fun evening with a good band and dancing. Great idea! Plenty of local girls would be there when we arrived. But first, there was dinner to be enjoyed.

Mother had dinner ready so of course, Roland and his friend joined us for fried chicken and turnip greens. Daddy, who fried the chicken, had insisted on serving the turnip greens. Mother had suggested earlier that she really didn't think young boys would like them, saying, "Boobie, Joe and Mary don't like turnip greens either and refuse to eat them."

It didn't matter to Daddy, knowing this was a Southern dish and that folks from the North probably didn't know about turnip greens. He would be the one to introduce them to a new vegetable; surely, they would find it most enjoyable.

While the young soldiers both enjoyed the chicken, they turned up their noses at the greens—a dish they had never heard of, much less tried. That night was the last time turnip greens were on the table when soldiers had their feet under the table. Mother won out, as she so often did.

Conflict cannot survive without your participation.

—Wayne Dyer

Uncle Henry

Uncle Henry Binkley, Daddy's brother, was a memorable figure, visiting our home often when I was a child and teenager. He was handsome and quite debonair, a well-known criminal attorney living in Louisville, Kentucky, where he had attended the University of Louisville Law School. Uncle Henry was divorced from his first wife and remained single for a very long time. He loved our family, Mother included, and she certainly loved him as well. He had no children, but was very attentive to Joe and me. We adored him.

I remember well a Christmas gift he sent me that brought both laughter and tears: Mother's laughter and my tears! When I took the wrapping off the huge box and opened it, there stood a doll as tall as I was, maybe even taller, with lots of black hair. That doll scared me to death! Mother's laughter was loud before she tried to console me, hoping to change my mind by bringing that strange doll to stand beside me! Instead, I burst out crying and ran away. Mother kept it on the back porch for a while where the poor thing stayed—until she could find her a home. I've never since liked dolls with black hair.

Joe and Uncle Henry always enjoyed each other. When Joe was a teenager, he even took his uncle with him on his date several times. The fact is that Uncle Henry, as well as Joe's girlfriend, actually enjoyed these evenings, I'm sure having some beers or whatever, and "drag racing" any car's driver to take his bet. Daddy and Uncle Henry were not too far apart in age, Daddy being the older. However, they were extremely far apart in how they lived their lives.

Uncle Henry really was great fun and I loved it when he came to town. I recall our meeting him at Union Station, where often he would step off the train looking for all the world like a dapper Philadelphia lawyer, dressed in a handsome dark suit, white shirt and dark tie. Sometimes he wore a dark grey or black pinstripe suit, always a smart chapeau on his head, summer and winter. He smoked cigars and wore good-smelling cologne. Always, when he arrived he would be carrying gifts in his beautiful leather luggage for Joe and me. Nothing as unusual as that horrid doll! Thank goodness.

Uncle Henry later married a woman of some means, whose name was Dorothy. I thought she seemed to love Uncle Henry more than he seemed to love her. He wore a hearing aid and when he got tired of listening to her, he simply tuned her out or turned her off! I was a teenager when the two of them married and came to Nashville. I felt sorry for her, and told Daddy, "Uncle Henry is rude to Dorothy when he turns his hearing aid off while she's talking to him."Daddy responded, "Have you ever noticed her rather shrill, nagging voice?" Well, perhaps he had a point, but I still think it was rude. I found it shocking to my sensibilities that this well-educated, kind, handsome man chose to be rude!

When Joe made the decision to go to law school, he also knew that he wanted to become a criminal attorney and sought advice from Uncle Henry. He discouraged him, saying, "Joe, think a long time before you decide on becoming a criminal attorney. It's the most difficult form of practicing law. I've found it at times so heartbreaking that I can't leave it in the court room, but have to bring it home with me. This sort of thing after time will play games with your brain."

I grieved and thought back on those words when I learned our beloved Uncle Henry had taken his life. What a tragedy!

Later, Daddy spoke of his brother, telling me of his devotion to family and his many friends when they were growing up. He told of Uncle Henry's kind heart, helping total strangers with the law, knowing they had no means of paying for his services. I felt even greater adoration and respect for this man who played a big part in my younger years. He was triumphant in the end:

"To laugh and love much; to win the respect of intelligent persons and the affection of children, to earn the approbation of honest citizens and endure the betrayal of false friends; to appreciate beauty, to find the best in others; to give of one's self; to leave the world a bit better, whether by a healthy child, a garden patch or a redeemed social condition; to have played and laughed with enthusiasm and sung with exaltation; to know even one life has breathed easier because you have lived—This is to have succeeded."

—Ralph Waldo Emerson

Uncle Henry Binkley

Courtship and a Wedding

Daddy's plans for me to continue my education at Peabody College for Teachers were shattered when I announced I would probably marry Thurman when he completed officer's training school in Miami. Before he left, Thurman asked that I accept his ring, which meant I would not be in circulation any longer. I was so young and so unsure of everything that I asked him to keep the ring and to give us time. My Daddy was influential in my saying that; as I remember, I used a direct quote! Daddy talked to us many times about the pitfalls of marrying at this time.

Thurman wouldn't keep the ring, so I wore it on my right hand or on a chain around my neck and waited. This meant I wasn't committed and left me with the freedom to enjoy time with what friends were left. At this time the churches and civic clubs were opening their doors for the soldiers who were in the city, many stationed at Fort Campbell. The USO was begging for help from families in entertaining servicemen.

Thurman enlisted in the Army Air Force in hopes of becoming a pilot. After screening and testing, he was selected as a candidate for Officer's Training School in Miami. We were thrilled at the prospect of his becoming an officer, although it was known to be a very difficult task and many candidates found themselves unable to complete the course. Thurman persevered and was commissioned a 2nd Lieutenant. His phone call reflected satisfaction in his accomplishment. He was excited about the upcoming graduation, thinking I could be there to share in his honor. Bless his heart, he had everything planned.

Lynn Williams and his wife Lorene were Thurman's good friends for years. Lynn and Thurman went through Officers' Training School together. Lynn would be graduating with Thurman. While I had met them and had dinner with them several times, I still referred to them as Mr. and Mrs. Williams, as they were at least ten years older. I'll never forget how excited I was when I hung up the phone to tell Mother and Daddy about the trip I wanted to take. I'd be flying with "Mrs. Williams" to Miami for the graduation. The plane tickets were purchased, and I went on a shopping spree to get together my wardrobe. I can still see the outfits I bought to *wow* this good-looking man. Then, simply during conversation, Mother and Daddy discovered Mrs. Williams was NOT Thurman's mother! My calling her "Mrs. Williams" had unintentionally misled them. My parents felt badly for me, but they absolutely refused to let me go. I can still feel the terrible disappointment and disbelief. This was the only time in my relationship with my mother that I was truly resentful. Thurman consoled me saying, "Perhaps it was a wise decision on their part."

Thurman and I were still not engaged. I was dating two others at the time. It was not unusual at the time to enjoy the company of more than one suitor. It suited all parties involved. I haven't thought of Barry Pierce in a long time, but feel I should mention him. A good friend and faithful Church of Christ man, Lloyd Scobey, was insistent that I should meet his best friend who would be in town from the Naval Academy. Along with Lloyd and his date, Barry and I enjoyed several really lovely evenings dining at the best places Nashville had to offer.

I think the problem was the time in which we were living. Everybody had the feeling we had to live life in a hurry because you simply didn't know what tomorrow would bring. I think Barry was in love with love. He was every bit a gentleman, a son of a brigadier general and obviously from a family of wealth. He kept in touch by phone and letters. He told me of a handsome diamond ring his grandmother gave him before she died. His third visit back to Nashville he brought it with him. He offered it to me on bended knee, as a sign of our engagement if I accepted. Scared me half to death—so unexpected!

I, in fact wasn't in love with any person at all. I was simply in love with life! I then shared the story of the other ring which I still wore on my right hand. This didn't faze his confidence at all. By this time, he had favorably impressed Mother and Daddy. The three of them had a delightful relationship, that is, until Daddy learned about the ring. Daddy seemed to stay in a state of confusion, worrying about his son going to war, and his daughter considering marriage. Each, to Daddy, was equally devastating.

Barry insisted I keep the ring until his next visit. It was beautiful, but I never wore it. On his next visit I emphatically returned it, but that didn't deter Barry either. He continued to visit Mother and Daddy and to send me gifts.I continued to wear Thurman's ring on my right hand, or around my neck.

Surely, I was caught up in the frenzy of this unusual time in history. Those carefree days before the war were fading fast, and my Daddy had visions for my future, as well as Joe's. I was expected to attend the Peabody College for Teachers in Nashville. Thurman had a different vision for us: to marry after my graduation from high school and his from Officers' Training School. These were days of excitement and unrest. After war was declared, our boys were enlisting with great fervor. Our life as we knew it was falling apart and we were forced to grow up much more quickly than those before us. At that time, I was becoming more attracted to Thurman, as the boys my age began to seem less mature. After he received his commission, Thurman was sent to Maryland by train with a short layover in Nashville. I would see him at the Union Station, as the servicemen could not leave the depot.

Thurman's sister and her husband, Matt and Lonnie Glymp, were to meet me at my house in the wee hours in the morning, maybe one or two o'clock. We would go to the Union Station and get a quick glimpse of Thurman, maybe a quick visit as well. Thurman was adored by this older sister and by her husband. I think he might have been the child they never had.

Mother and Daddy insisted I run upstairs and get some sleep. Daddy would set the alarm clock and wake me in time to dress. I'm sure Daddy was getting more and more concerned about me getting serious. To this day I wonder why the alarm didn't go off! From upstairs I heard talking: Matt and Lonnie! I threw on my clothes I'd laid out, grabbed a brush and lipstick and flew down the steps, practically falling in their arms, saying "Let's go!"

I was completely bowled over when I saw Thurman in his officer's uniform. Keep in mind he had trained in Miami beach, so not only was he deeply tanned, but was straight as an arrow and walked briskly with determination. I was swept off my feet! In the little time we had together, he asked if I would now consider wearing his ring, as a sign of our engagement.

I waited a few days before telling my parents that I had accepted Thurman's proposal. Daddy was not pleased, but neither was he unhappy about it. I know now he actually thought it would all go away and I would get on with my life. I did get on with my life, when after a few weeks I received a call from Thurman saying he was sending a recorded message by mail, and to call him immediately after playing it. The recording was of his upcoming leave, and of asking me to make plans for what he thought would be our upcoming wedding. Didn't take me long to reach him by phone and tell him that my head was spinning, my mind whirling, but in less than two weeks I would get it together. My joy was tempered by sadness, for my brother Joe and best friend Jim Davis were already serving in the military and could not be a part of this special day.

So many friends from East High School had already married their high school sweethearts. Many newlyweds had left town together, awaiting the time when the husbands were shipped overseas to be engaged in combat duty. It was a frightening time with emotions running rampant. Excitement, sadness, fear, love and anger all were raging high, higher than the seas to be crossed. It was felt deep in the hearts and souls of all of us who had to move quickly out of our happy-go-lucky teenage years into maturity, much too early.

On Friday, March 13, 1943, I walked down the aisle at Scales Chapel, West End Methodist Church. Harrison Brothers Florist (family on Mother's side) did a beautiful job decorating the chapel. Willard Collins, the minister, held the impressive ceremony. There were still some close friends in town who were part of our wedding. Fred Waller sang so beautifully my two favorite wedding songs: "I Love You Truly" and "Because." The 200-seat Chapel was full and overflowing, with some friends standing outside. It was a simple wedding, but I was pleased with its beauty. Our wedding dinner was at the Hermitage Hotel, where Thurman and I spent our first night together, pledged forever.

Begin doing what you want to do now.
We are not living in eternity.
We have only this moment,
Sparkling like a star in our hand—
And melting like a snowflake.

—Francis Bacon, Sr.

War Bride

The Day After

The Hermitage Hotel, Nashville

Marriage vows, wedding dinner, Mother and Daddy's tearful goodbyes, our wedding night—all behind me as I greeted the day as a newlywed. My new husband and I were having a lovely, quiet breakfast in the dining room of the Hermitage Hotel. It was the morning after our wedding and our "honeymoon" night spent in the beautiful wedding suite. Soon we would leave for Langley Field, Virginia.

Thurman was the adored youngest of five sons, and we sighted two of Thurman's brothers, Charlie and Jake, headed toward our table. Bless their hearts! They, Thurman knew, had been denied their plan to decorate the car, which his best man Johnny Garrett had hidden! Johnny had followed explicit instructions and it was safe in the hotel's garage. He would pick it up later after we had driven it to Union Station. Now Charlie and Jake were up to more mischief. I thought these brothers had done quite enough by calling us off and on throughout our first night together! Not so. They joined us to heckle their baby brother further. They ordered champagne and waited with us until our luggage was brought down. Charlie saw fit to help the valet load the car parked at the front door and pulled out what

I knew would be an ample tip. The brothers kissed us each goodbye; I couldn't turn my head quickly enough and those devils landed kisses on my lips to aggravate Thurman further. But even he was laughing *at* me, not *with* me. For sure, I grew to love my new brothers Charlie and Jake so much! A photographer from the *Nashville Banner* newspaper arrived and snapped a shot, all a part of their plan. Today I'm grateful they did. I love the picture of the "Newly Weds" sitting in the car in front of the Hermitage Hotel, ready to drive off, en route to the Union Station a few blocks away. There we would board our train, (the *Hummingbird,* as I remember) and embark on our journey into an unknown future together.

I felt deep and varied emotions at that moment: excitement, adoration, fear, wonderment, happiness, sadness. I thought of one of my mother's quotes, "Faith is the bird that sings when the dawn is still dark."

I couldn't help but think of my brother Joe and Jim Davis. How I missed them! I knew they too would have devised some off-the-wall scheme at the expense of Thurman. But you, know, maybe Thurman had had enough?

Union Station

Thurman and I drove the short distance to the Union Station. This was wartime. Servicemen were all over the lobby; lots of noise and activity was going on at this now "historic" train station built in 1900, fifteen years before the building of the Hermitage Hotel.

Was it the sparkle in my eyes, my beautiful travel suit, my handsome new luggage, or what? I'm inclined to think now that it wasn't about me at all, but the striking figure of the handsome young lieutenant to whose arm I clung. Everywhere I turned were smiling faces and nods from total strangers. I whispered to Thurman, "Do we look like newlyweds?" I hoped not! Several high-ranking officers were boarding and one would have thought Thurman might have been a son of theirs! An Army Air Force major turned to him and asked, "Are you traveling Pullman or Coach?" Thurman had already warned me that a mere Second Lieutenant wouldn't have a chance of getting Pullman reservations and I'm sure the Major knew this. A big grin came over his face as he and Thurman were talking. He, Thurman told me later, asked, "Are you newlyweds?" *How in the heck did he guess this?* That kind, thoughtful man offered us his ticket which included an upper berth on the Pullman. He said, "I don't mind at all traveling Coach all night. I can sleep on a rock right now!" Well, I had traveled several times by train early on but only once with Pullman reservations and then in the *lower* berth.

Have you ever climbed the ladder to an *upper* berth on a Pullman Car? Today if you found yourself in this predicament you would at least be dressed more appropriately, in jeans and tennis shoes. Picture this: I, like every other female traveler, was wearing silk hose and high-heeled shoes. The skirts in the 1940s were knee length and heaven knows if we didn't don a coordinating hat and white gloves for traveling. To top that off, an internal debate was raging. Was it more proper for Thurman to climb up first and extend his hand from the berth to pull me in, or should I go first and he push me up from behind? To tell the truth I've forgotten which I decided was more ladylike. Neither! That proved to be the easiest part of the whole night. Spending our second night of our honeymoon in the upper berth of the Pullman car was not ideal. The berth is hardly wide enough for one person and it was hilarious! Say no more...

I stop to dream about what is now an antiquity in this modern world. Nothing is produced today that begins to compete with train travel's old charm, grace, beauty and solidarity in yester-year. After a long six-hundred-plus mile ride by rail we came to a stop in our new town, close to Langley Field in Hampton, Virginia, where Thurman was based.

The privilege of a lifetime is being who you are.

—Joseph Campbell

My brother, Joe Binkley, and me on our Russell Street Porch

Joe Binkley

Jim Davis and his friends

The Davis Family
Standing: Lucille, Eva, Smith, Dick, Mildred, Sam, Sarah.
Seated: Martha, Papa, Mamie Lou, Jim.

The morning after our wedding, leaving the Hermitage Hotel.

YOUNG MARRIEDS

The Prices
Hampton, Virginia

Arriving in Hampton, Virginia, we were met at the shockingly small train station by Mrs. Nell Price. Thurman had prepared me for meeting these new friends of his; we would also stay with them until we found an apartment of our own. I was feeling a little lost and homesick, overwhelmed with so many changes. I was realizing this when I heard a booming voice shouting, "Hello Darlings!" A very heavy, plain woman with a remarkable smile approached, grabbing Thurman and giving him a big hug and kiss, calling him "Lieutenant" as she always would, even after the War. Then she turned to me and said, "Mary, so you're the one the Lieutenant always talks about as 'My Beautiful Mary!'" I longed to veer away and get to our destination. But Mrs. Price leaned back to scrutinize me better and declared, "You're such a little thing! We'll have to fatten you up." I, nor anyone else, had ever thought of me as little, and thin? *I don't think so. Maybe by comparison?*

Mrs. Price's laughter and jovial spirit was quite disarming. She was a spirited lady who sang in the choir at the Methodist Church where Thurman, on his first Sunday in Hampton, attended church services. She told me how they had met. "I spied him immediately, as he was so handsome and he was singing with great heart! I rushed out of the choir loft as quickly as my heavy frame would allow and hurriedly went up to him, saying, 'Wait until I can get Claude. You're invited to go home with us for Sunday dinner!'"

Thurman had told me he was shocked when he saw her leading this well-groomed, handsomely dressed man, her husband, toward him. Thurman did indeed go home with them, where he had a marvelous dinner. Nell was an excellent cook, as I was soon to discover. While they talked that afternoon away, Mr. Price learned that Thurman's watch was broken. Before it was time for him to leave, Mr. Price went to his room and brought down an expensive watch, telling him he would take his to be repaired. "Please keep this watch until the repair is done," he offered. They drove the young lieutenant back to the base and invited him for dinner on the next Sunday. In the meantime, the couple's only child, James, was introduced. This boy of eighteen years was huge, slow and obviously not in possession of a quick mind.

Since Thurman had briefed me what to expect, when I met the Prices I wasn't that surprised. Nell was so excited about having us stay with them in their home until we could find an apartment! Still laughing and talking loudly, we pulled up to her house–a two-story, attractive colonial. There was a screened porch on the front and a pretty yard with a flower garden not yet in bloom. I found it most appealing.

It was a little later that I met James, their son, and I was not ready for that! He kept staring at me in a peculiar way and I didn't feel at all comfortable around him, that evening or ever, as a matter of fact. The dinner was cooking, the dining table set with a cut linen cloth, stunning china and a fresh floral arrangement. Now, it was time for Mr. Price to be coming home from the shipyard, where he was an executive. The contrast in these two people was simply amazing! In all love, for I surely came to love her dearly, Mrs. Price was best described as "dowdy."

At dinner we had a rather strange seating arrangement, but I soon discovered it was to Mrs. Price's advantage to be on the side closest to the kitchen, rather than in the traditional hostess seat. Mr. Price made so many demands of her and she could more quickly get to the kitchen to take care of his many needs! James occupied the seat next to me and was nearest to Thurman, who occupied the hostess seat. So I felt almost lonely at the table the first time I dined in their home. The dinner was scrumptious, and I began to feel more comfortable in the company of this strange family. After we arrived from the train station, and before dinner, Mrs. Price took us upstairs to "our room." It was spacious, light, and airy. The first thing I noticed was a fragrance which turned out to be a hand soap in the bathroom just across the hall which was "our bathroom." We always used Ivory or Yardley Lavender Soap at home. I had never smelled any quite so delicate and fresh, nor had I even heard of Sweetheart Soap. To this day I'm still reminded of that home and the two people who became and remained such a special part of my life. Mr. Price treated me as the daughter he never had and along with Mrs. Price, I grew to love him so much. Except for missing home and family, our time spent in Hampton was most enjoyable. Mrs. Price's father, "Captain Skidd" and her mother lived across the street. We met them very soon. Their home was not a Southern Colonial as many on the street were. It did have a porch with rocking chairs, so it reminded me of home.

We were constantly looking for apartments and moved into one—for only one night. Mr. Price came over to bring some things and saw the undesirable neighborhood, which was to him not acceptable at all. The ugly décor also bothered him. He hugged me and said, "I'm taking you two home with me! We'll start over looking for an apartment because I couldn't sleep knowing you were in such a place as this." Well, I was only too happy to get back to our room with the delightful fresh aroma. Before we had time to follow the leads we had gotten, Mrs. Price's mother died suddenly of a massive heart attack.

Immediately following the funeral people flooded into the home, bringing food. So much food that it even began to be stacked on the back screened porch. So many people were there that every room plus the front porch was jammed. In the midst of all this, Nell Price came to me saying that she had already worked out a plan for Thurman and me, "You can move across the street! My dad can take the upstairs and have all his meals with us! You'll have the downstairs to yourselves." Actually this house had three bedrooms upstairs and one down. Thurman and I happily accepted, and we moved in with Captain Skidd.

We lived on LaSalle Avenue, one mile from Chesapeake Bay, where in the distance we could see US Navy ships docked. After a bit, the view was void of the ships altogether, as they had shipped out sometime in the night, a convoy to protect troops on other ships. I would watch the same scene slowly began to build again, knowing it would change in the dead of night. They would ship out and serve our country as protectors. Early one morning, leaving home with my book, a sandwich and a drink, I was sitting on my bench and missing the ships. I felt sad and prayed that God would protect these Navy men and bring them home safely. The library was a short walk from the house so I kept always at hand a good selection of reading material. I was lonely at times, but happy in anticipation of Thurman coming in from Langley Field.

The Field was very beautiful and the officers' homes were rows of old ivy-covered brick, standing side-by-side. The property was manicured beautifully with aging trees and bright flowers. I often wondered why Thurman had no desire to live on base! Perhaps it was the advantage of our neighbors, the Prices. We attended church with them. (Yes, I was a good Methodist while living in Virginia!) Or perhaps it was the Sunday dinners around their exquisitely set dining table. The fact was that Mr. and Mrs. Price afforded a great sense of family and belonging, and that meant a great deal to Thurman. We were their "children"; I was their only daughter and Thurman was their older son.

'It doesn't happen all at once,' said the Skin Horse. 'You become. It takes a long time. That's why it doesn't happen often to people who break easily, or have sharp edges, or who have to be carefully kept. Generally, by the time you are Real, most of your hair has been loved off, and your eyes drop out and you get loose in the joints and very shabby. But these things don't matter at all, because once you are Real you can't be ugly, except to people who don't understand."

—Margery Williams Bianco, *The Velveteen Rabbit*, "Becoming"

Best Ever Boyfriend, Part 2

After Thurman and I married, we continued our friendship with the Davises. And thus, more stories. Each time the following story was told, we laughed hysterically as if it had happened last week. We were in our eighties on the occasion of our last telling of what happened while Thurman and I were young, in love, married, and living in Hampton, Virginia:

Thurman was then a lieutenant in the Army Air Force stationed at Langley Field, Virginia and we were living in a wonderful old house off base in Hampton. One night, he and I were fast asleep when we heard a knock on the door. We both were shocked at the sound so late at night. Together we got up, he in front, and opened the door. There was my friend Jim, shivering, in the cold, damp night air. He was stationed at Camp David and was on a short leave. With our address in hand he had found us without any trouble.

There was so much for Jim and me to discuss, wending our way to the parlor. Thurman excused himself and crawled back into bed. There was only one bedroom downstairs, but there were three upstairs. Mrs. Price, the lovely lady who owned the house, charged us almost nothing, asking if her father could sleep upstairs. He and her mother had just moved into this house, and then her mother had died within weeks of a massive heart attack. The widower was now living there alone. This elderly man was called Captain Skidd, why, I have no idea! The arrangement was that Captain Skidd would sleep upstairs, and then cross the street and go to his daughter's house for all his meals. This was fine with us. He actually spent all the day across the street. His room had a comfy bed; however, the other two upstairs bedrooms were used as storage rooms. One did have a most uncomfortable daybed.

In the wee hours of the morning Jim and I were literally exhausted and said goodnight. Of course I wasn't sending Jim upstairs to that uncomfortable daybed to listen to the Captain's snoring, which at times had awakened us downstairs. The solution was easy, as I said, "Jim, you go crawl in with Thurman in our comfortable bed and I'll take the daybed upstairs, 'cause I'm smaller than you." Jim didn't argue but was happy to put his head on the pillow for the rest of the night.

I trudged upstairs, and put the pillow over my head, listening to snoring and waiting for sleep that never came. Finally, I decided I'd had enough. I went downstairs to our bed where they were both sleeping peacefully. I nudged Thurman enough to tell him that I was sleeping with them. When he opened his eyes he tried to whisper but the words were pretty loud: "That's fine, but I'm sleeping in the middle." Very soon on the outside of the bed, I was asleep with my best boyfriend Jim on the opposite side.

I had thought it was a hilarious tale to share until one night Thurman said, "Are you really going to tell that story again?" A friend once asked if I thought Thurman might have resented Jim's and my relationship. "Oh, for heaven's sake," I replied, "You really don't understand our relationship! It would never occur to Thurman to think of Jim and me as other than brother and sister." I would admit I don't have a friend who happens to be as fortunate and they would probably find it a bit strange or unusual. Many times friends did remark on finding it unusual, this relationship we both treasured. Of course, I had to tell Thurman about the remark and we both laughed heartily about it. Every time we told the story of our night together in Virginia, Jim and I laughed harder.

Jim continued to play a part in our lives...

Thurman and I with our baby boy came home to Nashville in 1945. Mother and Daddy graciously invited us to stay with them. We spent two years there until Mike was born. Jim was living next door with his mother, and the two of us were again neighbors, close as before. We'd sit on the comfortable porch at Mother and Daddy's house until midnight, talking. His mother Mamie Lou said that Jim never spoke about his time in the service, but he talked to me. We always had a very special relationship.

Jim was still using my nickname, based on my middle name, McClelland. He told me about his new girlfriend, Martha. "Mac, you will love her, I want you to meet her soon."

He was right. When I met Martha I loved her immediately and I was thrilled to attend their wedding in 1951. Joe was his best man. On Jim's eightieth birthday, Martha found several of my letters to him. She loved them.

After that wedding, Jim, Joe, and I were each married and the three of us and our spouses were great friends. Joe afforded us exciting nights on the town, along with great restaurants where we would be together. We accused Joe of inventing holidays for a celebration where we would be together, still the Three Musketeers from the old days. How we enjoyed dining at each other's homes, laughing together about hilarious moments from the past. I wonder now: Were the others bored?

Jim and Martha were gracious host and hostess. In their home, often Jim arranged the flowers for the dining room table or made the dessert. He always had a flair for the beautiful. Even as a child, wanting the tree house to be decorated in the best I could manage to drag out of Mother's house!

How I loved the years of our growing old together. Years pass, and so they have as I am completing these memories. I have outlived the both of them now, and shed a tear for the loss of the men I loved so completely, Joe and Jim, along with the loss of my sweet Thurman, who loved me and put up with the three of us telling the stories of our childhood spent together. How many girls have been lucky enough to own an eighty-three-year old relationship with her best boy-friend? My cup runneth over!

Hold a true friend with both hands

—Nigerian Proverb

Wifely Chores

The two of us being on our own, away from Nashville and apart from our families was, in retrospect, a good experience. My one anxiety was a practical one. *Today, I've got to come up with supper for my new husband, and I feel so inadequate!* I had not learned to cook. What was my mother thinking? I suppose she knew that after I married, I'd quickly learn. That's exactly what she had done so well. Her own family had a cook, so the story was, "None of Papa's wives had to learn and so the children weren't taught." Mother, on the other hand, had become an excellent cook. Starting as a newlywed and even after, I would have given much to have been in the kitchen, learning, rather that forever enjoying my footloose and fancy-free life. *Every child and teenager should be so lucky*. Or so I had thought. A few short years later, and this new bride had no idea how to cook a meal!

When I married, I'm sorry to say, I had never cooked a meal. Or anything else. My learning to cook was an experience Thurman survived and did so gracefully. I would arrive at the grocery and stand there and stare, at a loss. In this mood I would call Mother! She knew exactly what to tell me. I anguished over pleasing my husband—I can still feel a knot in my stomach thinking about it. On one occasion, cookbook in hand I tried what appeared to be a delicious recipe, only to have it turn out less than palatable. At another meal I thought: *I can't eat this mess I've made! Just look at that polite man forcing it down!* With that I began to cry. Thurman rose from his chair, held me in his arms, and declared, "Hey, it's not so bad. Anyway I didn't marry you to be my cook!" Was he in jest? No matter, it was so comforting.

I learned gradually by tasting, and never followed a recipe verbatim. When a dish didn't turn out so well, Thurman praised my effort, not the dish. When I apologized for a crummy meal, he would again say, "I told you I didn't marry you to be my cook!" That was a good thing. Eventually I learned to love cooking, and made things festive by adding a few flowers, candlelight, and music. I also knew not to panic when there was not enough time to both cook and clean house. When I had company, I put the cooking first, changed to low-wattage bulbs in the light fixtures, and filled the house with candlelight!

It was a very good thing that Thurman wasn't counting on me as his laundry woman, either. Bless the man's heart, he really didn't learn of my deception until after the fact. On this beautiful, warm, breezy, late summer afternoon I was on our porch reading, when the phone rang and I was excited to hear Thurman's voice, but not for long. "Honey, I just received orders to fly out in three and a half hours! I'll be gone for five days and I'm sure I don't have enough clean shirts to take." My mind began to whirl: *It's too late to go to the laundry!* His request followed: "Please, Hon, do up four of my dress shirts, and I like medium starched collars. You can go ahead and put them in my suitcase, because by the time I get home I'll have little time to get back to the Field to board my plane. I wish it were possible for you to go with me."

I hung up that phone thinking: *I wish it were possible for me to go* ***anywhere*** *right now!* I'm not proud of the fact, but I'd never ironed anything, much less laundered by hand a shirt. And starch? Well, how does one go about making starch? And what does he mean, *medium starch*? I rushed into the bathroom, opened the new white wicker dirty-clothes hamper and found the shirts. I looked at them, panicked, smelled them. Then I began to feel hopeful. They actually smelled clean, even fresh, I was convinced. It must've been his good-smelling deodorant. *Okay, I got this thing whipped!* I drug out the ironing board and filled a pan with cool water. I laid the shirt on the ironing board, and went to work. I wiped down the shirt with my damp rag, going over the underarms and sleeves twice. I gave these shirts a complete sponge bath, using a facecloth and cold water. They looked and smelled fresh, so now for the ironing! My husband had asked that I fold and pack them in the suitcase, as he would be in a mad rush on his way to the Field. Well, I declare, they looked like they had just come from the dry cleaner's!

As Thurman packed the remaining articles he glanced at my handiwork and praised me for doing a great job. *Should I confess?* I decided that now was not the time. Honestly, I did, much later. Thurman's laughter then was loud and long, while I begged him not to tell this story. "Please, especially not to your family!" I knew how well he would enjoy telling this one to anybody who would listen, and laugh with them over and over. What could I do then, but join in their laughter while I was dying of humiliation?

Unlike my learning to cook, I never mastered the art of being an outstanding laundress. This turned out in my favor because my husband decided it would be to his advantage, for the rest of his life, to just drop his shirts at the laundry! He said he loved me anyway; my cup runneth over.

"Every day is an opportunity to make a happy ending."

—Mary Williams

Life in Hampton—Langley Field, Virginia

There were several occasions like the one that occasioned my starched-shirt panic, when Thurman would have to leave for a few days. The Prices were forever there for me and counted it their pleasure, taking me under their wings when he was gone, but I missed him so much! I would have loved it, could it have been possible at these times, to be with Mother and Daddy. Even though I was happy, there were the times I felt lonely. I missed my girlfriends. I longed at times to know some girls near my age, which would've been possible if we had lived on base at Langley Field, where there was socializing among the wives. I knew a few girls at church, but unfortunately they lived miles from me and none of us having a car, we were limited to a "Hello, how are you?" at church on Sunday morning. Men don't long for these relationships, I'm convinced.

While walking on the beach one day, I asked a young woman if I could walk with her. She agreed and I hurried along to catch up to her. She was the wife of a captain in the Army Air Force, stationed at Langley Field, so we had something in common. They too chose to live in Hampton rather than on base. We had lunch together a few times which was very nice. Soon I met another Army wife who was excactly my age and simply adorable. Her husband was a sergeant, I learned.

When I planned the three of us would get together with our husbands, I was informed, "Officers in the Army Air Force do not fraternize with non-officers nor do their wives." How ridiculous! I wanted to verify this as quickly as possible and found—it was true! I did not give up my newest friend. The sergeant's wife and I continued getting together and the captain's wife refused our invitations. Well, the two of us looked at each other, laughed and enjoyed each other's company until her husband was relocated. Of course, I realized the captain's wife was following orders, which was only proper.

By this time, Mr. Price asked if I would like to come with him to meet the staff who worked at the Draft Board where he was chairman. What he was really interested in, I'm sure, was if I wanted to have a job. *Well,* I thought, *Why not?* The interviewer from the government met with me. He asked at least one million questions, the answers to which he was jotting down on a one-million- page form. This was a nice, young man just doing his job. However, I don't think his superiors would have been pleased at what happened next.

He asked, "Can you type?" I was quick to answer, "No." The nice young man looked at me and said, "You understand there are two jobs available, that of file clerk and that of typist. What you don't understand is that a typist is paid considerably more than a file clerk. I'll bet you can type your name, right?" He then took me to a typewriter where I, with one finger, typed "M-a-r-y B-i-n-k-l-e-y W-i-l-l-i-a-m-s", even laughing while he observed. I remember distinctly saying, "I think you had better answer that one *NO*!" Much to my utter dismay I learned I now was a typist employed by the Federal Government at the Hampton Virginia Draft Board. *How could he?* But actually, I began working as a file clerk.

One of the women in the office had been listening the day of my interview. Fully aware of the situation, she opened fire! Mrs. Bovey insisted that if I was designated as a typist, just as she was, then certainly I should be helping her carry the load. BIG MISTAKE. She gave me my first job, which sounds easy enough for a novice or even a very young child who knew the alphabet. I was to fill in the government forms to be mailed, setting up the date and time for the recipients' physicals at the local doctor's office.

The forms were placed on my desk, which I then completed, placed in the envelopes, addressed and mailed. All seemed to have gone well. However, it was soon to be learned that on all the forms, in the space provided for the designated day and time for these draftees to meet their appointments for physicals at the doctor's office, I had inadvertently typed in PM rather than AM! Can you imagine the havoc it wrought when they all showed up at 8:00 PM?

The morning following that debacle, I walked into the Draft Board office, where I felt reduced to the rank of "Village Idiot." Naturally, Mr. Price had already been informed of his protégé's mistake. You can only imagine how I dreaded going home after my most humiliating day, continuing to hold back tears so as not to endure further humiliation. I stopped at the drug store for a Coke, fortifying myself for the encounter. I lingered as long as possible before catching the street car home. I comforted myself with the thought, "Well, I told that guy from the Federal Government I wasn't a typist!" When I found myself at the stop at the corner of our street, I reluctantly stepped off.

Mr. Price was already home, waiting for me. I drug myself up the steps, ready to step on the porch when the door flung open, and there he stood! What I didn't expect was that he stood there smiling, with a twinkle in his eye. After a big hug, he said, "Now don't you worry. Mistakes are made daily at that office and all's been taken care of." With that remark, my tears began to flow and in seconds I found myself joining him in his uncontrolled laughter. Hysteria? I think so.

By the time Thurman arrived from Langley Field, I fell in his arms laughing rather than crying. The atmosphere I had left at the Draft Board was quite a switch from that around our dinner table. We all found humor, rather than disgrace, in my predicament.

"Never let success go to your head,
and never let failure go to your heart.

—Unknown

The Smell of Coffee

On one occasion I wanted so much to go to the Officer's Dance at the beautiful Chamberlain Hotel, just across the Bay, and spoke of my longing to Mrs. Price. The next morning, on the seat of our car lay an envelope with my name on it. While I've forgotten the amount of money it held, I remember her note telling me to buy a formal gown at the exclusive dress shop in Richmond, because I was going to the dance! No doubt she had talked Thurman into taking me.

I had the most wonderful evening, meeting the wives and dancing the night away. During dinner, the smell of coffee bothered me and I felt slightly nauseous. The next morning, I experienced the same feeling, without a clue as to why. I thought that the Beech-Nut gum in my purse would help. It only caused me to feel more ill. After a few days of this, the light dawned in my nauseated brain. I spoke with Mrs. Price, explaining that I suspected I was pregnant.

She was absolutely ecstatic and from that moment on spoke of her "grandchild."! It seemed I was the Prices' only daughter, and Thurman was like a son. Mrs. Price could not do enough for me. She and Mr. Price hovered over me to such an extent that the only time I could get away and dream of my baby was when I took walks to the Bay. Most days I went twice!

Walking four miles a day and having a hearty appetite, I was the picture of good health. I had regular pre-natal care. At one appointment, my obstetrician called in part of the staff and said, "Mary, how did you get that tan?" I sunned every day possible until the birth at the end of April. The doctor warned me of gaining too much weight at every visit, but I just kept on eating until I resembled the fat lady at the fair, an allover gain of weight!

My reading material varied considerably as I began looking for books concerning babies and childcare. As the time grew close to having my baby I longed for my mother to be there and contribute her first-hand experience. We talked every day and as this was her first grandchild, she was too excited for words. All her family and friends, (my extended family), were overjoyed at the coming of my baby. Poor Mrs. Price was feeling a little left out. When I told of mother's impending visit, Mrs. Price insisted, "Tell your mother there's no need for her to make the trip, because I am here and can take care of everything!" Naturally, I never mentioned this to Mother. Thurman and I made the decision that we would wait and call Mother immediately after the baby was here. We also decided to not call Mrs. Price as she had many times asked us to do, but that just he and I would go it alone. All new mothers know the feeling of awe, disbelief, overwhelming excitement, thanksgiving and many more emotions experienced at this time.

When Charlie was born, we called Mother with the news. Can you believe I was in the base hospital for two weeks? My room filled with flowers from Nell Price and her friends. Then I brought this little one home. I called Mother, and she took the train to Virginia.

Meanwhile my Virginia mother, Nell Price, took over just as soon as we hit the front door, hovering over us like a mother bird. She couldn't wait to get her hands on my baby, and I truly was glad to have her taking such excellent care of us all: baby, Thurman and me! Mrs. Price cooked a delicious meal, had placed fresh flowers all over the house, and enjoyed to the fullest being a "grandmother" for the first time. In the middle of her rapid-fire greeting she glanced over at me, took a breath and interrupted her own monologue, saying, "Oh darling, I meant to tell you! The church is having a bazaar and so we need to get together all your darling little clothes to take. Heaven knows you'll never get in them again after having a baby—all you have to do is look at me!" With a flourish she gestured towards her once-upon-a-time-waistline.

Oh my soul, my heart went to my heels. *What is she saying? Of course I'll wear my clothes again!*

After finding my voice, I responded, "Let's wait till I talk to Mother. She and I will do this for you, but you know, I'd like to wait before I give up on being able to fit in my clothes again."

Days before the bazaar was held, I was wearing them. After starving myself and listening to my mother complain that I wasn't eating enough to keep a bird alive, they fit! Mother stayed with me three weeks and by that time I was enjoying wearing all that I'd brought in my lovely trousseau. I actually weighed one pound less than the day Thurman and I married. I waved goodbye to Mother at the train station while wearing one of my best outfits.

Before we left Virginia, Charlie became "Bugsie." When his two upper teeth came in slightly protruding, Thurman and I started calling him "Bugs Bunny." Later we shortened it to Bugsie. He was a beautiful baby growing to be a beautiful little boy. The entire family, and especially the childless Annie Gary, doted on my child.

Mr. Price did business with a gentleman, Manny Hettleman, from Baltimore, who owned a scrapyard there. He bought scrap metal from the shipyard where Mr. Price was employed, and the families were close. Thurman had been in Mr. Hettlelman's company several times before we married, even visiting him in Baltimore on several occasions. He enthusiastically told me about this Jewish family whom he found fascinating. Mr. Hettleman was a self-made man and had become quite wealthy. He talked with Thurman often about the possibility of his coming to Baltimore and working for him after the war. This scared me, because I knew I would be dying to get back home and be near family. When the time presented itself at the end of the war I found that Thurman, while very much interested, was as eager to return to Nashville as I was. We kept in touch with the Hettlemans for many years and were sad to later receive a letter from Sarah, Manny's wife, concerning Manny's fatal heart attack.

I visited Nashville as often as possible and while it was sad leaving the Prices and my first home with Thurman, I was very excited when we could return after the war.

The principal thing in this world is to keep one's soul aloft.

Gustave Flaubert

Homecoming

World War II was coming to a close. Thurman had his discharge papers in hand and we were heading home to Nashville, one mile at a time.

Thurman and I, along with our beautiful baby boy, were loading our maroon-colored 1942 Pontiac. Actually Bugsie was sitting in his stroller, jabbering, not being much help at eighteen months. We were experiencing a roller coaster ride of emotions. How many times down through the years I found reason to cry out of one eye and laugh out of the other. This time, because we were heading home, but also leaving our first home as newlyweds and the birthplace of our baby son.

Our much beloved adopted Virginia family, Nell and Claude Price, soon stepped across the street, Claude to help and Nell to cuddle "her" grandchild for the last time. The men were keeping up a good front, but Nell and I simply let it all go. When the time came for me to take Bugsie out of her arms, the show of love between us simply exploded. When Claude, who claimed me as his only daughter, hugged me with his head resting on top of my head, his tears were wetting my hair. Oh my soul, I was completely drained when I closed the door of the car to begin our long ride home.

Thurman drove, I beside him, my head turned backward to watch Bugsie, who was swaying gently in the hammock strung between the back doors. Though not as safe as the car-seats that would come later, it made a wonderfully comfortable ride for babies of that era. I felt a crick in my neck developing, so swung my long legs over the seat, over the hammock, landing on the back seat where I curled up and continued my watch. Thurman laughed and asked, "Why in the world didn't you ask me to stop the car, where you could have made that move a bit more ladylike?" As if anyone was there to care, but him. But then, that was my dignified husband. Such a gentleman!

Riding along through the beautiful Virginia landscape was breathtaking, no interstate then, mind you. My mind whirled at a future prospect: all of us beginning our civilian lives together, deciding where to live and whether Thurman would further his education or get a job. I was much in favor of school, however this had to be for him to figure out himself. But, the closer to Nashville we got, the lighter my heart became. After many miles, we turned the corner onto my street. I laughed and yelled, "Home Sweet Home!" While Thurman never laughed as loudly as I did, he was quietly laughing with me—or at me.

Late as it was, all the lights were shining, both inside and out, and Mother and Daddy were in the porch swing waiting. What a welcome! Mother grabbed Bugsie, Daddy grabbed me. I'm quite sure that Thurman didn't care at all, if nobody grabbed him; he was all too happy just to get out of the car. We started unloading, unbelievable all the stuff we had to find a place for in their house, not even including all left in the trunk 'til morning. Now as I reflect on this homecoming, I have to wonder, "Were these two gracious people as thrilled as I believed them to be?" If not, surely they never let on. Then, I was only mindful of how happy I was. Perhaps I'd not quite yet gotten over being their "little girl."

I promise: we did very soon begin looking for a house... well, probably not as enthusiastically as possible. Both Mother and Daddy insisted we take our own good time looking; we were welcome to stay as long as needed. It was such a special time enjoying the bonding of family, especially Bugsie with his grandparents. I was overjoyed seeing Daddy beginning to bond with Thurman. Daddy had desperately tried to convince Thurman to forget marriage until I was through school and the war was over. It hadn't worked, and I knew that was still in Daddy's mind.

Thurman very quickly found a job, or rather his older brother who was a banker located the job, even though Thurman had not given up the idea of furthering his education through the GI Bill or going to Nashville Law School at night. He received such discouragement from his brother, who was several years his senior, he abandoned the idea altogether. Daddy, on the other hand, was standing in the wings, hoping to see a different conclusion to Thurman's dilemma.

The days moved into months, so beautifully peaceful that before we knew it, we were celebrating Bugsie's second birthday, still no house, a fact with which everyone concerned seemed to be quite content. Daddy's voice still echoes in my ears, saying, "Sugar, don't fret. There's room and we love having you here." *Really?!? For sure?!?*

Not long after we settled in, high school friends began to call. These were close friends who had married their high school sweethearts, and were the same as we, rearing their families. Our relationships picked up where they'd left off before the war. All of us had help on Fridays, so we could have "Girls Day Out." We'd meet at Cross Keys on Sixth Avenue for lunch. If the money held out, it was on to Candyland on Church Street for dessert. My mother was teaching and unable to help out during the day. So Aline Tomlinson, my new friend and help, entered the scene—she sat at the big round table in Mother's kitchen, getting to know Bugsie and me. I liked her immediately, and knew we would be good friends. I didn't like being called "Miss Mary" or "Mrs. Williams" by her, so I asked her to call me what all my friends called me, just "Mary." I loved that she agreed without any argument.

Aline never ever disappointed me in any way, except when it couldn't be avoided. On the very few occasions when she called saying she was under the weather, I was immediately so very sorry she was not feeling well, even though distraught that I would be at home all day while the others were out on the town having a jolly good time. It's a known fact in my family that we all felt exactly the same way about her. Bugsie loved Aline. She loved him, and I loved the fact that I could leave my child in the hands of this good woman, who took perfect care of him.

It was April, Bugsie's third birthday. He grew by leaps and bounds, but his brain seemed to develop at an even greater rate. It had to be all the attention from Mother and Daddy, with their passion for teaching. Even as a very young girl, I had dreamed of marriage, a home…a cottage with a white picket fence, and five babies, yes, five. So far I had the marriage and one baby!

We were pregnant.

"Honey, you do know with the baby on the way, we really do have to diligently work toward finding a house."

But Mother and Daddy kept singing that same old song, "Stay a little while longer!" They reasoned with us, "Stay until after the baby is born. You can keep saving toward that down payment on the house." Our own home eluded me again.

As with the first pregnancy, I flew through nine months without problems, gained lots of weight, ate lots of chocolate. I walked every day with Bugsie riding his tricycle in front. When I felt the need for longer strides, I'd push him in his old stroller, which he thought was really funny: a big boy like him, riding in a baby stroller. We both enjoyed those jaunts. I sensed Aline was just as excited as the rest of us about the new baby on its way! And then, there he was!

Mike was as dear to us as his big brother, almost four years older. Mother and Thurman arrived at the hospital to bring us home. Aline and Bugsie, at home, were anxiously awaiting our arrival. Mother had brought with her a beautiful baby boy's day gown, sewn by a seamstress who specialized in babies' clothing. I loved watching her dress him, talking baby talk superbly to him all the while. When he was dressed in his finest, it was time to go home.

As Thurman parked the car in front of the house, Bugsie and Aline came running out the door, down the steps, out to the car to get their first view. I'm not sure who was the most excited, Aline or Bugsie! She carried Mike in, but first she gave Bugsie a vase of flowers to carry, always so mindful of Bugsie in any situation and more so now that he was no longer the only child. She was intent on assuring Bugsie that "big brother" was the most important person in this baby's family. It's unclear in my mind how long Aline stayed to help me with the baby, but I know it was several days. The basinet stood on the hearth in our bedroom. Aline gave Mike his first bath.

When I say "our" bedroom, this was Mother and Daddy's room, the largest by far in the house. Mother turned it over the night we moved in, so we would be comfortable with the little room (the nursery) and the bathroom close by. They moved their things upstairs to the room I'd had before I married. As I'm reliving those bygone days, I keep wondering: *Surely these two selfless people are counting the days until they would hear we've found a house.* If this were true, again, they never let on. Really now, how could they have not?

Finally, we moved.

"Music in the soul can be heard by the universe."

Lao Tzu

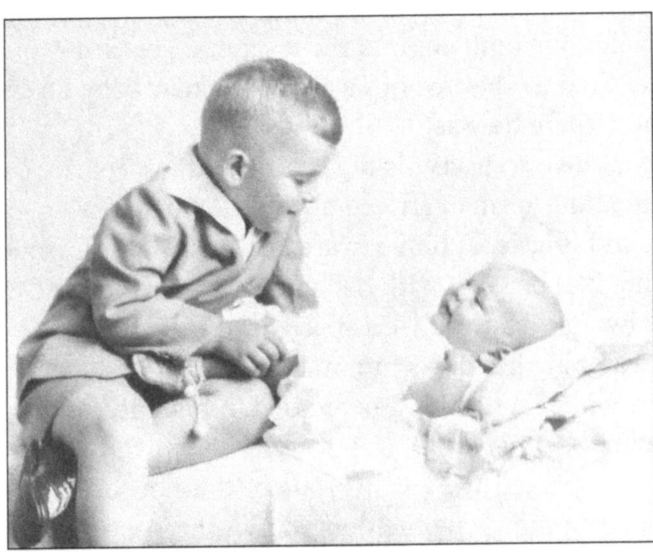

Charlie and Mike

New Neighbors, Old Friends

Our first home was in a little neighborhood where in every house lived young families just like us, which was a lot of fun. The houses were modest, putting it mildly, but adequate. Every house on Huffine Street, it seemed, had a fenced-in yard, and every neighboring family seemed to own a puppy and have little children.

Aline Tomlinson moved right along with us, continuing to come every Friday, as well as times in between when needed. She was indeed my loyal friend. Bless Aline's heart, she could never get over the pile of un-ironed clothes that were packed to the ceiling in a little closet, which served no other purpose. I'm not to this day sure how this could happen when I myself ironed every day! I was pretty persnickety about how my children looked when in school or in public on any occasion. They may have had the freedom to wallow in the dirt or mud when playing at home, but my expectations were high when they left the backyard and playtime. It was true, however, as Aline always said, "I don't care how hard I try, I can't get ahead of this pile of un-ironed clothes." She knew for sure that I did not expect that she would or ever could. We were always of the same mind: the children's care came first.

The ironing could wait.

One of my most endearing memories of my friend has to be the times when I would come in from my Day Out with the Girls, expecting Aline to be ready to step out the door to walk the half block to the bus stop. The time it took for my bus to reach the end of the line and return, allowed enough time for Aline to gather her things together and walk the half block. She could get on the same bus I had gotten off. On more than one occasion, I found her in the kitchen ironing the white, collared Eton shirts to be worn on Sunday with their navy, short-pant Eton suits. She would say, "I'll catch the next bus, 'cause I'm afraid you will never get them ironed in time for church." She wanted them to look their best every bit as much as I did, you see. That wasn't difficult. Both the boys had outstanding blue eyes, a gift from their granddaddy and daddy both. I always loved the sun and so these two joined me in a dark tan. With their blue eyes and blonde hair, they were crowd stoppers!

Our little neighborhood with the house, minus the picket fence, proved to be a really fun place to be with my boys. Several boy playmates lived close by, whose parents Thurman and I enjoyed. So there were cookouts whenever the weather cooperated (even during mid-winter). We all brought our own steaks, and the hostess would provide salad and twice-baked potatoes. According to how the hostess's day went, it could be just a once-baked potato! Every house had a swing set, and one, a tree house. The boys played while the parents enjoyed each other's company. A few fights cropped up occasionally among the boys, but we soon always managed to agree on a manner to settle them. Our second-door family had lovely parents and three mostly well-behaved boys. On one occasion the oldest boy became angry at Bugsie and hit him in the face with a metal truck. That was the first incident of any consequence, and I didn't handle it "cool, calm, and collected"! The darling mother was so apologetic—crying and reprimanding her son to such an extent that I pulled in my horns and got over it, almost. Although the scar on Charlie's face never faded completely, it was a good lesson on forgiveness for all of us. The child's mother was so upset when she saw the wound that it took some persuading on my part to help her forgive. I don't think I was 100% successful, to tell the truth.

I was conscious that: *Life is good. God is good. I'm in love with a good man. I adore my boys. But something's missing.* Not to worry—we were pregnant again! Would we round off the family with a girl, the baby girl I'd always dreamed about? For the life of me, I can't remember why Aline wouldn't be with us for this event, but I keenly remember my devastation at the news.

Third pregnancy, and except for the heat, I had smooth sailing for nine months. I was ecstatic when I brought Marilyn, my baby girl, home to Bugsie and Mike.

Unfortunately, however, I wasn't happy with the person I employed to take Aline's place. Mother picked up on the fact that I was disgruntled and said, "Just let her go and I'll take over." The boys thought that was the grandest idea, and it really was. Two adorable boys, eight and four, and now my precious girl— I knew the angels in heaven were smiling down on me saying, "Your prayers are answered." They then sent me another angel on earth, for Aline returned. She was thrilled over our baby girl, but I could see she was wondering how in the world she would add *baby dresses* to the ironing!

Our little house shrunk with our new family addition, so we were on the lookout for another house. Maybe a cottage with a white picket fence? The time spent in looking went much quicker than last time, and soon we were moving.

"I have found that if you love life, life will love you back."

—Arthur Rubinstein

Friendship and Care:
Ties that Bind

Marilyn W. Switzer
Blog, March of 2012

Yesterday, my mother had a luncheon for her old friend, 98-year-old "Miss Aline" Tomlinson. Their friendship began as employer/employee. Miss Aline knew she was there to iron the clothes and watch over the children, and if she could not do both, watching over the children was the priority. One of those children was me, Marilyn. All those children who are still living are in this picture. The child Miss Aline remembers best is my brother Charlie, who died almost six years before this was taken. She called him Bugsie. It was his family nickname.

Although Aline worked for my mother, it is not in my mother's nature to be a hard task master, she could not consider herself above anyone else. Aline is not of the nature to consider herself beneath anyone else, so, a beautiful relationship ensued.

Despite the obvious differences, the sameness is the basis for the bond. We knew we were to obey Miss Aline as if her commands came directly from my parents. She often covered for my brother Mike when he, in his own words, would "act the fool." She was not so inclined with me and my infractions. I remember a day specifically when Miss Aline was keeping me, at our home on Moran Drive. I did not know where the boys were. Had they been home, I probably would have behaved a bit better for I knew they would go straight to my parents if I did something wrong.

My daddy thought I was perfect, so was highly unlikely to take seriously any negative reports from my brothers about my alleged bad behavior. But Mother was a bit more likely to give credence to their reports. Knowing how Miss Aline protected Mike from punishment for his shenanigans, I was out playing with the hose pipe. Yes, we called it a hose pipe. It was a hot summer day and the windows were open, allowing every little passing breeze to blow through the screens, giving a bit of relief to those inside.

That day, Miss Aline set her ironing aside and opened the window to tell me it was time to turn the water off and come in. Well, I took a notion. I guess I thought Miss Aline needed cooling off. I do know I was not ready to come in, so I turned the water on full blast, pointed the hose at Miss Aline behind the screen door and sprayed her for all I was worth! I'm really not sure why I did such a thing. Had I any sense about me, I would have said, "The devil made me do it." After soaking Miss Aline, everything in the room, and causing her to put the ironing away, 'cause she had to clean up the mess I made, I was still quite confident she would not tell on me. I was living under a terrible misconception. Miss Aline ratted me out.

When Mother asked Miss Aline, "Did you have a good day?" Aline chose not to shield me from my misbehavior. She told my mom, and then my mom told me that she was really disappointed with me, and she would have to discuss with my daddy how to handle my misbehavior. Man, I thought I was golden. Discuss it with my daddy, who thinks I'm perfect...I had it made. Not so.

Picture this: my stinky old brothers, my loving daddy, my mother and me, who had this little secret we would be keeping. Imagine my surprise: when asked how her day had been my mother launched into a detailed description of my rebellion and defiance! My brothers were having the time of their lives. Daddy was furious. He marched me from the table to the snickers of my brothers, marched me to another room, spanked my bottom, and made me go back to the table. I thought my mortification complete. It was not. At the end of the meal, my mother brought out a beautiful porcelain plate and cup with Bambi hand-painted on them, which she had bought that day. She was probably paying for it with money she had not really had at the very moment I was spraying Miss Aline. "I bought them for you, because you are my precious, good, little girl," she shared. The welling tears of remorse flowed. I suffered every emotion possible from that little prank.

At the luncheon Mother gave for Aline, her niece Joanne came from her home in Dallas to be there. Joanne was eighty-two years old, spry and so full of personality. I just wanted to hug her, so I did! Also, there were two ladies from Miss Aline's church—two ladies who have taken exquisite care of her. She has no blood family in Nashville, but she has her church family. Her pastor, Reverend Harris, dropped by with two other men from his church. One of those was the brother of Edith, who takes such good care of Miss Aline. He himself admitted he is a bit of a backslider, but no one seemed to care, least of all the

Standing: Marilyn, Mary, Doree, Mike
Seated: Sam, Aline Tomlinson at age 98
Armistead Place, 2012

Reverend Harris, with whom he arrived. I loved watching the love between all of these people, related by the blood of Jesus. I also loved the way they called each other brother and sister, like we used to years ago.

There was a period of time when Miss Aline and my mother lost touch with one another. When my brother died, they somehow reconnected. The friendship flourishes once again. When Miss Aline had to be moved to a nursing home, my mother became her "help." She makes sure someone visits, her clothes are clean, possessions are not stolen, the special treats are bought, the holidays are remembered. She makes sure that needs are met. Mother reminds Miss Aline that she can not be fussing at the helpers or residents where she lives. Miss Aline needs a little help with that stuff.

I'm so grateful for family. It was lovely being at my mother's with my siblings on a Tuesday afternoon visiting an old friend. Several times, by several different people, the words were uttered: "God is good. Blest be the tie that binds."

Blessed are the happiness makers.
Blessed are they who know how to shine.

—Henry Ward Beecher

Oops—I'm Mortified!
Fall, 1947

Words can't express that thrill and excitement I felt when we bought our first home. Never mind it was a small little clapboard house with Williamsburg green shutters, very much like all the others on our street. To me it was my castle, my dream come true! Thurman talked his mom out of the lilac bush he loved in the yard at his home. This was not a small bush, rather a very large, old bush which had been moved from his grandparents' yard in the country. I had my doubts as to whether this beautiful bush would survive the move when Thurman planted it outside our bedroom window. Not only did it survive, but it grew like wild fire as though it was determined to erase my doubts and fulfill Thurman's desire to have it in his own first yard. The joy I found in cutting those lush full blossoms to bring into our home almost brings tears today. We put up window boxes and planted petunias in shades of pink and lavender.

I was beginning to inject my own personality into the look outside, so now I was ready to begin on the interior which was best described as "drab." So, my husband and I were off to the paint store where we were bordering on coming to blows over shades and colors of paint. I leaned toward "bright and colorful," a look that obviously went against every fiber of his being. Thurman stated, "I like the neutral shades like in mama's house."

Laughingly I suggested, "Well, what would you know? You're extremely colorblind, so I'll choose."

We brought our buckets of paint home, all off-white, but

arms loaded down with tubes of color to mix in with the white. Maybe we both won?! Thurman began painting first in our bedroom after I oversaw the mixing of paint to suit my taste, which turned out, quite by chance, a soft robin's egg blue. He commented, "Hey this is really pretty." At that moment I breathed a sigh of relief.

Watching my husband on the ladder, painting away, I thought, "This doesn't look too difficult. With two working we can go twice as fast." At this point the ladder was free because he was now painting the lower half of the wall using a pan-like thing to dip his brush in. Thurman didn't hesitate to point out the location of the second paintbrush. I grabbed the ladder and a half empty can of robin's egg blue paint, plus a smaller container to hold paint. Now I was all fixed to begin my very first painting adventure! I climbed close to the top rung of the ladder with a half empty can of paint at its foot, readily accessible. Then came a knock on the front door.

I suggested, "Thurman, go see who's at the door. I'm up the ladder." It was Ollie, Thurman's mom, a woman who was very neat and organized, and the woman I had grown to love because she was my husband's mother. She still inspired awe in me. Looking back, I wonder, *Did she think it odd that I wasn't dressed for the job I was doing, even to having on beautiful new shoes?* Hardly appropriate, to say the least. To this day, I don't know whether I was nervous, trying too hard to make a good impression, or what! But in order to appear gracious I decided I must come down off the ladder and welcome her with a hug. Bad mistake! Remember the half-full bucket of paint at the foot of the ladder? My foot went smack dab in the middle of the can, turning it over, of all things. What can I say? Certainly I was humiliated in front of my mother-in-law as I looked down at the hardwood floor now a beautiful robin's egg blue! Even worse, when I pulled my foot out of the paint can, it was dripping robin's egg blue paint. Daddy had bought me that expensive pair of Pennalgo shoes just a few days before. What a mess I'd made! As the whole episode turned out, Thurman and I both knew we weren't born to be painters. He helped me clean up the mess, uttering half under his breath, "I know why men who paint for a living drink. I may turn to it myself before this is through." (Daddy, after learning the fate of my beautiful new shoes he had purchased after hearing me mention a desire for these, immediately wrote a check for me to replace them!)

At this point Thurman and I agreed it would be wise to employ a professional painter. After contemplating the cost, however, we decided together to finish painting the rest of the house ourselves. Looking back—with all the woodwork painted white, living room and bedrooms finished in airy pastels—we were so proud. We then rewarded ourselves with dinner at the Hermitage Hotel!

The kitchen, pantry and breakfast nook were left for me to finish after I decided wallpaper would be charming in this area. My husband turned it over to me! After wrapping myself in wallpaper a few times and cutting the paper too short many times, I was determined to finish. Do you know, the room came alive and was indeed charming?

Down through the years of our lives together this story, among many, afforded us laughter, mostly at my expense, not his!

Whether you think you can or whether you think you can't, you're right.

--Henry Ford

The Adoring Dora Binkley, Grandmother

When Charlie and Mike were little, my mother was teaching at Jere Baxter School (a favorite among neighborhood schools at that time). On Friday afternoon Mother, who was "Mae" to my little ones and "Dotey" to Joe's, would come by and get my boys for overnight visits. It became the Friday night ritual. Thurman and I would have Friday nights to go out on the town with friends—whether we could afford it or not.

Joe had two children. Bink and Lou were very near the ages of my boys. On Saturday Mother would have Joe's children come over and spend the day together with my boys. They can tell you stories about how they played outside, bringing furniture outdoors as backdrop for their plays. Mother didn't care! She was so wonderful with children.

Then Joe's children would go home, because they were going to their own church the next morning. Mother would keep my children again Saturday night. She would take them to Chapel Avenue Church of Christ. Thurman was Methodist and couldn't bring himself to go there. But I would take the bus and go to church, joining Mother. She would have Charlie and Mike dressed in their Sunday clothes. At lunchtime, Thurman would arrive and we'd all have Sunday dinner at Mother's.

How could she do that? I had weekends off! She invited the children, so she must have really enjoyed it, but I do wonder. The only explanation is *she had to love it*. Mother used to say, "The bad thing about my keeping my grandchildren is that they have to go home, and then I'm so sad." Is that not something?

This gracious mother and grandmother always went the extra mile to bring joy into her own life as well as into the lives of those who were blessed by being a part of hers. Reflecting on Dora Binkley, my mother, I can quote:

"The difference between ordinary and extraordinary is that little extra."

—Jimmy Johnson

James Smartt

What a darling man! After Thurman and I came home at the end of WWII and lived with Mother and Daddy a couple of years, we moved into the little house in Inglewood. Charlie was five and Mike was one. We had great neighbors and those were happy years.

Two blocks away on the corner stood the greatest grocery store in town, east or west of the river. This was where I met James, son of the owner, Mrs. Smartt. The butcher was Mr. Akin and the three of them ran the market. James was the buyer and did he ever know how! The produce he selected was superior to that of all the big stores. The meat was the freshest and of the very highest quality. So widespread was the reputation of Smartt's Grocery that people came from miles to trade there. Nothing was packaged in advance. The meat was cut in front of his customers and to their distinct specifications. The store carried the best labels of canned goods.

I was forever spoiled. I've never since enjoyed grocery shopping as much. The store went out of business a good many years later, and for sure I've never grilled a filet mignon that was in the class with the ones James cut for me. There was another reason for customers gravitating to Smartt's Grocery: the man.

James Smartt greeted each customer with a smile and treated everyone alike while serving them. The windows were sparkling, along with the floors, and it truly became a special place for me. I was probably his most frequent customer because on a whim I could cross the yards to the back of his store and arrive in just a few minutes.

I could have been the advertisement for the Goo Goo Cluster Candy back then, which was the product of the Standard Candy Company downtown. It was founded by a Nashville family and at the time sold only in Nashville and surrounding towns. For the life of me, I don't know why I didn't buy several Goo Goos at a time! After putting the children down in the afternoons and asking my neighbor to watch them, I'd slip across the yards and buy one Goo Goo, to enjoy a cup of coffee and my Goo Goo all by myself. The boys didn't like them because they had peanuts in them, and besides, I didn't want them to eat candy every day. James found it amusing and Thurman found it outlandish! It's a wonder I didn't put on some pounds. However, even if I had, it wouldn't have made any difference. I loved my Goo Goo!

The boys enjoyed trading with James and often took their nickel or even a dime to do their shopping. I'm sure James made them feel like one of his special customers. Thurman became one of James' friends as well because he stopped in frequently when I'd forgotten something I needed, more times than I like to care to remember. But I learned later that they both enjoyed good laughs when discussing my buying habits and how much I bought. Thurman assured him we didn't eat it all. It was the friends and family I entertained.

One day I had a list a mile long and James was helping me find some things, as I was in a hurry. Several friends were in the store and it seemed to be more confusing than usual. I had two basketfuls that James carried out to the car. Sometime later that day I opened my checkbook and saw the check I'd written, for well over a hundred dollars. It had not been torn out! I called him and I'm sure he wondered why. I said, "James, thank you for that great amount of groceries you showered on me, I'm so grateful." There was a long pause. Finally, I said, "James, I didn't pay you for all those groceries you took out to the car."

He said, "Mary, when you come in the store we all get confused." I know he meant this statement in the kindest way, because just a short time ago he was bedridden when I was visiting him. We got a good laugh sharing these memories.

Later, we became neighbors when James, his beautiful wife and their two children moved a block up our street. Josephine and I became good friends, and their son Jimmy and my son Mike became great buddies. One day, Josephine drove Jimmy and Mike to get their physicals for junior high football. When they came out of the building, the boys were reeling with laughter. Jimmy's explanation was, "Mike simply couldn't urinate in his little vial, so I just poured some of mine in it."

Losing James was difficult for all who loved him, and there were many. Josephine and I are still close and see each other often. My good friends of many years are valued beyond any words to express.

Time spent laughing is time spent with the Gods.

—Japanese Proverb

The Mosby Family

I dearly love the nostalgic feel of summer in the South. But this summer of 2010, the heat is over the top! Still, I can't imagine why we could complain in this era of air conditioning. Looking back, it was 107 degrees in 1952, July 5th, the Saturday Marilyn, my third child, was born. There was no air conditioning, not even at the hospital! I chuckle to myself as we all complain about the heat, knowing full well that the complainers will be soon voicing a different tune: "It's just too darn cold." The older I get, the more I realize: *Why spend time complaining about something we have no control over?* Besides, the Good Lord knows what He's doing and probably is a little weary of us all. Just as he became weary of the Israelites on their march to the Promised Land. Their murmuring and complaining caused us to find them a bit disgusting, yet we sound equally ungrateful on many occasions.

In June I lost two friends very dear to me, Alice Mosby and James Smartt. Let me tell you about my beautiful Alice. She was a godly woman who later in life I found to be quite as wise as my mother, whom I thought to be the wisest person I ever knew. Alice was buried last week on her 100th birthday after living a long and fruitful life.

How I cherished the time we spent together, first in her home in East Nashville, then in her son Ronnie's home in Franklin. When I first knew Alice, she and her husband Frank often visited his parents, the Mosbys, who were our next door neighbors on Russell Street. They lived on the right side of us, as one faced our house; the Davis Family lived on the left. After Mr. Mosby died, Frank and Alice and their two beautiful children, Mary Frank and Ronnie, moved next door to my family in the old Mosby home. I never knew Alice was truly not happy with this move until she was older.

Frank and I had a special bond. As a young girl I would slip through the hedge dividing our property and join him on the Mosbys' porch swing. This usually occurred when Alice was doing dishes, after suppertime. Mary Frank was a precious child who would join us, sitting on her daddy's lap.

Alice and I connected after Thurman died. Our many visits revealed news about ourselves that we both found fascinating. How I loved hearing Alice reminisce about my family! She loved my mother dearly. I learned Alice had often sought Mother's advice on things important to her. Alice shared many cute stories from memories of watching Joe and me playing outside her window when we were children. She was right on target when she remarked, "Mary, you did everything Joe told you to do, didn't you?" After asking her, "Why do you think that?" she told me her story.

"One very cold snowy day we were visiting Frank's parents and I was sitting looking out the window. You and Joe were out playing, and I watched you wring your hands, stomping your feet, trying to get warm, I'm sure. You walked off a few feet I could see, to run home. I could see Joe's face and it was obvious Joe wanted you to stay and play. This happened several times and you kept returning, to make him happy, I would guess."

Alice was so correct. No wonder Mother nicknamed me "Pollyanna" for I tried to please and make happy the world. We all enjoyed the classic children's book by Eleanor Porter that inspired my nickname.

Alice also recalled the mornings she watched Joe and me walking to school holding hands. We weren't always so lovey-dovey when we were older. However, he was my hero growing up. As punishment for endless bickering when we were around eight or ten years old, we had to put our arms around each other for five minutes. How cruel was that? I'd rather have a spanking!

Later, Alice met all my boyfriends as they came and went, and critiqued them as well. When she met Thurman she declared, "He is the best yet!"

When Thurman and I came back to Nashville at the end of the war, we were graciously asked by Mother and Daddy to live with them in my childhood home. They seemed to love having us there and they got to spoil their beautiful grandchild. Thurman and I evidently enjoyed being there as we stayed until after Mike was born. Thurman and Frank Mosby had become friends even before we married and moved to Virginia. During this time, living next door, they built a close relationship.

I loved kidding Thurman and Frank about playing croquet at Centennial Park. Wasn't that an older person's pastime? But I was set straight on this subject, finding it to be a much more professional approach. The croquet grounds at Centennial Park were covered and beautifully manicured. The state tournaments were held there. They were quite exciting!

Frank and Alice's daughter, Mary Frank, was seventeen and looking forward to graduation from East High School, enjoying her days of being the senior who was voted "Most Popular in the Class" and Homecoming Queen. Frank and Thurman were playing croquet when Frank got word to go to the hospital—Mary Frank had suffered a fall horseback riding in Percy Warner Park. The two of them rushed there together. When I received a call from Thurman, he was pleased to pass on the good news that the doctor was reassuring concerning her recovery. Never will I forget the second call, listening to a voice I hardly recognized say, "Mary Frank died just moments ago."

I wanted desperately to find my voice and ask, "What in the name of God went wrong?" But the words were caught deep in my throat. I was in such pain that I simply laid the phone down and sat till Thurman walked through the doors.

How many times in our lifetime together did I fall in his arms, staying there until my sobs were quieted and I could finally remove myself from his warm embrace? Toward the end of his illness, he had become so weak I recalled the emptiness I felt when I could no longer expect to be consoled by him, at a time I needed it most. I was losing him. A few weeks before he died I so longed to be in church Sunday mornings that I asked a family member to come occasionally. As I drove there, thoughts of life without him overtook me, and I wanted to scream. On entering church, I still have an image of a friendly, broad-shouldered man putting his arm around me and asking, "Is there anything I can do to help you?"

"Lend me your shoulder when I need it, if you will."

When the time came for Thurman to leave us, I drew my strength from the word of God and found my peace. In the hard times even today, I long to fall in my husband's arms and stay there until my sobbing ceases.

Mary Frank's funeral was held in the auditorium of East High School. Every seat was filled by all who knew and loved her. Her death was so unnecessary. While Mary Frank was still unconscious from the fall, the attending nurse turned her on her back and left the room. She strangled. Her death was so difficult for me to grasp. So young, so beautiful.

After the funeral Alice fell into my arms, distraught. Except for my brother Anderson's death when I was five years old, I was untouched by tragedy. I had no words to console her. When Frank sought me out as I was leaving, I was still at a loss for words, feeling guilty when nothing came out of my mouth.

❦

There came a time after Thurman and I found a house, leaving the old neighborhood, getting on with our busy lives. The time came when the Mosbys moved out as well. Even though the love was strong as ever, we were caught up in our own lives and drifted apart. Frank Mosby passed away, leaving Alice with her one child, Ronnie. I remember him well, delivering his newspapers by bicycle. While Mary Frank had looked so much like her father with dark hair and brown eyes, Ronnie inherited his mother's beauty—blonde with exceptionally beautiful, light blue eyes.

It was at Thurman's funeral when I found myself gazing into such eyes, wondering where I had seen them before. Then I saw the older woman with the young man. I was so glad to see Alice and Ronnie again! Our friendship took up right where it had left off, which left us several years to enjoy the special relationship of old neighbors of years gone by. Alice remained active into old age, tending her flowers, enjoying Bible studies, her friends and family.

I am so thankful for this good Christian lady being a part of my life once again. Our visits took place at her home in East Nashville, and then in Franklin, where she moved at the end of her life, to the home of Ronnie and his wife. There, Ronnie built Alice her own addition, with a view of beautiful flower gardens. She deserved the love and attention she received until her death, on her hundredth birthday.

And he answered, "You shall love the Lord your God with all your heart and with all your soul and with all your strength and with all your mind, and your neighbor as yourself.

Luke 10:27

Thurman and the Girls

My days were happy with the man I loved, our two cherished boys and our precious baby girl. Our family was complete. Marilyn was the apple of her daddy's eye and she played it for all it was worth. The boys were great with her, but certainly she got away with everything when her daddy was around. Marilyn was a precious child, sweet and cooperative. I loved dressing her in the prettiest little girl clothes. She experimented and found that a little whining got her everything with her daddy, and so she became a big whiner around him. I always thought it odd that he never caught on or found the whining annoying. She clung to him like glue.

I recall an incident that was typical of many others. In our first home we had a floor gas heater. Marilyn walked across the hot grill barefoot, leaving the pattern burned on the bottoms of her little feet. Of course, I was killed with her pain, and cried while calling Doctor Overall.

I got the new medication that he prescribed and sat and rocked my baby in my arms all day. With each breath she moaned, "I want my daddy." In between the moans she would muster the strength to even scream, "I WANT MY DADDY!" Lord knows, I was getting unnerved. I called Thurman and told him, "You have to come home right now." I held the phone where he could hear the pitiful sounds. Of course, he rushed home. His baby girl needed him!

Marilyn's last moan was when we were sitting in a rocking chair in front of the door, waiting. When she saw him it was like a faucet being turned off. With arms held out toward him for him to take her, she was giggling and her pain was magically dropped. Even the print on her feet faded and I think her daddy did wonder what the emergency was! Marilyn had a wonderful disposition and as she grew up I know her relationship with her Daddy never changed. He was always in her corner!

Knowing how men are with their girls certainly came true with him. He once said, "If we have five children, I hope they're all boys." That was before Charlie was born. I think that back then he was afraid of girls, why I can't say! I never asked. The boys and I stood by watching their Daddy letting the girls wrap him around their fingers. Actually, we openly laughed at them! This "man's man," who early on felt he wouldn't know how to deal with having daughters, surely learned his way.

The relationship between Marilyn and her Daddy was repeated fifteen years later with Doree Ann. He delighted in having this beautiful little girl, whom he thought might be mistaken for his granddaughter, charm him beyond what he expected. Doree was a daddy's girl while staying attached to me, as well.

I watched him react when she began bringing the many injured creatures home to be cared for. His generous offer was to allow her the freedom to take the dogs and cats to our veterinarian immediately for instant medical care. If being spayed or neutered was needed, that too was covered, including a trip to the dog groomer. Guess you know who was left at home to care for these animals and eventually find them good homes! It was worth it all to both of us to see her eyes light up when it all ended favorably. If the outcome was ever unfavorable, Thurman always consoled Doree in his special paternal way, bringing her acceptance and comfort. I never loved that man more than while watching him display his love for his children.

Zip-a-dee-doo-dah, zip-a-dee-day,
my oh my, what a wonderful day!

—Uncle Remus, created by Joel Chandler Harris

Resurrection

Awakening very early in anticipation of the full day, as is my custom, I lingered longer than usual. Thanking God for, among my many blessings, the ultimate blessing, that of Jesus' resurrection, giving us all hope of life after death. I'm looking forward to getting to my church, Otter Creek, listening to the heavenly voices of the *a cappella* chorus on stage as well as the congregational voices, quite as lovely, lifted in praise to our Holy Father. This Easter, 2012, I am settled in my pew listening, as well as joining in at the appropriate times to the "Hallelujah Chorus." The stage is banked with an abundance of beautiful Easter lilies and I feel my eyes filling with tears just as they have for well over fifty years on Easter mornings, when my mind reverts to a poignant, precious memory tucked away in my heart.

It was Easter morning and my little house on Moran Drive was full of activity with the five of us, Thurman, Charlie, Mike, Mell (Marilyn's nickname), and me making preparation for getting to church on time just as we were in the habit of doing every Sunday. However, because there would be many more visitors than usual on Easter, we had to get there early in order to get a good seat. Everybody was dressing except for me. I started breakfast, ham and biscuit, scrambled eggs and fresh fruit, along with milk and a hot pot of coffee with Hot Cross Buns, always a must at Easter then.

All of a sudden, I saw the boys rushing out the back door, jumping in the car, tires screeching. *Oh, for heaven's sake,* I thought, *What in the world do they think they are doing? Breakfast is almost ready and they're not here?!* I'm sure I was probably a bit disgruntled. The children had already opened their Easter gifts which I loved to shop for in anticipation of seeing their pleasure while opening them. I am very sure among them there was one for me, *always* from my thoughtful Marilyn.

I can read the boys' minds now: *Whoops, we didn't get Mama anything!* As if I would have been upset! I'm sure they were discussing where they might very quickly find something suitable for me as they headed out Gallatin Pike in the direction of Spring Hill Cemetery. I'll never know which one spotted the Easter lilies on the side of the road and decided this would be a quick transaction and just the perfect gift for Mama. When they rushed in the back door, faces beaming, I thanked them profusely and placed the pot of lilies in the middle of the kitchen table, so we could all enjoy our beautiful centerpiece. I of course recognized the fact that this was not a living lily, rather an artificial one designed for sale to people visiting the cemetery on Easter morning—where a sunrise service was being held.

My well-intentioned, unthinking husband leaned over, touching the flower and proclaiming in front of God and everybody, "I don't think this is real." What?!!?? Actually, it was said as though certainly this was inferior to "live." In a flash I grabbed my lily off the table, caressed it, and hugged the boys.

"How wonderful!! This special lily will be enjoyed time and time again on Easter morning in its place in the middle of our breakfast table. I'm so thrilled I won't have to pitch it in a few days because it died! Thank you so much for being so thoughtful, you two. I do love you for it." Of course, their daddy chimed in, praising them as well, so it all ended on a happy note.

I can see that pot of fake cemetery lilies as though it were right in front of me as I write, sitting here at the dining room table fifty-two years later. After having brought it down from the attic on Easter morning for several years, it was slated to find its permanent home in the attic among all my many treasures, too precious to discard. These tangible memories had to finally go when the attic was cleaned out before our move across town. However, until I close my eyes in death, my memories will always be "alive" and so will my resurrected Easter Lily. Thank you, Charlie and Mike! Thank You, God, for their lives and all the joy, love and excitement they brought to my life!

True wisdom lies in gathering the precious things out of each day, tucking them away in our hearts.

—Unknown

Maxine

Maxine and I were going to the same church, Riverwood Church of Christ. We were young mothers rearing our children, although mine were several years older than her two. Karen was four and Lisa two, little girls always "dressed to the nines." I sat in my pew for several Sundays admiring the family—not only Maxine and the girls, but the daddy as well, who was always "Buddy" Bivins to me, although most people called him George. I thought: *I must get to know this cute family.* I can't tell you why I didn't move faster to introduce my family. Our three children, Charlie, Mike, and Marilyn, were probably fourteen, ten and six. Then, of course, there was my good husband, Thurman. This was around 1958, over fifty years ago! It turned out to be a really lucky day when the spirit moved Maxine first, prompting her to ask, "Could you come over to our home for lemonade this afternoon?" I reflected on that day down through the years, watching and loving that same personality portrayed, as she reached out to people in any and every way imaginable.

Maxine is an only child. Her mom told me that when Maxine was a little girl she wanted playmates so badly that she would give them any of her toys to have them stay longer when they were visiting her. Don't misunderstand me. These days Maxine doesn't have to bribe her friends to have them stay longer. It's simply her love, warm hospitality, the good food she serves, and last but not least, the infectious giggle that keeps us coming! While sharing in the above, plus enjoying her condos in San Destin and Sarasota, Paulette, Irene, Bernie,

Maxine, and I were dubbed "The Ya-Ya Sisters" by Paulette, after the popular 1996 novel by Rebecca Wells. I suggested that we prick the palms of our hands and mingle our blood, like the characters in the movie, to be initiated into the sisterhood. My suggestion went unsupported. We consider ourselves lucky to be Ya-Yas just the same.

You must understand long before this melding of friends took place, Maxine and I declared each other "sisters" because neither of us have an "honest-to-goodness sister." Our secrets are kept; our tears are shed. Our laughter can actually burst out over something so silly, we can wonder ourselves about it. We engage in both frivolous and serious conversation with understanding.

Buddy and Thurman became close, and we enjoyed each other's children and being a part of their lives.

"Come over for supper."

"We'll grill out at one or the other's place."

"Let's spend the day together."

That meant going shopping or antiquing, going to the pool to swim, sunning on the patio, taking time to stop for a cup of coffee at each other's homes either in the morning or in the afternoon, making my famous cinnamon toast to go along with morning visits! We had dinner out on the town, celebrating birthdays together. We sat on Maxine's patio covered by the aluminum awning, listening to the rain, not wanting to leave although it was late. Thurman and Buddy counted heads at church, asking, "How many do we need this Sunday?"

Thurman was the only person I knew who called Maxine, "Max." I was mortified when the four of us were standing under a streetlight after Maxine had a few highlights added to her hair, when Thurman remarked, "Max, is your hair real?" I don't know what the answer would've been had the question been: "Max, is the color of your hair real?" I could have died, but my friend was cool, saying, "Of course my hair is real!" I don't think Thurman ever asked that question again in his lifetime after I explained later, "Don't you know better than to ask a woman such a question? You may as well have asked some woman if she's pregnant when she's not!" Bless that man's heart, he wasn't usually insensitive to what was proper!

In 1974, Maxine and Buddy moved all the way across town. And yes, of course, I was happy for them to move into a darling new house in a lovely part of the city, but how I was going to miss those impromptu visits! The new house was ready. The last day as Maxine was leaving our side of town, she called to make sure I wasn't at home before she left her house. Neither of us wanted the scene of a tearful departure. When I returned home, a package was on the step from my friend—a framed sentiment: "To a friend's house the way is never long." Even before I moved much closer to her many years later, the way was never long! We kept the fire of friendship burning and the road back-and-forth equally hot.

In 1980, I was recovering from rotator cuff surgery and had absolutely no use of my right arm. I was unable to drive. Maxine came to get me and drive me to our destination, a friend's house, for wine and snacks before going out to dinner. We drove up to the house. Maxine got out of the car, while I waited for her to come around to open the car door, because I sure couldn't! I watched Maxine leave the car and walk up the walkway to our friend's house, leaving me stranded. I thought, "Surely she'll miss me before she walks in the front door." Not true! She was enjoying her glass of wine with our friends when it dawned on her. She flew out the door and down the walk, mouthing her apologies and giggling at the same time. No harm done, it was just another funny story to share!

We spent beautiful spring and summer mornings together, either on her patio or mine, loaded down with anything and everything we knew would draw the sun to our skin and give us that wonderful healthy-looking bronze glow which was actually a status symbol back then.

Little did we know while we were working so hard to look drop-dead gorgeous, that one day we would both be paying for it in different ways. Maybe if all those brown spots the sun caused would run together, I would have that becoming suntan again. Today as Maxine is dealing with more serious effects from those days in the sun, she will remark, "It's all your fault you know. I would lie there on the patio, on the beach, or at the pool, watching you turn brown while I turned red. I stayed as long as you did in the hottest part of the day knowing the red would eventually fade and leave me a nice shade of tan." Oh, the havoc it played in the meantime! If we had only known! I don't think Maxine would say this, her condition being much more serious, but despite the ugliness it wrought, I wouldn't give up my days in the sun swimming, boating, or simply sitting absorbing the rays. Today when my girls and I go to the beach together you should see my beach attire—far from yesteryear! Of course, they are smart enough to protect their skin, hoping not to look like me, I would think.

My baby, Marilyn, was eleven years old when I shared my news of being pregnant, and Maxine cried. I'm sure she was thinking perhaps I would feel like crying. Nothing further from the truth! How we welcomed our new son, Sam! After the event, Maxine was our most frequent visitor and I would think the most thrilled, other than my mother. When I returned home from the hospital, Maxine came over carrying a gift for me, a really cute brown housecoat that looked more like a dress. So typical of Maxine, knowing my clothes weren't fitting all too well at that point and knowing I'd never be caught wearing a bathrobe. These garments were always depressing to me because of memories of seeing my mother, after Anderson's death, having one on all day for months. I've always associated sadness with bathrobes, no matter how colorful and cheerful the fabric. I loved that housecoat and the one thoughtful enough to select the perfect gift!

Maxine and Buddy enjoyed my children and were interested in what they were doing. We as mothers know how much this is appreciated. I have a cute memory of Maxine and her girls debating over who was going to hold Sam. I think Maxine would give my mother some competition in "who loves babies the most."

When we met in church, Maxine would snatch baby Sam away from me as soon as I was seated on our pew. One Sunday, unbeknownst to us, as we were passing my baby back and forth, a woman sitting behind us was thoroughly enjoying the scene. Now keep in mind, Maxine is only four years and a few months younger than I am, but she's cute and petite and I'm tall and rarely referred to as "cute." At the close of service, this nice, unsuspecting woman couldn't wait to get to us, remarking, "I so enjoyed watching Mother and Grandmother with this darling baby." It quickly dawned on me: *This silly woman thinks I'm Maxine's mother!* I must've sounded indignant when, in no uncertain terms, I let her know of her awful mistake. Marilyn was standing by watching it all and said, "That woman will never come back to this church again!" I have to think she was not planning to anyway. The two of us, along with Marilyn, laughed heartily afterward. I wonder if my heart was in the laughter, or if I faked it?!

Early in our friendship, Maxine and I found a common bond in so many facets of living, which is a strong force in keeping a friendship alive and well. Today, we're still sitting together in our pew many years later at a church far removed from the old church where we met all those years ago. Our friendship hasn't waned one bit, and among my many friends, I still call her my oldest and best friend, to which I can add, "and one of my greatest blessings."

Many people will walk in and out of your life,
but only true friends will leave footprints in your heart.

—Eleanor Roosevelt

Gainful Employment

I had never planned to be gainfully employed during my married life. My husband had never wanted that for me either. I had married this intelligent, personable, good-looking, ambitious man, voted "Most Likely to Succeed." I had planned to have five children with him, a life-long dream, who would be my life and my "career." But life took another turn, due to a little black suit.

It was the most attractive black suit I had ever worn. Mother and I bought the suit while we were together on a shopping spree. Mother needed an outfit to wear to a special occasion with my Daddy. She found what she wanted at our first stop, Tinsley's.

Tinsley's, an exclusive shop on Church Street, was founded by the Tinsley family in 1888. It was well known for dressing the elite in Nashville society. This did not include Mother and me, but after all, this was to be for a special date with Daddy. I had no such occasion in mind for myself, but browsed while Mother was making her purchase. I saw the little black suit. "Take heed and keep thyself from all covetousness," briefly crossed my mind. It did not deter me from exclaiming over the suit to Mother. We left the store, each smiling and carrying a big box!

I had not spent a dime of my husband's hard-earned money. Mother, as you might have guessed, could not say the same.

A few days later I reasoned that this suit must have the perfect hat to complete the "look." I reasoned further, "Since

Mother bought the suit there, I'll just wear it and retrace my steps to Tinsley's fine millinery department!"

Good decision. The fashion designer Alan Keck from New York was there. As I tried on the hat, he asked if I'd ever modeled. He added the fact he brought a professional model with him from New York and she would put me through a training class!

Actually, I had done some modeling in high school, but I hardly saw how this opportunity would be possible. Mother and Daddy encouraged me and Thurman said, "Well, go for it!" Mother was still teaching at the time and so I turned to Aline, the wonderful lady who had helped me before. She became a life saver through so many years, and a dear friend. She would watch the children for me.

This designer had a beautiful line of clothes and furs. He was New York City all the way and at my age I was a little in awe of him. I can't imagine how I found the nerve to speak up, but on a certain day after he selected my clothes to be worn, I looked at them and back at others on his rack. Timidly, I asked, "Mr. Keck, I will wear whatever you want me to, but may I select a few that I feel will be more appropriate for me?" He looked a trifle annoyed but said, "Show me." I slipped into the first one, watching him when he nodded, saying, "Yes, yes, that is perfect." A second and third time of modeling my selections for him and hearing back his "Yes, Yes…" and then he turned to me and said, "Okay, you Nashville girl with your southern drawl, you pick 'em from now on!"

I enjoyed modeling but oh, my feet hurt wearing high heels all day! The pay I received sounded pretty good, but after paying Aline and missing being with Bugsie, I left after four seasons. Mr. Keck came to me at the time I planned to leave to try to interest me in joining his group in Atlanta or New York. "Where the pay for models," he said "is greatly increased over the pay in Nashville." He never understood the fact that I had absolutely no interest in his offer. Had I not told him over and over about my two-year-old? And so I came home with a few lovely after-five dresses that I bought for a song with my money, and a good feeling that I was where I wanted and needed to be.

Years flew by with all the school activities and other interests, enjoying family and friends, but the time arrived when it became a necessity that I get a job. Thurman had bouts with depression that concerned me greatly and I felt uneasy, but couldn't make myself apply for a real job from nine-to-five.

Thurman learned of an opening at the telephone company located on Third Avenue and Church Street. I drug my feet getting dressed to go into town to apply for the job. I had an interview on the spot with "Mr. Smith," who was hiring, and for whom I would be working if I got the job. I immediately felt uneasy around this man as I answered questions I felt unrelated to my job skills or the position. I was praying he would send me on my way and that I would never hear from him! I couldn't believe my ears when he announced, not only to me, but to others around him, that I would be in his employ starting Monday of next week. I could've died and cringed when he hugged me and kissed me goodbye, which I thought to be very unprofessional. I was sure he was quite the womanizer. The tears flowed as I drove home and I was contemplating telling Thurman that I would have to wait to hear later about the job. All of my life I had a guardian angel and she was with me.

The Lord knew my heart and once again heard my feeble cry for help. A few days later I was at the right place at the right time and had an opportunity to step in and do TV commercials at WSM.

Life is what happens when you're busy making other plans.

—John Lennon & Paul McCartney

Our Children

Charlie

Our first child, Bugsie (Charlie) loved people and his face was so bright! Before we came back to Nashville, he and I rode the street car to Hampton frequently, and I pushed him in the stroller to the library, the market, and to the park several times during the week. He spoke to every person he saw. After we returned to Nashville at the end of World War II, Mother and Daddy often read to Bugsie, I suppose because they loved children as well as being professional educators. They spent much time not only reading to him, but seeking every opportunity available to turn it into a "fun" teaching experience. I can see him standing in the middle of the dining room table under the beautiful Tiffany chandelier, putting his hand on each fruit, learning not only the name of the fruit, but the color as well, just as Joe and I did as children. Bugsie's speech was not crystal clear that early, but he knew what he was saying and so did we.

In the first grade, his teacher, Bonnie Bayer, called me and talked for a long time concerning her observation of him. At first, she thought he was such an excellent student that it must be to the exclusion of everything else. So, she made a point of watching him closely on the playground. She found he excelled there as well. He was a leader, kind and helpful, and always for the underdog. This was an attribute all of my children possessed all of their lives. And so, all were well-liked by their peers.

At eight years old, Bugsie had a brother, Mike, and a sister, "Mell" or Marilyn. One might think he wouldn't be all that thrilled to be sharing the attention. Not so! After Mike was born, it seemed that friends and family came in droves and all were quickly caught up in Bugsie's sheer excitement. He took their hands and led them to wherever Mike was in the house, saying, "Come see my baby!" When Mell came into our family, Mike and Bugsie were equally thrilled over their new baby sister.

Charlie found success in everything he sought after with his good looks, his good heart, and good brain. He excelled as a child, a teenager and as a young man. His wife Carol and their three children, Annie B., Charlie Joe, and Anderson were left to mourn his death in 2006. I, his mother, and his siblings still feel his loss deeply.

Mike

When Charlie (Bugsie at that time) was four years old we welcomed the birth of our second beautiful baby boy. Mike was big, healthy and full of energy. He was fearless! At two years old he had a headful of blonde curls and light blue eyes that, yes, twinkled. Spring, summer and fall his skin was a wonderful bronze. This darling child afforded us laughter along with an unaccustomed fear: for his safety. He was not yet eighteen months old, riding on Bugsie's tricycle in the house. When he opened the screen door, I was conversing with a neighbor and to my horror, before I could reach Mike, he flew down six concrete steps, landing on all three wheels! This was the beginning of the lifestyle of our "Daredevil."

We moved into our new home, which at one end of the porch had a ten-foot drop. I was sitting in the swing, watching Mike, but again he was too fast for me. He climbed up on the tricycle and headed off the edge, landing on his face. It had to hurt! He cried and certainly he was never a crybaby, not even when it was expected. But this little episode did not deter Mike. He continued these shenanigans as he grew up on Moran Drive.

Thurman was not a fisherman, nor was Bugsie. But it was

evident even at five years old, that Mike loved fishing. I did my best, taking him to Shelby Park to fish in the lake. He couldn't get enough of it. As an adult, Mike and his son Michael, my first grandchild, succeeded in tournament fishing, affording them a substantial increase in income! Fishing was Mike's number one sport.

Because Mike looked angelic, as well as 99% of the time being a cooperative child, my mother could never believe it when I told her, "When Mike does get angry he's a holy terror!" The kids in the neighborhood rarely crossed him, having on a rare occasion seen this side. I honestly think Mother didn't believe me until one day...

She had the three boys, Bugsie, Mike and their cousin Bink, Joe's son, to spend the day. Bugsie and Bink were four years older than six-year-old Mike, but they played well together. Something went wrong during this visit. My phone rang and Mother said in a panic, "You've got to come over and see to Mike! Bink and Bugsie can't get in the house. Mike has his BB gun holding it on both of them at both the front and back doors, because he can outrun them!

I laughed all the way to Mother's house. When I arrived, Mother was standing in the front door pleading with my youngest. Sure enough, the two older boys were standing back, not daring to venture any farther to enter the house—Mike still had gun in hand, daring them to try. I couldn't be too upset with Mike—it was sheer comedy!

I hollered at him, "You either put your BB gun down this instant or I'm having Mae call your Daddy!"

Mike threw the gun down on the ground and stalked off in a huff. I knew in my heart this was not all Mike's fault, so I brought the three boys together on the front porch, lectured them, had them shake hands, and sent them on their way to enjoy the rest of the afternoon together. Secretly I was still laughing when I turned my back to leave. The moral of this story? Mother was made aware her lovable grandchild could actually lose his halo now and then!

Hunting was high on Mike's outdoorsman's list as well. He was about twelve years old when he got his first two beagle hounds. I can't believe that I let him keep those two puppies in his bedroom at night and many days. These dogs were too spoiled by the family to ever be well-trained hunting dogs, the stated reason for getting them.

Mike became every inch a man, strong and still fearless, rugged yet tender. Two anecdotes reveal the man by telling about the boy. When Mike was young, three or four, he asked for a doll at Christmas. His Daddy was against any son of his getting *a doll!* I settled this by consulting with our pediatrician, Dr. Overall. He explained that this showed tenderness, adding, "He will be a good father and love babies." So, I placed that doll behind our other gifts, against the trunk of our Christmas tree. Thurman and I were standing there together on Christmas morning, watching as those sturdy legs trampled over all the other gifts to get the doll. She lived in Mike's room with all the stuffed animals and was never mentioned again.

Dr. Overall's prediction was right on target. The adult Mike loved the babies in the family: his own and his siblings' children. In contrast, he spent two years in the Marines during the Vietnam War after his high school graduation. Mike excelled in sharpshooting and earned an award for it when graduating from Boot Camp. I was there at the ceremony. One of his fellow soldiers was a teacher and several years older than Mike. This soldier came to sit beside me at the airport as we waited for the Marines to embark for their assignments in Vietnam. He said, "Mrs. Williams, if I find myself in a foxhole anytime in the future, I hope your son will be beside me." He spoke of Mike's strength of character and bravery, his expertise, and concluded that Mike was a credit to the Marines. These words gave me some sense of peace and I dwelled on them often until Mike returned home, safe and sound.

During high school, a beautiful girl won Mike's heart. We first met when I needed young people to dance on Dave Overton's *Five O'Clock Hop* show at the WSM television studio.

Later, Vickie was everything a mother could wish for as Mike's wife and our daughter.

This strong, uncomplaining man suffered several years from pulmonary fibrosis, before his death in April of 2015. Vickie and their children, Michael and Amy, along with their children, were all a source of joy in his life. His face lit up when he recounted their accomplishments. Little Anna, Amy's youngest child, won her grandfather's heart when just a baby. He offered to keep Anna when her mother went to work so her daddy could further his education. Seeing the beautiful bond these two had brought back memories of the Christmas when Santa brought Mike a doll, and our pediatrician predicted a tender father.

The terrible heartache of losing Mike and Charlie will never go away. I think of them daily, thanking God for their lives, along with the joy they brought to their Daddy and me.

Marilyn

How I loved and enjoyed my boys! Bugsie was eight and Mike four when I learned that we were expecting another child. I was excited and filled with anticipation: would this one be a girl? Yes! This one was welcomed with open arms by her brothers and her mother and daddy. I felt so blessed, recognizing that God's angels were smiling down on me. Surely this baby fulfilled my dream of a large family, and would be the last.

I had an exciting job offer when Bugsie was twelve, Mike eight and Marilyn four, to work in television, and my family encouraged me to accept it. With Mike and Bugsie settled in school my only concern was Marilyn. I'd placed her in what I thought to be a really fine nursery school—Miss Ruby's. For fear that she wouldn't enjoy being there through lunch and naptime, Mother and Daddy picked her up each day and she had lunch with them and that was their time together. After Marilyn attended Miss Ruby's that first year, with my thinking she was enjoying being there, I was excited in the fall as we prepared for the second year. Then I heard her crying in her room. I was shocked to learn that she hated being there and really didn't like Miss Ruby one little bit! She was hateful to her and to all of the children. Well! It took all of a very few minutes to get Miss Ruby by phone and let her know that Marilyn would not be returning. She let me know that she thought my child was spoiled and asked what I would do the following year when she might balk and not want to go to school. I told her I would deal with that when the time came; I was not concerned that Marilyn would not want to go to school, she simply did NOT love her nursery school at all.

What fun Marilyn and I had together the entire year. She went with me to work at WSM and on several occasions was included in commercials. She has expressed, more than once, that year was the happiest of her childhood.

Marilyn was everything I imagined she would be and truly contrived to be all of her childhood. In her Daddy's eyes, she was the perfect child. She was a joy with a remarkable disposition. She sailed through school with the love and respect of her teachers and peers.

As her life unfolded, Marilyn's creativity became evident in several areas. Her tour company, "I'll Take Tennessee," that she designed foremost for fourth grade students in private and Metro Schools has proved extremely successful. Marilyn Switzer's walking tour with historic coverage of Old Nashville has proven popular with students and their parents alike for more than thirty years.

She creates table arrangements for her own grandchildren's birthday dinners that are worthy of magazine coverage, as are the meals she serves. The greatest compliment I can pay her is to tell her, "You are so much like Mae." (Mae is what my children called my mother.) I longed to be more like my mother myself, only to find my daughter is much more like her. For this, I'm sure, I love her even more.

Sam

Sam came into this world surrounded by love. My mother adored him and my daddy, Samuel Herman Binkley, was so impressed that he finally had a grandchild named for him! All of my friends, whose children were now growing up, adopted him. My best friend, Maxine, and her girls were so attentive and showed their joy over this adorable baby. Sam was six weeks premature and was so small. Dr. Overall, my pediatrician, let me bring him home early because he said, "You have had three babies and I know you can take care of him." Mike, Marilyn, Charlie, and their friends seemed to really enjoy this precious little one. Mike wanted to babysit when Thurman and I joined a square dance group, which I thought was the cutest thing ever! Thurman and I both trusted Sam to his care completely. These two formed a strong bond. Bonds between siblings always gave me such joy. On occasions when I think about it now, it warms my heart more than they know.

I watched Sam excel in so many varied areas. Even though he was small for his age, he tackled a sport with a vengeance—until he grew tired of it and moved on to a new sport—where he again excelled until he grew tired of that one and found a new sport to conquer. Even as a little boy he loved music and would sit at a piano for hours, assembling chords, creating harmony. It was evident he had a flair, but Sam absolutely refused to take piano lessons. It was not long before his interest transferred to drums and again he excelled in self-teaching. In elementary school, Sam was invited to join the private Goodpasture High School Band, which was a first and last. His interest in art took off at Goodpasture School, where the art teacher became aware of his talent and spoke to us about getting him enrolled in Art School. This child refused formal instruction, period.

Sam grew to love to read, accumulating a library of books containing material foreign to my ability to understand. His interest became far and wide and his desire to learn seemed to flourish. His next desire was to write, and his writings grew and became intriguing and so beautiful. He had no interest in being published, insisting it all was just for his own pleasure.

At this time in Mother's life, when she was not in the classroom teaching children, she loved being with Sam. She felt that he was much like her child, Anderson, whom she lost at age thirteen. She wanted to be with Sam as much as possible and the feeling was mutual because Sam surely loved her as well! Many mornings I picked her up to spend the day with us. Daddy spent days mostly reading and chauffeuring Mother and her friends to wherever they wanted to go. So many times Mother would call and I could detect that she was lonely. I would ask if Daddy was there and she would say, "Well, yes, but he has his head in a book, so there's no conversation." I would laugh to myself because I knew it was true! Whenever possible I would stop and get her. It gave me such joy because she was happy just to be in my company—and the feeling was mutual.

Sam was fun and handsome. I used to think he looked like the other three children, all "Binkleys." Before Mike left for school, I would sit and rock Sam, something I loved to do. It was just natural that I was singing lullabies while I rocked and one morning Mike said, "Mama, your singing is terrible! Could you tone it down some?" I knew he was not kidding. I continued to rock and sing every morning, but a little softer.

Today, I love when the phone rings and it's Sam on the other end. We can easily find ourselves buried in conversation for well over an hour. I find him and his lifestyle fascinating, with few changes in his personality from when he was just a boy.

Sam seemed to be growing up as an only child. Before long his older siblings would be getting on with their lives, and he would be truly alone as far as having a brother or sister to grow up with. But life turned out differently.

Doree

I was forty-two and Thurman was forty-seven when I found another baby was on the way to join the Williams family. Hooray! I was now blessed with five children, the exact number I dreamed of having well before I married. We had lived next door to the Davis family—Mama, Papa and nine children—how I had adored the noise and laughter coming from that home!

We were both a bit apprehensive when we headed off to the hospital for another birth, calling ourselves, laughingly, "old people." We were only kidding when we said "old" because we knew we weren't! The nurses marveled as they saw that I was so tanned and asked the same question I had heard from nurses when Bugsie was born: "How did you get your back and the backs of your legs so brown with your fat tummy?" Thurman and I remembered the same question was asked before and got a big laugh out of it. I now had three sons and one daughter, so I was thrilled when our fifth was a girl! Never mind that Marilyn would be fifteen years older than her sister. I knew in my heart that they would be close. I now had my second family which everyone enjoyed.

When I think of Doree as a two-year-old, I see her on the day she picked up a yellow butterfly off the picnic table in our backyard. For the first time I witnessed that sorrowful look with tears brimming over, hands outstretched, holding the wounded butterfly, asking for my help. How many hundreds and hundreds of times has this scene been played over during her lifetime? It's difficult to describe my youngest child's personality, but the foundation is that Doree loves people, just like Sam does. Even though Sam was even more demonstrative than she was, Doree Ann loved everything alive: dogs, cats, horses, butterflies, and bugs. She has such a sensitive nature. She was always in pain over any creature that was hurt.

Doree was so excited and upset one day, sobbing loudly, trying to open the back door, that by the time I got to her I was a nervous wreck. I knew something terrible had happened! I didn't know whether to laugh or shake her when she explained, still wailing, mind you, that our little dog, who had a habit of sleeping in the middle of the street, was almost killed! Never mind that Pepper was running merrily along behind her, totally in one piece. As Doree became older, the number of stray animals that this child brought home was unbelievable. I wouldn't even begin to stagger a guess as to just how many!

With each story I got about the neglected animals she had the same expression on her face as when she was just a very little child and her heart was broken over a "butterfly's broken wing." I loved her sensitive heart, but many of my friends came to dread the phone calls when I tried to place those animals in good homes. While they hated to turn me down, they did! However, my prospects became greater as I learned about families who owned farms. After visiting them, usually with Doree Ann in tow, how could they refuse? Doree's passion for troubled animals is still very much in evidence. Her husband, Stewart, has taken over my role as the bewildered one. God bless him! What a good man he is!

Her sister Marilyn says, "Doree is an intensified version of Mom." It is true and family and friends are well aware of the fact. I love that Doree and Mell, fifteen years older, are good friends. Mell is more like my mother and you must know from reading this memoir, that is the ultimate compliment. However, Doree not having the years to know Mother as Mell did, seems perfectly happy to be called my clone. Bless her little (big) heart!

The child was reading the newspaper at four years old. Even though, of course, she didn't understand what she was reading, she sounded out the words quickly and correctly, much to Marilyn's disbelief—until she came home from college and witnessed it for herself. Her little friends' mothers were astounded when she was riding in in the car with them, reading aloud the billboards and street signs! Learning was Doree's childhood past time. While most little girls would be playing with dolls, she was dragging a tablet and pencil around. She happily watched the children's learning programs on TV. If the alphabet was being taught she followed instructions, forming the letters at random, then bringing the tablet to me, asking, "What does it say?" Doree became frustrated until I stopped what I was doing, sat down with her and formed words from the letters. When she entered school, I received a call questioning me. I had to tell the teacher and principal, "She actually taught herself!"

I don't know what hold the girls in our family had over their Daddy but we were all aware that although Doree was not the persuader that Marilyn was, she had her own tactics. She adored her Daddy throughout his lifetime. I used to say, "If I were jealous-hearted, it would not have been of 'other women' but of my own precious girls." Their relationship with their Daddy I found touching, and while the boys made fun of them, I think and hope that they got a kick out of it, too.

I really wasn't shocked to find that I was the oldest of the mothers whenever I joined Sam and Doree's school and extracurricular activities. One would think I would be intimidated, but it was interesting and when folks say having children late in life keeps you young—it is a true statement. I joined in all the children's activities and had the energy to do it along with meeting new people and making new friends. It kept life fun and exciting! I wouldn't have changed it for the world.

All my children's lives are woven with my own and so are featured in many of my stories.

Having children—the responsibility of rearing good, kind, ethical, responsible human beings—is the biggest job anyowne can embark on.

—Maria Shriver

Thurman and me
Easter Morning
Hampton, Virginia

Nell Price

Charlie and me
Hampton, Virginia

Channie Raymond Williams and Ollie Jane Sellers Thurman's parents

The Williams Family, 1949
Standing: Don, Matt, Jake & Stine, Charlie & Nell, Doug & Ruth. Seated: Lois, Frankie, Channie Raymond "Papa", Ollie Jane, Me, Thurman with Mike. Floor: Gayle, Barbara, Charlie.

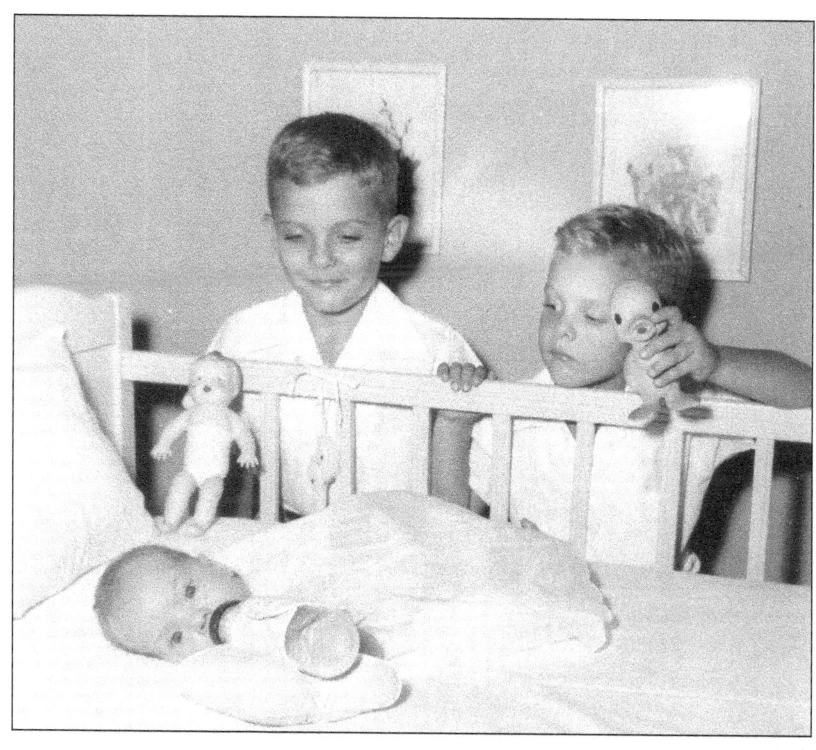

Charlie, Mike and Marilyn, Huffine Street, 1952

Playtime in the Huffine Street backyard

Our Happy Home on Moran Drive, Flag Flying!

Charlie

Mike

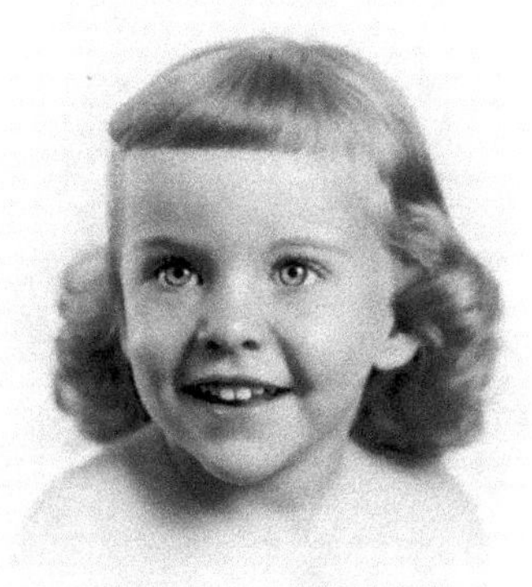

Marilyn

Mike, Thurman and Charlie
circa 1960

My friend, Mary Frank Mosby

Thurman himself shot this photograph, his favorite photo of me during my modeling years.

MID-LIFE

The Return of Pollyanna

I loved my new house, a cottage with a front porch. I found appealing rocking chairs, later a swing and hanging baskets. Pots of colorful flowers. Although not so large or spacious, it was reminiscent of my childhood porch. Certainly, the rooms weren't high ceilinged or very large, but oh, how I loved our little house! With two bedrooms, living room, dining room, kitchen and den, it was my castle. I went about making our little, far from perfect house a home that I later learned each child found to be a place of refuge and love. I learned a lesson while living in this house to which I think every wife and mother has given thought.

Surely, you haven't concluded, reading my story thus far, that I remained through my adulthood forever "Pollyanna", the optimistic child from the novel of the same name. The one and only bathroom in my little cottage was beginning to get on my nerves. The banging on the door by one of the children demanding access to the room immediately, or there would be an accident outside the door! That put an abrupt end to my plan for a long, relaxing, hot bath to begin the day or end my long, work-filled hours before crawling into bed. Without realizing it, I was building a resentment: WE NEED A BIGGER HOUSE!

Mother and Daddy were aging before my very eyes, needing more and more of my care and attention. Thurman's bouts with depression caused my heart to ache for him. "Oh, Dear Lord," I prayed, "I'm losing my usual fun, optimistic way of coping with life. God, Can You help me, please? I pray what's happening to me doesn't affect my precious children." I did not want to be indifferent, to become less kind or understanding.

Looking at my calendar I found I had an appointment with Dr. Scott Bayer, the wonderful man who was not only my gynecologist and obstetrician, but a dear, wise friend and mentor. As usual I dressed so as not to appear frumpy and sad, managing a big smile when I walked in and sat down in front of him. Bless his heart; he took one look at me and said, "Tell me what's wrong." I answered, "I don't know what you're talking about." Dr. Bayer replied, "You are smiling, but your eyes are so sad."

The words he spoke opened the gate of a flood of tears held back for weeks. That sensitive man excused his nurse, saying he needed more time with me, while offering me his handkerchief. It was not my style to open my heart to anybody concerning my problems. However, I let go with a flow of words explaining the sadness in my eyes. As I talked it became evident to him my greatest concern was my guilt in not maintaining a peaceful household. He saw through it all. "You are aware that you, as a wife and mother, are responsible for the atmosphere created under your roof. Not your husband, not your children. You! I see the pressure you're under, and it may be you need medication to help you through it, which I'll prescribe today."

I refused medication and dried my tears. I determined to change my attitude by stopping to enjoy my blessings. I determined to laugh at the compliments I would receive on getting to church on time with all of us looking our Sunday best, from friends who knew I needed a second or even third bathroom! The mere fact that I became calmer, kinder, and less critical was like a wash of fresh air under our roof. I smiled an honest-to-goodness smile, remembering my past when I was more like Pollyanna, and on the spot vowed to become like her again!

Life is a shipwreck.
But we must not forget to sing in the lifeboats.

—Voltaire

This is the day that the Lord has made,
let us rejoice and be happy in it.

Psalm 118: 24

May the words of my mouth and the meditations of my heart
be acceptable in thy sight, O Lord, my strength and my Redeemer.

Psalm 19:14

Live Television
1956-1966

Bugsie was twelve, Mike eight and Marilyn four, when I became a pioneer in food commercials and live television. As always, I was deeply in love with Thurman, and in those years I was also very happy in my work!

This was live television–no video yet–which meant having a spot on the Noon Show. I arrived at between 11:15 and 11:30 and readied to go on air, afterwards heading home. Then it was back on the road for a spot on the *News with Jud Collins* at 6:00 PM. The income from commercials, even with the schedule, was by far the most lucrative thing I could do and I loved completely this new job! The new concept of food commercials took off with a bang. The George Doyne Advertising Agency, for whom I worked, bought time on WLAC and on WSIX, while WSM was adding more and more time. I had plenty of work.

I first demonstrated live for advertisers during the *Million Dollar Movie* on WLAC which began on the air at 10:00 PM and was off the air about midnight. My commercial would come at 10:00 PM or at any time until midnight. I was never afraid to drive to downtown where the studio was located, on Fourth and Church Street in the Life and Casualty Building.

This was a life separate and apart from problems and anxieties that I was going through dealing with Thurman's terrible depression. I never felt I should share these problems with the world and so even my family was unaware of the severity of what was happening. I worked hard to shield my children. I prayed continuously on the way to the studios, day and night, for some relief for my husband. It broke my heart seeing him so miserable. I didn't like his doctor at all but could do nothing to convince Thurman to change and so we weathered the storm together and eventually things became normal again, all while I worked in television. I always worried what effect those years had on our children's lives and I never really knew, nor do I know now.

The food commercials were highly successful and more and more TV time was bought by the companies I represented. This became a lucrative occupation and I was not stuck in an office nine-to-five, the most important perk of what I do. WSM offered me more commercials, and that boosted my income considerably, as well as affording me the opportunity to meet so many interesting people in the industry. I loved working with all the WSM crew from the producers down to the stock boys—loved them all! Frankly, I was having so much fun I could hardly refer to it as a job.

For a while all my commercials were with WSM, however the two other local channels, WLAC and WSIX came into the picture as my companies branched out, buying more advertising time. I knew full well there soon would be an overlapping of commercials airing live, and I certainly wouldn't be able to do them all. My job expanded into interviewing and training new people while continuing to choose those commercials I wanted to do myself.

Being a pioneer in the field of food commercials, I was expected to create a way to show food in the best, most enticing way while it held up under the extreme heat from the lights overhead. Trial and error, trial and error! I soon learned one cannot believe everything viewed on TV. Nobody had ever done these kind of commercials before, ones that showed food as beautiful and tempting. The food had to be false. It was a challenge for me to do it. Take ice cream: Common sense says that you can't show ice cream under those hot studio lights. I styled the Purity Dairy commercials. How do you show strawberry shortcake with whipped cream and keep it looking delicious? I tried a few things and lit on shaving cream. It worked! It looked just like whipped cream. It was just one of "my tricks" for making the product look delicious on-air.

The WSM (We Shield Millions, owned by National Life and Accident Insurance) TV kitchen was in a corner of the studio. Right beside the kitchen was the control room. There was a counter there. Ralph Christian, the newsman (anchor) was getting ready to do the news and was going into the control room. I noticed they always waited till the last minute, then rush into the control room.

This time I had the shortcake with its fake whipped cream on the counter as Ralph came rushing in. Before I could stop him, he took a swipe of that shaving cream and put it into his mouth. Then he was foaming at the mouth; he was spitting; was he ever carrying on! The cameraman and I just died laughing. But when he came out of there…!!!

My older children were all on live television at WSM-TV. If there was something to produce and the station needed a child, certainly I had one to fit! Marilyn was asked to be on Eddy Arnold's Telethon for Cerebral Palsy. Dave Overton hosted a dance show, Five O'Clock Hop, every weekday afternoon. Charlie and Mike, along with their girlfriends, were there to dance the afternoon away!

One of my craziest shoots was because of a busy schedule. I had a huge number of people for dinner on Thanksgiving. We all had tickets to the Thanksgiving Day Clinic Bowl football game, which I simply couldn't miss. It was an annual event with the best two Nashville teams competing for the title. Yet I also had to be at WSM-TV for a live commercial, and host Thanksgiving dinner at home afterwards. Marilyn remembers that—she wanted to be in that commercial, and I wanted her to be in it too, playing part of a family gathered around a beautiful dining room table.

We left the football game for WSM to be on camera for the live commercials, then rushed home. I had everything ready to put on the table! I gave my best friend, Helen, the list: when to light the candles, where the matches were, etc. I wrote it all down and had the food ready to the point that it would be hot. We would arrive home about the time everyone was coming for dinner. I didn't want my guests to wait. How did I do that? I don't know, but I did.

Jud Collins at WSM was Nashville's most popular announcer and I did commercials on his noon show as well as his six o'clock news show. We became good friends. While engaged in idle conversation, he learned that I had modeled off and on for several years. Jud suggested that I should do the commercials for Cain-Sloan, our major department store. Because he was the person asked to interview the aspiring young models, guess who got the job? I found it to be much more relaxing preparing my food for the camera's scrutiny than that of my face and hair. Going downtown to select the clothes, hats, shoes and accessories was time-consuming. However, I did continue to model in the Cain-Sloan commercials as long as they continued to run on television.

When I look at my hands today I simply shake my head, wondering: What happened? Because in the past, my hands had to be perfectly smooth and nails perfectly manicured as the cameras zoomed in on them. I had to keep them ready for the next appearance. Have you ever on TV seen a hand pulled through a silk stocking, showing the superior quality of the silk? That silk should refuse to tear, and yet be transparent. I shudder to think what these hands could do to that stocking today. Oh well, it was fun while it lasted! I truly would not enjoy going back to pulling on rubber gloves every time a dish was washed or a flower planted.

I found it a real challenge to shop at the finest stores for background accessories and props. Unfortunately, I learned the hard way not to bring any of this from home. Lost in the shuffle early on were several pieces of my own sterling flatware. After this, I purchased a place setting, adding the cost to my expense account. I broke the cost down to include part on each client's account since it was used on all. My advertising agent thought this was very acceptable. Never was I questioned concerning a submitted expense, except on one occasion, when this particular client did indeed question the amount submitted. As I remember, I was pretty incensed when I met with someone from the company to discuss the matter. I'm not usually a cold person, but you could have cut the ice with a knife in that room; a method of defending my integrity. This man was seated at the desk when I entered the room. After I introduced myself, the poor man wasn't given a chance to open his mouth until after I had my say:

"Sir, I have enjoyed working with your company while doing your TV commercials, very much. I'm sorry you are displeased with the cost of my executing these commercials. When I am holding the copy in my hand, I can go only one way with it and that is to produce the most beautiful, mouthwatering, enticing picture of your product imaginable at any cost. I find I can do it no other way myself. However, you may want to find someone who can, and that will be perfectly fine with me."

This man listened and when I had finished he reached across the desk, took my hands in his and offered an apology, saying, "I do understand, having met you and listened to you. I will continue reviewing our commercials with a greater appreciation than before. Can I take you to dinner?"

Seven Years Later...When Marilyn was eleven years old, Mike fifteen and Bugsie nineteen, I was still enjoying completely my TV work and the perks that went along with it. Life was good and oops! I'm pregnant!

Jud Collins had approached me three different times about the possibility of furthering my TV career in different facets. I was mulling it over in my mind and getting excited over the possibilities of what might come of it. Even so, I was not upset at all when I knew there was a precious baby on the way. I simply closed the door on a career that I knew I would've loved, in exchange for the excitement of holding and rocking my baby, for it had been a long time since the last baby in our family!

During the first months of my pregnancy, I continued to work. During the ninth month of my fourth pregnancy, videotaping was perfected. WSM called and offered me the opportunity to demonstrate a product in the first pilot commercial on video tape. I accepted! When I left the studio everybody came out and I was overwhelmed at the sendoff from producers, directors, cameramen, announcers and stock boys. They had planned a surprise party, and thought I'd be back to work in a few months. I didn't think so. I would have gone back when it went to tape but I had started my guide business.

I felt my calling in life was to be for the Lord to lead me as a wife, mother and homemaker. I was aware my friends felt sorry for me, but I was happy! I think of all the children Mike was the most thrilled. We decided to tell him first and swore him to secrecy. You see, he had said several times that he would love having a baby brother. Well, the secret was out almost immediately—when he ran down the street to tell his friend! I knew Marilyn would be the one most impacted by the news as she had been our baby for eleven years and was at the age my presence was wanted and needed. I honestly can't exactly remember Bugsie's reaction, but I know it was positive.

I had one more part to play in Nashville's media history, when Hollywood came to Nashville. Director Robert Altman came here to make a movie. Actors and musicians were trying out for a part in the movie at a hotel. "Mary, why don't you go audition for a role in that movie?" my friends at WSM were insisting. They kept after me until I went, just for fun. And I got a part in the 1975 movie *Nashville*. The home where we went on location, a horse farm on Old Hickory Boulevard, was great fun!

WSM-TV was sold and became WSMV-TV in 1982. Everyone I worked with there is gone now. Dave, Jerry, Ralph Christian. I have heard from the previous head cameraman, Joe Adair, who was younger. All the others I knew are gone, and so are the days of live commercials. It all seems like a fairytale. For ten years, it was a great experience and loads of fun!

All the world's a stage,
And all the men and women merely players;
They have their exits and their entrances,
And one man in his time plays many parts...

—the character Jaques

from *As You Like It*, Act II Scene VII, by William Shakespeare

Marilyn's Television Debut

In the late 1950s, Eddie Arnold was to be the spokesperson on a WSM-TV Telethon for Cerebral Palsy. Marilyn, he thought, would be the perfect little girl to play the part of the child he would be speaking about—a child who was able to enjoy a normal childhood, versus a child suffering from cerebral palsy. Eddie Arnold with his gentle demeanor and soothing voice was the perfect celebrity to deliver the plea to remember these children by sending a check for further research. Eddie had seen Marilyn at the studio with me many times. The year before she started school, she went with me every day for the noon show commercials.

I was thrilled when the producer asked me for permission. I was given a sketch of a child skipping rope. The drawing showed her wearing a darling dress, Mary Jane shoes, with a huge bow in her hair. This was the picture of the child Marilyn was to portray, which meant I had nothing to purchase. I selected one of her prettiest handmade dresses, and what little girl did not own a pair of black patent Mary Janes and an array of ribbon bows for her hair?

The day for Marilyn's studio appearance started out wonderfully well. Although it had rained earlier, the sky was clearing. Marilyn was excited, dressed, looking the perfect model. She was holding her new jump rope when I heard the phone ringing. Next door neighbor Josephine was calling. "Was Marilyn dressed yet to play her part for the TV commercial?" She explained she had rollers in her hair and therefore, could

Marilyn come over and model her outfit? Josephine loved my children, and with two boys of her own but no girls, she found a special joy in her relationship with Marilyn.

We had plenty of time to spare, so out the door went Marilyn, down the hill to Josephine's back door. As she started up the wet concrete steps, she somehow someway took a terrible fall! She scraped her face badly on the concrete, cutting a deep gash in her forehead, and completely destroying the dress. Josephine carried her inside, placing her on the sofa. To this day Marilyn remembers her own concern that the blood gushing so profusely from her wound would ruin Josephine's sofa! So like her to think of others before herself.

My mind went into gear: I had to quickly call WSM Studio and tell them what had happened, assure them they would have a replacement, and find that replacement for the part. So, as many times before and after, "Thurman to the Rescue!" Thurman walked in, ready to take his girl to Emergency to get stitches, while I was still on Josephine's phone trying to locate the substitute child. A brainstorm occured, and I called the downtown professionals at Pauline's School of Dance. They quickly found a child. Dressed, jump rope in hand, she arrived in time for the scheduled spot on the live telethon.

I felt sorry for my child but assured her, "I know there'll be other times when you will be asked to appear on television." Indeed, there were. As mothers, we never want to see our child disappointed or hurt, emotionally or physically, but truly—isn't it a growing experience for both in living this wonderful gift called "Life"? I'm just thankful Marilyn was brave, because I'm prone to panic when one of my children is hurt.

I love those who can smile in trouble, who can gather strength from reflection. Tis the business of little minds to shrink, but they whose heart is firm, and whose conscience approves their conduct, will pursue their principles unto death.

—Leonardo da Vinci

Bloopers

When television was live and not taped, you could never tell what might happen on the air. Unexpected turns of events that went out over the air were called bloopers, and usually were quite funny to all who watched. They were not always funny when you were the one creating the blooper!

Although the commercials were live, I did have a script, and could read the copy by looking into the camera lens through a device still used today, the teleprompter. Of course, I read the script and prepared well beforehand. Nonetheless, participating for ten years in live television commercials led to quite a few bloopers, and here you can read of two, revealed from behind-the-scenes at WSM-TV.

Jersey Farms Dairy

Being on live television proved to be both exciting and nerve-wracking. My very first blooper was on a Jersey Farms Dairy commercial.

I arrived at WSM Studio as usual, ready to walk in and begin setting up for the commercial on the *Six O'Clock News with Jud Collins* (WSM-TV's first, and principal anchor for twenty years). Lo and behold, I found the doors to the studio closed, with the red light on, indicating they were on the air and no entry was allowed. Political speeches were in progress. *What in the world,* I thought, *do I do now?*"The dairy item being featured was chocolate milk in the carton. I knew this would be stored in the refrigerator inside those closed doors in the studio's kitchen area. The Pyrex pan I was to use would be on the stove, where the cameraman was to zoom in to show the convenience of simply pouring the cold chocolate milk from the carton, taken from the refrigerator, into the invincible Pyrex pan, ready to make a delicious cup of hot chocolate in just a matter of a few minutes. *How would I get to the demonstration kitchen in the studio?*

Thankfully, one of the crew appeared and took me back to the stock room, which had been made into a temporary set. I found Jud set up at a desk in a corner of the room for the news show, as well as a table across the room ready for my commercial. The Pyrex pan awaited me on the eye of the hot plate, ready for its close-up. That shot would be especially tight, so that it would look like a stove to the viewing audience.

The copy was written to show that Jersey Farms chocolate milk could be used in multiple ways, so there were three scenes, or setups, within the same commercial. I was keeping an eye on the teleprompter while the Jersey Farms Dairy spot was in progress on the air. The first setup showed a child's lunch box with items: grapes, an apple, a sandwich, and the small matching thermos, ready to be placed inside the lunch box. All went well during this first setup, while the milk was being poured into the thermos. Thankfully, not a drop spilled, making "a delicious child's lunch box treat!" A pretty picture.

Next the camera had to pan over to the next set up, which was to show how one can make a quick cup of hot chocolate. First the cameraman showed a wide shot, featuring a dining table with flowers, linen napkins, china, crystal, and silver, again a pretty picture. Now he was ready to zoom in on the Pyrex pan sitting innocently on the eye of the hot plate, with a big plump marshmallow to the side, ready to top it off after the hot chocolate was poured into the fragile cup. The marshmallow never made it!

I was keeping a pretty close eye on the teleprompter as I began to pour the cold chocolate milk into the Pyrex pan, when all of a sudden...

A terrific noise of breaking glass, along with a blackout of dark clouds of smoke filled the screen on the teleprompter. Smoke was also filling the TV screens in living rooms all over Nashville and surrounding areas. WHAT HAPPENED? was the question, along with shock, on every person's face in the stockroom. In an instant I realized the hot plate had been plugged in much earlier by someone who had no idea it was simply for staging, not heating. It was, of course, by this time extremely hot. *But what to do next? It was LIVE!*

Jud, ever the professional, moved quickly into adlibbing some bit of news, motioning to one of the cameramen to turn toward him, leaving the mess I'd created. I had already made an attempt to signal the cameraman to pan across to the next setup for the commercial, wondering why in the world he didn't. Later he explained, "I was in such a state of shock, it took me a few seconds to recover." It seemed much longer than seconds that the screen was covered in black smoke! I'm sure it wasn't. The entire commercial was only sixty seconds.

For us, this was no laughing matter. It was a horrible disaster. As the news show closed, the cameramen, the stock boys and Jud quickly turned their attention toward me, as they were concerned I would be fired by Mr. Doyne (Doyne Advertising Agency). This man was known to expect nothing less than perfection on these commercials. Considering the amount of money paid for airtime, it was understandable. I was not surprised when the door opened and in walked the lobby receptionist, looking rather stricken herself, as I'm sure she had seen the disaster on the TV in the lobby. She seemed a little reluctant to say, "Mary, you have a telephone call." We all looked at each other, thinking the worst.

I picked up the phone to the sound of uncontrollable laughter on the other end.

Oh yes, it's Mr. Doyne! Rather than hearing "You're fired!" I'm sure I was smiling as I heard him say light-heartedly, "Mary Williams, you've managed to leave the name 'Jersey Farms' on the minds of the listening audience for a very long time. I'll take you to lunch so you can tell me what happened. I'd love to know!"

We all agreed this was a grand ending to this TV blooper. Instead of being fired, I enhanced the products' name quite unexpectedly. Isn't this, after all, what commercials are all about?

Tender Ray Meat

Tender Ray Meat was a Kroger grocery item starring in all the dinner table commercials tonight, with the first one shown on the six o'clock newscast of Jud Collins. The dinner table was set for a wide shot, showing a view of the table set with a center flower arrangement, silver candelabra, fine linen, china, crystal, and silverware. The script copy concerned the absolute tenderness of this prime beef roast, shown on the dinner table ready to be served, along with appropriate side dishes. The picture was very appealing to the eye and would prompt many buyers to try Tender Ray's roast.

Once again I had, well beforehand, experimented with how to show the meat under the piercing TV lights to best advantage. This was one of what I called "My Tricks." I had come up with these to help each product look its best on television. (Keep in mind these little revealing stories happened over fifty years ago! Surely, other methods are being used today.) That big beautiful roast had been seared only, and rubbed with a mixture of liquid Banquet Gravy Seasoning, mixed with red food coloring. Before it was placed on the table ready for a close-up shot, another layer of Wesson oil or olive oil would be quickly added to give it a sheen. It really did look scrumptious. My eye on the teleprompter, I felt pleased so far with the look of Kroger and Tender Ray's commercial.

The next shot was on a second roast. It had been cooked to perfection, ready to be carved, showing its extreme tenderness. There I was on live television, new carving knife in hand, attempting to cut the first serving. The knife refused to cut into the meat! Watching the live shot on a monitor from the corner of my eye, I began to panic. The veins in my wrist began to protrude as with continuing force I bore down on that knife, *until the roast slid off the cutting board, falling to the floor, with the camera still on the now-empty board.* The cameramen were laughing so hard that even though I was mortified, I found myself laughing hysterically with them. That was one tough piece of meat!

It was interesting that I was in no way held responsible for this blooper by the ad agency. I think this was a lesson for the copywriter. Never, ever attempt a feat even resembling this one again on live television.

Thurman was watching the news at home. He had not yet stopped laughing when I walked in the door. His comment, "I hope you choose a different cut of meat for our Sunday dinner!" sent me into hysterics again.

With the advent of videotape and later, digital memory, bloopers remain only on the few live shows, not commercials, for the added enjoyment of the viewer.

Sometimes we let life guide us, and other times we take life by the horns. But one thing is for sure: no matter how organized we are, or how well we plan, we can always expect the unexpected.

—Brandon Jenner

Too Modest?

Early on during my days of live commercials I received two calls that gave me cause to ponder. Betty McMillan, Doyne Advertising Agency copywriter, had become a good friend. She had no idea I would balk after reading the copy sent to present Frigidaire on-air. Reading further into the copy I saw where I was requested to stand beside the Frigidaire refrigerator, wearing a swimsuit, as I made gestures toward the appealing features found inside when the door was opened.

When Thurman came in that evening, I handed over the copy to get his reaction. He immediately said, "Well, it wouldn't bother me as much as it will your church people." In fact, one of the sisters in the congregation had recently questioned seeing WSM's Weatherman Bill Williams and me dancing in the corner of the studio kitchen to the music of the WSM Noon Show Band. This shot was not intended in the format, simply done because Jud quietly signaled the cameraman to turn his camera on us. To this day, I have to wonder why this was a problem to a few of my sisters in our church! After Thurman reminding me of this, I decided to refuse the job. This was probably the right choice to make, and I heard nothing more about that commercial.

The second refusal was related to a request by WSM related to the country music industry. Even though my memory wavers on the exact client, the copy remains vivid in my mind. This too was offered to Thurman for a second opinion. As the model, I would be lying down on a leopard rug wearing a sexy, slinky black gown. After looking at the picture enclosed, I didn't have to ask if anybody thought it was appropriate. Today, it might appear almost modest. However, I never in a million years would have been caught in the revealing black satin gown sprawled out on a leopard skin rug! Thurman's reaction came quickly after reading the copy, "You know the church would excommunicate the entire family with one airing! You don't need my opinion, because you already know the answer. I hate the very idea! Think about your sons—do you think they might be embarrassed?"

A few days later I walked into the studio and found the beautiful young model rehearsing for the commercial. The dress was a perfect fit—for a quick moment I felt a twinge of envy. I recovered quickly, happy with the choice I'd made which left me in good standing with my church sisters, my husband, and my boys.

The standard of modesty was much higher then. Even so, unwanted approaches and advances abounded as much throughout my lifetime as in that of a woman born later. The "Me Too" movement of 2017-18 has brought much attention to these problems for the women of today. In my day, however, one did not reveal these problems. Fortunately, I was able to keep my dignity, honor—and modesty.

If the society of today allows wrongs to go unchallenged,
the impression is created that those wrongs have
the approval of the majority.

—Barbara Jordan

Annie Gary Bentley

The story of Annie Gary spans my life's stages. Throughout my childhood I could see Mother's sisters, some of "The Draper Girls" and Annie Gary—lifelong friends who lived on the same street. Mother and Annie Gary attended the same schools from third grade all the way through Hume-Fogg High School, which was the first public school in Nashville.

Annie Gary's husband Bob Bentley owned a drugstore in Hillsboro Village, on the corner of 21st Avenue and Blair Boulevard. Their comfortable, attractive home was nearby on Blair Boulevard. The Draper Girls whom I knew and loved were Ollie and Bess. They lived on Gartland Avenue in East Nashville, within walking distance of my house on Russell Street. In summer the younger Draper sister Kate came with her only child, Mary Jo, to spend the summers. Kate was divorced from Joe de Rhoulac. In order to receive alimony, she had to live in Phoenix, Arizona, but came here to escape the heat of their summers. When we in Nashville were sweltering in the heat and high humidity and without air conditioning, I used to wonder just how hot it did get in Phoenix, Arizona!

Life was happy. Mother was again planning her dinners and little luncheons. She made up for lost time and planned picnics in Shelby Park. They were out under the trees on picnic tables set up on the lush green grass; sometimes the picnics were at the now long-gone Sycamore Lodge. Even in the middle of the day or in the evening when it was cooler, there we would enjoy playing ball, the playground, and free movies on Saturday evening. I had two favorite people. One was my mother's sister. I was named for Aunt Mary. Her husband was David McClelland and I was destined even before I was born to be Mary McClelland.

The other was my mother's best friend. Annie Gary spent at least one day a week with Mother all of my life and often more than that. She was my second mom. Every time she came, she brought a gift for Joe and me. She must have spent a lot of time shopping, as she wanted a designated boy and girl gift. When we each opened our gifts, Joe would many times like mine better than his. Mother would say, "Oh, Mary won't care if they swap gifts." She was right and Joe and I both came away from the transaction very happy. The person who didn't come away happy was Annie Gary. She began to bring gifts that were alike. She shared this many years later with me. She was shocked to find that I really hadn't cared about the swap, "just as long as Joe was happy."

Maybe this was why Mother nicknamed me "Polly," for Pollyanna, the heroine of the novel written years before I was born. Pollyanna was portrayed as a persistently optimistic child. Later a movie was made, and I remember how I loved the movie. While I haven't lived up to the nickname of the persistently optimistic child, Pollyanna, I must have been, and am today still by all standards, optimistic!

Joe and I occasionally would talk about the fact that we got along so well as children, even though he was definitely in command and I was a willing pawn. Annie Gary never really understood this relationship. This wonderful woman along with her mother and daddy and her many animals grew up in Mother's neighborhood. She moved there when she was eight years old, and Mother being the same age, they became inseparable. Both families owned cottages at Monteagle, a summer resort on top of Lookout Mountain, close to Sewanee University (University of the South).

All of my mother's friends told me that Mother was a beauty as a teenager. Annie Gary was in every snapshot and she was adorable as well. She explained to me that one snapshot shows a particular young man. He was the doctor in Nashville that Mother was engaged to marry at the time she met my Daddy. I think the vacation cottage had been sold by the time Joe and I were born, perhaps after Mother's papa had died, as there are no photos including us there.

Annie Gary and her husband had no children, so she adopted us, playing a huge part in our lives. After our parents died Thurman and I adopted her as a grandmother to our children. All five of our children dearly loved her. Charlie's first child, Annie Bentley, was named for her. Her first name is actually Anna, but the name Annie B so suited her that it stuck.

There were lots of visits with Annie Gary when I was working at Channel 4, WSM-TV. The tower and studio were located off Acklen Avenue in the general neighborhood of Annie Gary's home on Blair Boulevard, in the Hillsboro Village area. Many, many times she would invite me for lunch after I had done my noon show commercial. Annie Gary had lived in this home for many years and I had fond memories of it, so I always accepted her invitation and we sat down to a delicious meal prepared by her cook (whose name I can't remember).

One afternoon she said to me, "Mary, I think I need to make a plan for my future years." Annie Gary was eighty-four then, and had no family. She had already spoken to the owner of an assisted living place in one of the large homes in the area, and wanted me to visit with her there. I would meet the people and give her advice as to whether this would be the right move. We decided she should keep her place and enjoy it as long as possible, going back during the day and entertaining her neighbors and friends with little luncheons her cook would prepare. She would then drive over to the home in the evening and spend the night. This worked for a period of time and she enjoyed her porch, visiting neighbors and friends.

One day after lunch in her home, we were again seated in her living room surrounded by her beautiful furnishings. She had made her plans; she needed more care than this place could give, and had already visited the nursing home in the neighborhood. "Mary, I have no family to speak of," she began. Her husband's two nieces who lived in Birmingham were the closest of kin. She continued, "I don't want one thing in this house sold, down to the dishtowels. I want to give it to people who will appreciate it. I know you will. And as I think of you as my daughter, I want you to go through the house and take all that you want first."

There were many things I would have loved to have, but just as when Mother and Daddy died, I lived in a small house. I said, "Annie Gary, you have so much I admire, but I have all I can manage to fit into my house just with Mother's things. So let's talk about this."

Charlie and Carol were newly married and would need several pieces that I put their names on. "Annie Gary," I said, "I do want the beautiful English dressing table in the bedroom upstairs, where I always slept when spending the night with you. I loved it even as a child." She was grateful that I would have this particular piece in my home; she loved it as well. It was in her home as a child. She said, "It is as good time as any to share with you the fate of this lovely piece of furniture."

It was a Saturday morning, and I was so excited. Thurman and I had already moved a piece out of our bedroom to make a place for the dressing table. Charlie had borrowed a friend's truck. He and his daddy headed across town to load this prize. I truly could hardly wait! Out the window I saw the truck turn into the driveway, and hurried outside to get the first glimpse. I noticed a strange look on both fellows' faces. When I looked into the truck bed I understood why. My beautiful English dressing table was in shreds! I cried, "What have you done?"

They looked at each other sheepishly, each hoping the other would speak up. "Oh Mama, we're so sorry, but we were on West End Avenue in front of Vanderbilt University when, I guess, a gust of wind blew it out of the truck."

I screeched, "Didn't you tie it down? Didn't you secure it with rope or something? Was it just standing there on its delicate curved legs? Couldn't you have laid it down, or **something**?" They just looked scared as I vented all my disgust on the two of them.

"What do you want us to do now?" one ventured.

The beveled-edge mirror was strewn in pieces all over the truck bed, and I turned and suggested, "Pick up every sliver of wood and mirror and pack it in something and take it to the attic. I'll call my friend who repairs antiques and see if it can be salvaged."

Alright, alright, I thought later, *it's over. At least it wasn't one of them who flew out of the truck ending up in fragments.*

That afternoon I was waiting for Thurman to come home. He opened the door and had a twinkle in his eye. He didn't come in, put his arm up and acted afraid. I said, "Don't worry, I'm over it."

He said, "I was afraid to come home, you were so angry this morning."

"I'm not angry anymore, but I do suggest you use a little better judgment the next time in moving a piece of furniture."

That night after supper we got the biggest laugh out of it and my husband said, "I don't recall ever seeing you angrier than that!" But it was all over and done with.

I did call my friend on Monday, sounding desperate. He came by that afternoon. I'll never forget the expression on his face when he advised it was a lost cause and truly beyond repair. After that piece of furniture had been moved, I knew Annie Gary would look for it when she visited. She continued coming to our house for all occasions: birthdays, holidays, and special times in-between.

So when she came in next, I said "Annie Gary, I just have to tell you what happened…I was ugly to Thurman, ugly to Charlie, and I could have killed them! You gave me that beautiful piece, the one piece I really wanted to remember the happy times spent in your home. And now, I don't have it."

She said, "Oh, honey, don't be ugly to them. That was just a mistake they made. Don't ever be ugly to them over something as trivial as that." What a wonderful woman. My grown children were always delighted to see her, of course, and Doree and Sam adored her. They doted on her because she was their grandmother figure during several years after Mother had passed away.

Oh, I'm so grateful for having these wonderful people in my life. The influence of these special friends over the years continues today in my children's lives.

Every time you are able to find some humor
in a difficult situation, you win.

—Unknown

Charlie and Mike, each at age 18, above
Sam and Doree, below

Our Family Portraits by Henry Schofield

Our Family Portraits

Our treasured family portraits are the centerpieces of my home. They came about because of my work for Henry Schofield's commercial and wedding photography studio. Henry was responsible for the photography and I planned, arranged and styled the displays for magazines. Henry and his wife Edna and I became good friends during the time we worked together in commercial photography.

Mother's creations, effortlessly produced in her kitchen on Russell Street, became my source for the yeast breads, cakes, pies and cookies to be photographed. Henry and Edna were thrilled with the perfection found in the baked goods under the scrutinizing eye of the camera.

One particular occasion Henry requested several pumpkin pies, because a slice would be removed to show the texture of the filling. I was in a state of panic—Mother was out of town! I cannot begin to tell you my suffering as I slaved over baking twelve—yes, twelve—pies to transport to the studio! The Schofields were impressed with my effort, and the resulting photograph was quite acceptable. This was a fun but tedious experience.

There were times when Charlie would help me transport the food to be photographed, picking me up many hours later at Schofield Studio, then located on West End Avenue. When Edna met him, she thought he was so handsome and asked if she could do his portrait for display in the studio's big picture window. She explained that down the road she would charge only a minimum fee for the portrait. I was more than thrilled to be able to afford this portrait! Charlie was eighteen, Mike was fourteen, and Marilyn ten years old. Edna promised that if she were still living when the others turned eighteen, she would do their portraits as well.

All of these portraits are in full view on my walls and I enjoy them every day.

Little did we know that down the road a few years, Edna would produce two more portraits! When Marilyn was eleven years old, Sam joined our family, and three years later, Doree Ann. We didn't wait until these two children turned eighteen to have their portraits done, because Edna and Henry said they would not be living by then, which turned out to be true.

When Sam was two, before Doree was born, I walked into the studio to do some setups to be photographed. I had Sam in tow, as Mother wasn't able to sit with him that day. Edna gasped, "He's such a beautiful child!" and made a plan on the spot to surprise me.

The studio had moved to Hillsboro Village and on that block on 21st Avenue there was a book store and a ten-cent store. Edna gave me a little list and asked me if I would mind picking up a few things for her, which of course I was glad to do. Sam was enjoying the surroundings in the studio and Henry was busy explaining to him about the cameras. So Edna suggested I leave him with them.

You can imagine how shocked I was when several weeks later Edna called and asked me to drop by, for she had something to show me. What an adorable portrait of my child, framed in an antique gold oval frame! It had been shot while I was sent on those errands. Tears filled my eyes. I can still see Henry standing there with the cutest grin on his face and a twinkle in his eye. He was so very talented in his field of commercial and portrait photography. He was one of the top two wedding photographers in Nashville.

After having done Sam's surprise portrait, two and a half years later I brought Doree to Schofield's for hers. She was a darling child, but she didn't have the strong Binkley features her four older siblings had. Henry and Edna teased me unmercifully: *Where did this one come from?*

It was some time later that Thurman commented on the fact that I had so many pictures of my family, but he didn't even know what his parents, Mama and Papa, looked like when they were young. It didn't take me but a few minutes to reach out to Frankie, Thurman's sister, and have her find a picture of them. She began to sort through some old photographs and found the most adorable picture of the two of them together. I wanted to surprise Thurman at Christmas with the gift I knew he would cherish, and I surely did just that! I couldn't wait to give it to him. So a week early, when just he and I were at home, getting dressed to go out with friends for the evening, I brought it in, wrapped for Christmas. Thurman was pretty good at hiding the fact that he might be sentimental, so when I saw a tear in his eye and felt his finest bear hug, I knew I had scored. The first thing he said was, "Doree looks like my mother!"

Of course, Edna Schofield did the work using oil on canvas. When I first took the photograph to Edna she took one look and laughing, said, "Now I know Doree is yours and Thurman's." Ollie is beautiful in the portrait, and it thrilled Doree and her daddy to see the strong resemblance. I loved Ollie and Papa and enjoy viewing this picture placed on our wall of ancestors. I find that visitors are drawn to the family pictures, which thrills me. I had begun to fear that if I kept adding to the walls my ten grandchildren and seven great-grandchildren it would become overpowering. But the joy and curiosity shown by visitors has extended to my growing family.

There was a time when interior designers would tell you not to have a portrait in your living room, but to make a gallery in your hall with them. I try to place some things that are not family with the family pictures, to balance it. But I have to see my family pictures. They're not just hanging there; I really enjoy them. And I'll admit there are a lot of them!

I began to doubt my judgement when Maxine asked, when

I first moved to Armistead Place, "Why don't you get rid of those? Give the portraits to your children and invest in some good art." Maxine is my best friend and we are very free in expressing our ideas.

I meant every word when I answered, "Maxine, I love your paintings. I know they're lovely. To me, my children's faces are so beautiful and they are what I love surrounding me."

Of course, we laughed about it.

When I moved to Armistead Place in my seventies, everything here I brought from home. But I needed a tall, slim lamp for one space. I began to search for that lamp. I loved to browse. In some ways this has been therapy during my busy life. I might browse a museum, an old home, an antique shop or whatever struck my fancy, taking my own rare, sweet time. Some owners of those places became my friends, not because I was a *big spender*, rather that I would visit and convey visible and vocal delight when impressed.

I recall a warm summer day getting an urge to run out and look again for the lamp. My adorable grandchild Maclellan was spending the day, so she was with me. A pleasant day and a pleasant memory ensued.

The antique store on Harding Road knew me well. I looked but never bought anything. When we entered the shop, it was late in the day so there were few shoppers. The owner greeted us with enthusiasm, especially the little girl with the bright expression and big smile. But she had a bit of trouble pronouncing my granddaughter's name, Maclellan. When she got it, she asked, "Maclellan, what are some of your favorite things?"

Maclellan had her little hands behind her, just like I had told her to keep them. She thought a second, and said, "Nunny loves angels." The lady took her by the hand and off they went to browse and find all the angels in the shop.

After my long search, I found the perfect lamp there that day, even though it was somewhat out of my price range. The interior designer, a man with whom I had talked many times while browsing, was helping me. After I made the purchase, he asked, "Can you get this in your car?" When I realized that indeed, it wouldn't fit, he said, "I'll follow you and bring the lamp." He walked into my home with the lamp in his hand, froze, and said, "Who did this? I love it!"

"Even with all these portraits?" I asked.

"Yes, I love it!" said the experienced, pricey designer. I wanted to hug him on the spot for laying to rest all my fears about overloading the walls!

What a happy ending to a profitable day.

A man said to Buddha, "I want happiness."
Buddha said, "First remove 'I', that's ego,
then remove 'want', that's desire.
See, now you're left with happiness!"

—Attributed to Gautama Buddha

A Daughter's Dilemma

Thurman was forty-seven; I was forty-two, pregnant with our fifth child, Doree Ann. Sam was three, Marilyn fifteen, Mike nineteen, and Charlie twenty-three. Actually I'd always said I wanted five children but hadn't planned the age gap. What a blessing and added bonus Sam and Doree have been!

Mother was showing signs of not being able to keep clean that wonderful old house where I was born. The persons we hired to clean the house weren't showing up—or if they did, doing a poor job. Daddy was losing interest in his yard and flowers for the porch.

I was making more visits to bring food. On one visit I found Mother in her bedroom on her bed, unable to speak. Daddy was in his chair in the living room reading, seemingly unaware that Mother had suffered a mini-stroke. I was devastated. Mother was seventy-nine and Daddy eighty-three, and it seemed like almost overnight they had become old. It was a scary thing for me, these two precious people had always taken care of me. I still felt like Daddy's little girl, whom he still called "Sugar." I knew I would be back to spend the night. This was the beginning of the changing of the roles. Joe and I would be taking care of them. He and I decided to move them out of the house to a smaller house close to me.

Joe was at the peak of his profession as a very popular and successful lawyer. "Nobody could try a case like Joe Binkley," David Raybin, author of *Tennessee Criminal Law*, wrote in the Nashville Bar Association's Memorial Resolution. Joe was recognized too by the Nashville Bar Association when he received posthumously in 2002 the Jack Norman, Senior Award for outstanding, ethical criminal lawyers. Certainly Joe loved our parents, but I was to learn very soon that as their daughter, I would be their sole caregiver. As I told them over the next three years when they expressed concern that I was overdoing: "You simply can't live long enough for me to do everything I want to do for you." I meant every word. Joe supported me in every decision I made and was a great moral support when I needed to share my concerns. I had to work fast as the months were gaining on me and I was showing my pregnancy bigtime.

Mother recovered from the mini-stroke, and though she certainly wasn't well, we had fun making decisions together later. She loved my being there, dismantling the house. This was after we had to approach Daddy about moving, which I knew would be quite a chore. I knew Mother would do anything that I suggested. I thought it would be best if Joe did the talking and I would go with him for moral support when he would talk to Daddy. Joe had prepared his speech as though he might try this case in court. Certainly, he had the reputation for swaying a jury. I was impressed with his speech and just knew he had won Daddy over.

So it was a shock when Daddy said, "Well, son, that all sounded mighty fine. But you come back and we'll talk when I get old." At this point all we could do was leave, defeated.

I told Joe, "We'll come back in a day or two and you sit in the rocking chair and be my moral support."

If my brother, the well-known attorney who had gained the reputation of "never losing", couldn't win this case, I must have been crazy to think I could. We walked in together and Daddy was sitting, as I knew he would be, at the library table, reading. I knelt beside his chair, placed my hands on his knees, and said, "Daddy, do you love me?"

He chuckled and said, "Sugar, you very well know the answer to that!

"And you do know, Daddy, how much I love you. Right?"

Again, that little chuckle.

I hadn't rehearsed so I didn't know which way this was going now that our love had been declared. I think my guardian angel stepped in when I asked, "Daddy, do you believe the Bible is true?" He looked at me like that was a pretty dumb question, but I kept talking. "If you do, you believe, 'Once a man and twice a child,'" I quoted. I wished I had looked up the book, chapter and verse! Of course, he was right there for me with the proverb. "Well today, you're the child and I'm moving into the role of the parent." He was beginning to smile. "Daddy, I tried in most cases to make you happy because I loved you, do you agree?" He gave a little nod, his smile getting bigger and bigger. "Look at me, I'm pregnant. I have a three-year-old, a teenager who needs me, a husband, and a house to keep! It's impossible to keep help at this old house. So, do you love me enough for me to find a smaller house closer to me, where I can look after you and Mother like you have looked after me?"

And he answered "I'll do whatever you think is best, but I don't want a little house with no porch and cramped spaces." I would worry about that later. At least I had my answer. And as Joe and I walked out the door, Daddy was chuckling, bigtime. I was giving Joe a hard time because I had accomplished our mission where he had failed. Probably the first and last in our lifetime.

How many times my guardian angel appeared during my lifetime! There were times I am sure God's angel was worn out with my frantic pleas. After many prayers asking for answers to my dilemmas, do you know the house three doors down from us became available for sale?! Of course I called Joe. Bless his heart, as usual he agreed to any of my suggestions concerning the care of Mother and Daddy.

Let me stop right now and tell you that Thurman was my rock during these days. Right at my side, pitching in to do whatever was needed. I've never known him in our lifetime together to leave me stranded. Never mind that I'm pregnant, dragging Sam my three-year-old along every step of the way every day, praying my precious child Marilyn, fourteen, wasn't lost in the shuffle. My sleeves were rolled up and I was on a mission. I had no time for tears when our old house, where I was born, was sold. The little house to which they would be moving, by the way, had no big porch, and did have cramped spaces!

What in the world was I going to do with all the furniture and collected junk in this house where Mother and Daddy had lived for over fifty years? Decisions had to be made, and quickly at that: What to keep, what to let go? Mother and I worked well together, and even though I knew she would question some decisions, she never complained. The Birdseye Maple bedroom furniture (along with a stunning diamond ring) was given to her by Papa when she graduated from high school. It had been in her home before she married. It was the bed where all three of her children were born. Everything was too large scale to even think about taking to the new place.

Then there was the outstanding, signed, Tiffany chandelier above the dining room table where Joe and I had stood as little children, learning our colors and the names of the various brilliantly colored fruits in the middle of the mahogany table. Mother and Daddy went through the same teaching ritual many times, obviously finding great joy the in the second time around. This outstanding chandelier was too large for the small dining room. Many, many other things had to go as well. Our neighbor knew the value of the chandeliers. He said, "I want something out of this house and I've always admired the chandelier." He had been very close to Anderson, my brother who died: they had been Eagle Scouts together. I was happy to give it to him. He insisted on paying $100. Had I not accepted the money, it might have been easier for Charlie to have bought it from him later, when he realized what I'd done. Charlie really loved this piece and wanted it more than anybody. How many times have I thought, Why didn't I think to give it to him? I thought it was going into loving hands which made me happy, and I could move on. Charlie approached this neighbor later and offered any amount to have it back in his hands. The only reason he was able to stop his offer at $1000 was because my neighbor's wife was there. She thought the deal was heartless and immoral. She said, "Stop it!" And he took Charlie's check, which made me think he wasn't as interested in his love of the family as he was in the monetary value, which would be thousands. Actually, to know it's still in the family and still loved makes me happy.

I wish I felt as happy about the fate of other pieces I had to add to the let-go groups. The whole thing was overwhelming. Daddy had a built-in-cabinet in the kitchen with his tools and such, which I proceeded to clean out. He could not keep up with me as I sorted through, having a big pile I referred to as The Dump—which I carried out to the end of the lot, by the alley. The trash was growing. The only time I stopped to cry was when I looked up and saw him looking so pitiful, retrieving things I had labeled as junk back into the house. I didn't cry, I sobbed. Daddy heard me, and walked into the bedroom where I was sitting on the bed. He put his arms around me and said, "Sugar, what's wrong?"

I'm sure I told him. "I don't know what to do. I can't take all your stuff to the new place." He and Mother had never seen the place I was moving them. Nor would they until I had finished it all. Once again, he came through for me. "Oh, Sugar, don't worry, I understand. You do what you think best. I'll take back to the trash what I brought in just now. We sat there together a few minutes, me with my big tummy, dirty clothes, and tear-stained face. We hugged and laughed, with my tears streaming down my face. I was spent when I loaded up Sam and a few small pieces I would keep for myself and headed home. I must have looked unkempt and tired. My kind husband took one look at me and told me to rest while he fixed supper. I soaked in a tub of hot water until I could feel the heartache as well as the body ache subsiding. As this point I felt like eating, falling in bed, getting a good night's sleep and start back with the moving the next day. That would be the last of my tears, and from then on the three of us made a fun thing about being together with Sam, having lunch together and generating some excitement about the upcoming move.

Now, how in heaven's name was I going to take care of getting the big objects out of the house and placed? I know in hindsight I made a terrible mistake in my decision. I went through the Yellow Pages and found an antiques dealer who was located on Dickerson Road—Binkley's Antiques. I thought the name Binkley, my maiden name, might be a good omen. So I made an appointment with Mrs. Binkley to come over and appraise the furniture. Looking back, I now can understand why she was eager to quote me a price which I accepted without further advice. Thurman's sister, Matt Glymp, had been a successful antique dealer of fine furniture and accessories for a number of years. A few days after the deal was closed and the papers signed, I learned from my sister-in-law I had made a big mistake, having sold at a much lesser price than I could have to someone else. There was no going back, and Mother and Daddy were not aware of my mistake in moving too fast with my decision. So we moved right ahead with our plan. Everybody happy?

I moved out everything except the bare necessities, leaving them literally two chairs and the TV. They ate off paper plates. I was still insisting, "This is fun, you're almost camping out now! Only be a few more days till you move so close to me. I found a wonderful African-American lady to be your friend as well as cook and clean for you. Mother, we can have more fun days together soon." I'd already employed the painters and selected light airy colors. White marquisette, ruffled curtains would be hanging in every window in the house. There was no time to have anything made. Then one day before they were to move I ran downtown to the five-floor Castner Knott Department Store on Church Street, and bought it all in one afternoon: curtains, white bedspreads, throw rugs for the bedrooms. The next day I flew to the furniture store and bought twin beds for one bedroom. The rather small-scale Jenny Lind bedroom furniture which was mine when I was living at home would be fine for the other bedroom.

My baby was growing; I was beginning to slow down just a bit. While the painters were at work I ran down to the house to hang curtains. I was on a ladder when one of them said, "Lady, I don't think you should be on that ladder. I'm a union man and I could be fired, but just don't tell anybody and my buddy and I will get this done for you," which they did. Things were coming together. My beautiful guardian angel was working overtime.

The day was approaching for me to tell Daddy the new house was ready, and have them leave the old house. I explained to them that I would have the TV picked up that morning along with the bedding and anything else that needed to be moved. The cleaning crew would come the next day. "Don't worry about running the vacuum. Just close and lock the door and don't look back. Look forward to your new life. A new baby is on its way, and our three-year-old will want to spend many hours in your new place with you." They adored Sam, who was named after Daddy.

Daddy was still driving so I was at their new house, waiting. Talk about anxious! What would Daddy's reaction be when he realized there was no porch, and, indeed, cramped spaces? I'd gone to my florist and bought several bunches of flowers so there were flowers in every room. I'd lowered one leaf of the dining room table that had been in the old house and pushed it against the wall and had it set for lunch for Mother, Daddy, Sam and me. The table and chairs were all I could bring, as the China cabinet and buffet would never have fit in the room. I have to say the place looked very inviting. The question was: What was Daddy going to say? I held my breath. They stepped through the door. Daddy walked through the house, looking everywhere, then through the kitchen, and out to the garage without uttering a word. My throat was going dry and I was terribly uneasy when he turned around and looked at me and said, "Sugar, I like it."

Halleluiah! Praise the Lord!

Sally, the cook and housekeeper, came the next morning and she proved to be everything I had anticipated. She was there with them for three years. These were happy, relaxed years and they felt loved and very needed. I would ask them to keep Sam from time to time. He loved to ride his big wheel the short distance down the hill, park at their front door and join them for breakfast many mornings. They both seemed happy and content in their new little house. My prayers were filled with Thanksgiving to God who had brought me through with flying colors.

Gather the crumbs of happiness and they will make you a loaf of contentment.

—Unknown

Last Journeys

1966

Daddy was eighty-three and Mother was seventy-nine. They were living three doors from me now, on Moran Drive. Even before Daddy was older, there were tales told about his driving that stemmed from the fact that he was known as the absent-minded professor. Mother never learned to drive; she came from an age when most women didn't. However, she was Daddy's co-pilot when they got older. Joe and I were beginning to get concerned about their safety and the people driving down the road as well. Mother and their housekeeper on Moran Drive, Sally, began to divulge little harrowing experiences that weren't laughable. After one incident involving his not stopping at a four-way stop in a school zone, while driving Sally home, his license was revoked. Unbeknownst to me, my brother was able to get it reinstated, and lo and behold, Daddy was back on the road. I was more than a little upset with my brother Joe, even though he explained, "Mary, I did it for you because you would be the one responsible for all the driving."

My answer to that was, "It's much more stressful knowing he's endangering the lives of children when he's taking Sally home. That's when children are being let out of school! I'd much rather add to my responsibilities." So I prayed without ceasing when I knew Daddy was heading for the car.

It was during these days that I knew Daddy had taken his car to his nephew across town to have some work done. This particular area of town was not the safest or most desirable to find yourself in. Daddy was very fond of his nephew and didn't want to deal with anybody else who might be closer to where he was living. I knew he left right after an early lunch. I took Sally back to her home that day. I hurried back to my own home, as I was having dinner for our close friends Maxine and Buddy. Around suppertime Mother called, "Mary, I'm worried about Daddy, I haven't heard from him since he left home,"

To console her I said, "It isn't that late. Besides, you have no idea how much time it would take to fix the car." Mother would listen to me no matter what. I continued fixing dinner. It was getting dark when I called her.

Her voice sounded so strange as she said, "No, I haven't heard a word."

Then I called the garage and learned they had closed for the day. I called my oldest son, Charlie, and asked if he would drive to the vicinity of the garage and see if he could locate Daddy, which he did immediately. I didn't call Mother again, as I didn't want to alarm her.

We were sitting down to dinner when the phone rang. It was Mother and she was crying. I left the table and went down the street to bring her home with me. Charlie had found nothing to help to find out anything about Daddy's whereabouts. He called my brother, his uncle Joe. The two of them scoured the area together. At home, the four of us finished our meal and Buddy and Maxine left for home. Still no word.

They were hardly out the door when Joe called, "Don't tell Mother, but I've called the police to help us search the area." This was turning out to be very scary. The hours wore on. I made some coffee and Thurman and I sat with Mother while we waited for news. I thought: *Mother is seemingly calmer than I am at this point.* I was near hysteria. The phone rang at daybreak: the police had found Daddy.

Joe and Charlie had stayed in their cars while the men were in the area searching. It was decided it would be closer for Charlie to bring Daddy home so we continued to wait, much relieved. I'll never in a million years forget how I felt when Charlie helped him out of the car in my driveway. I took one look and couldn't believe my eyes: Daddy was black. Covered with coal dust! Now I know my uncontrollable laughter with tears flowing was "hysteria."

The story unfolded as Daddy spoke first, "I somehow got turned around when I left the garage. It was getting dark and I turned into what I found to be a coal yard. I drove around this huge coal yard again and again without finding an exit. I must have become a little disoriented and decided I'd simply have to wait until I was found. I hoped to find a security guard, but I was so tired I sat down on a bed of coal and fell asleep."

When Charlie saw him he recalled, "I couldn't do anything at first but laugh. It was a ridiculous state of affairs." He said to Daddy, "Granddaddy, why didn't you get back in the car? It's more comfortable than a bed of coal!" Charlie helped him up off the coal pile.

He broke up laughing when Daddy explained, "By then I couldn't find the car, it was so dark outside." The car was found about half a block away. The two had a confrontation over whether Daddy would drive it home.

Charlie had a new Volvo and insisted his granddaddy ride with him, finding something in the trunk to cover the seat. He assured him, "And I'll get your car taken home later."

When they arrived, we all had a bite of breakfast together, and it became time to pick up Sally. I would do that, but before I left the house I wanted to talk to Joe. He came to the phone and I must have been talking loud and fast. I remember him laughing after I said, "Joe, under no circumstance do you bring Daddy's car here. I'm leaving this for you to take care of, blow it up or whatever. Also you need to come over here as quickly as possible and explain to him that he has no license, no car, but tell him not to worry, because I'll take care of everything."

"Yes Ma'am! I'll take care of it this morning," laughed Joe, and he did.

Later that morning I went down for a short visit to see how Daddy was doing. He looked up with those beautiful blue eyes and said, "Sugar, they took my car away from me."

I could have cried but all I could softly say was, "I'm so sorry." Daddy never knew I was the culprit, not Joe. I decided to just leave well enough alone.

1970

The last three months of Mother and Daddy's lives were spent in Imperial Manor, the very best facility I could find to place them. For several months before this move had to be made we had nurses around the clock. A registered nurse who had retired from St. Thomas Hospital was with them during the vital hours and two home care workers came for the afternoon and night shifts. Sally stayed on as well. This arrangement worked for a while till we needed more skilled help. This wonderful woman, a registered nurse, moved in and cared for Mother around the clock. Until she explained, "If there was any way I could possibly continue taking care of your parents I would, but the time has come for you make a hard decision what to do next." She said it was not feasible that I would ever find anyone to take over her job. She had moved in because she was so disgusted with the sitters who didn't follow through after she left instructions. She did this expecting only the same payment as the sitters through the evening and night hours: "I've fallen in love with this family and it grieves me to leave."

One of the saddest days in my life was the Sunday that I went to Imperial Manor with Thurman at my side to make the arrangements for them to move there. We decided to get a double room, as I couldn't bear to part them. Daddy was not in poor health but was getting somewhat feeble. When I asked him about going with Mother, he said "Sugar, I don't want to stay here without her, I'll be much happier in the room beside her." And so the move was made.

My days became routine. I would see my fifteen-year-old Marilyn and my six-year-old Sam off to school after breakfast. I would then cook a good meal for Mother and Daddy. They really never complained about the food there, but I had eaten it—not good! When I would walk in before mealtime the residents were waiting for Doree. They were gathered in the big room, many in wheelchairs. Their faces would light up when they saw her; she really was adorable. She would go from person to person, enjoying all their attention. One man kept gum in his pocket which she would pull out every visit as he held his pocket open. When I arrived at the hall, they would take my food, put the cold things in the refrigerator and take food to be warmed in the microwave. When it was time for lunch, they would help me take it to their room. I would feed Mother and Doree first. Then Daddy and I ate together. After lunch Doree climbed in bed with Mother and they took a nap. Daddy and I spent the time visiting together and all in all it was a sweet, sweet time. I watched the clock so Doree and I would be on time to pick up Sam at school. Dinner would be ready when Thurman walked in the house at five-thirty or six o'clock, after which I went back to Imperial Manor, taking some snacks for Mother and Daddy's supper. I always stayed until bedtime, when I would lovingly tuck them in. When I got home the kitchen was clean; Sam and Doree had their baths and were settled in for the night. What a great Dad Thurman was, I could never have made it without him, my rock!

Three months to the day they moved in, every day was routine, like all the other days. But this evening fell out of the routine, when Thurman wanted to go with me, and suggested we leave the little ones with Marilyn and her friend. It was a lovely summer evening and only a short distance to the Manor from our house. So, I made Daddy a lime sherbet and ginger ale float. A close friend, Helen, walked over that evening. Daddy was on the patio outside their room and Mother was in her bed when we arrived. Mother had become very weak and was in bed most of the time now. We enjoyed a lovely time together as we sat there talking. Daddy enjoyed his sherbet float. He said two or three times, "Isn't this the most beautiful night? I've never seen the stars appear so close and be so bright." Twice during the time on the patio he said to me, "Sugar, I want to thank you for all you've done."

And as for the statements which he had made so many times, I said, as I had so many times, "Oh, Daddy, you and Mother can't live long enough for me to do everything I want to do for you." It was bedtime, around ten o'clock, when we stepped back into the room and I kissed Mother good night.

She opened her eyes and looked at me and said, "Sam." I'm sure she was saying she wanted to see him, for she absolutely adored that child, and would always comment how he looked like her son that she lost, Anderson.

Helen walked out of the room first, then Thurman and I were walking out together, when Daddy called out for the third time, "Sugar, I want to thank you again for all you've done."

Thurman and I drove home and talked of how Daddy was doing so well, and that I should fix him another sherbet float soon, because he enjoyed it so much. We both felt concerned about Mother, and felt I should again employ sitters for the nights, which I had done when they first went to Imperial Manor. We went to bed soon after we came in, but for some reason I was sleeping fitfully. At one-thirty in the morning, the phone rang. I jumped up and felt cold when I heard a voice say, "Mrs. Williams, please come to Imperial Manor." When I hung up the phone Thurman was standing beside me, and I fell into his arms, knowing of course it was concerning Mother. I prayed as we drove there that she hadn't died without me being with her. What a shock to find that it was Daddy who had died in his sleep of heart failure. My first thought was how strange his last words were to me a few hours before: "Thank you, Sugar, for all you've done." My second thought was of his great concern that he would more than likely be left to live the rest of his life without Mother, because she was getting weaker every day. His concern had been addressed by the Great Provider. He had talked to me about whether or not he would come to the little house close to me and live there after her passing. I would end the conversation with, "Daddy, please don't worry, whatever happens you will be loved and cared for."

I had not been home too many hours when Thurman and I were sitting at the kitchen table, having a cup of coffee and waiting for Joe, when the phone rang. The voice on the other end said, "Mrs. Williams, I hate to make this call. Your Mother passed away in her sleep." It was seven hours after Daddy's death. I suddenly felt so empty. No one ever again, I thought, would love me in the same way these dear people had. I know there are all kinds of love: love for your parents, love for your siblings, love for your husband, love for your children, love for your friends. I loved passionately all of these. I still do.

After recovering from the initial shock of losing them and planning their funeral to be held at the same time, I found myself dreaming again, seeing them in death. Caskets were always left open during this time, a practice I've never liked since the death of my brother Anderson as a child. I did want to see those beloved faces one more time, but I was praying I wouldn't react hysterically and cause everybody else pain.

What a relief when I walked in the room and felt at once, at peace. I smiled, knowing my guardian angel was right there. Rather than being saddened during those hours, it was like witnessing a wedding. These two who together lived in love for over fifty years were now leaving together to spend eternity with their Father. I had no regrets. I found myself enjoying the people who were there at the funeral. I simply couldn't fathom the numbers who had come to pay their respects. Dignitaries from the political and legal worlds, the Governor, the Mayor, and many others I knew indirectly, through Joe. Even in the rush of the crowd Joe found me and introduced his sister. Daddy, I felt, would have been impressed.

People also presented written stories. A testimonial about my father from the men in his Bible Class today hangs in the library of the East End Methodist Church. Many of Mother's former Sunday School students at Chapel Avenue Church of Christ wrote memorials which I have treasured. A very much older woman came to me, held my hand, tears flowing down her cheeks, "I'm not sure you even know what your parents did for me." Similar stories were repeated time and again by both men and women. I was impressed and grateful that they had come and knew how impressed and grateful Mother and Daddy would have been.

These two lived a good life, they loved God and their fellow man. The legacy they left will live on and on in my heart of hearts: I know I'm a better person because they lived. The precious family all around would miss them, but at the same time we would continue telling our humorous and serious stories, and enjoy reliving our lives with them.

I had no way of knowing that Thurman had already made plans for a trip for me to the beach where I could bask in the sun and feel the warmth and beauty of God's handiwork. There's no child of God who through a lifetime enjoys His creation of the ocean and sandy beaches more than this one. For all His blessings I'm eternally grateful.

To handle yourself, use your head;
to handle others, use your heart.

—Eleanor Roosevelt

Picnics in the Cemetery

When Marilyn's son Marshall was a little thing, maybe three years old, we decided we'd go out to eat, taking Marshall with us, and then take flowers to the cemetery. But Marilyn noted that my adorable grandson made such a mess eating out—so we changed the plan. Why not a picnic, with Mother and Daddy? They were resting in peace there in Spring Hill Cemetery. So Doree, Marilyn and I did that, talking about Mother and Daddy all the while. It was so relaxing. I shared stories that they had not heard. Marshall ran around the cemetery freely. What an adorable child!

There were many such occasions. The girls don't always go with me now, for they're so busy. But for a long time, the three of us would go to the historic Spring Hill Cemetery on Gallatin Road in East Nashville to visit my mother and daddy's graves, and those of my brother Anderson and my Aunt Mary. Thurman's grave is not in the same area but is a short distance away. We took care of them at one time, all going together. I didn't even go for Easter this year, when I usually change the fall flowers. I put red roses out at Christmastime, but I didn't go back and change them. I'll feel the need soon to go. Perhaps I'll go alone.

One Christmas, about three years ago, I had beautiful things created. Rather than put flowers, I would put a wreath on the monument. We worked so hard on the graves that Christmas. They looked unusually beautiful, and I couldn't have done it by myself.

We turned the corner as we were leaving, and there was a monument with a pitiful looking arrangement on it. Marilyn laughed and pointed to it and said, "Mom, look over there! I want you to know right now that we're not going to spend the time and money that you have on the cemetery. This is probably the best memorial you'll have. That little, half-dead arrangement of flowers." They were so cute, they just died laughing, as did I.

I replied, "I don't blame you. I'm so glad you don't feel the need or the urge to do it. But as long as I'm living, and I feel the urge, I'm going to do it." They never have had as much energy as I've had, they'll tell you that.

Back when Doree's children, Cole and Channie, were young, we would go to the cemetery. My grandchildren loved it; they loved to wander. Reading the markers at Spring Hill was a favorite pastime for me because it's a historic cemetery. So when we went, I took the children to the old section and read aloud, and we would speculate on the families. They were most interested in the baby monuments. They were beginning to read by then.

One day we were driving through the cemetery and Doree and Marilyn were with us. Channie said, "Aw, Nunny, there's a good man buried over there!"

"What?!"

"It says Goodman." Good man! Out of the mouth of babes...

Marilyn's son, Marshall, christened me "Nunny" when he was little. Mike and Charlie's children continued to call me "Grandmamma," but the other grandchildren and later, their children, call me Nunny. Both names sounded with love when they fell upon my ears.

A few years back, I was keeping the grandchildren, Doree's Channie and Cole, for the weekend. They both had to sit in the backseat with seatbelts, and they didn't get along that well at times. They would get bored and start fussing. They were just siblings, it was normal. But it made me very nervous because

I couldn't tend to them when I was driving. That weekend I said, "I need to go over to the cemetery, and beforehand to Geny's to pick out some flowers. You all would love to pick out the flowers for Gandy's (Thurman's) grave. Why don't we ride over there together and I'll do the arrangement?"

We went and had the best time picking out the flowers at the wholesale place. The children were so good! We drove over to the cemetery and they were still acting like angels. "So where would you like to go for lunch?" I asked my darling, well-behaved grandchildren. They wanted to go to Whitt's Barbecue on Harding Road, back across town, but there's no place to sit there. So many times, we'd pick up the barbecue and go down the road a short distance. That was where Belle Meade Buffet used to be located and where we had so many treasured memories. There was an alcove there and we would sit on the bench and eat. They were thrilled: Yes! We were going to do that. It would be fun!

We hadn't been in the car anytime at all when they started spatting, just picking at each other. I said, "Y'all just stop it! You've been so good, but now you're ruining the day. Cut it out right now!" They kept it up and I said, "Y'all are going to make me have a wreck! I'm going to stop this car and wait for you to stop."

Channie and Cole cried out, "We'll stop, we'll stop!"

But they didn't. I found myself going down a one-way street, the wrong way! It made me so mad that they had distracted me to the point of danger. A car was coming toward us. HONKING! Once that was taken care of, I said, "Don't expect to go to Whitt's. I'm not going out of our way to go. Instead, we'll stop at Mrs. Winner's, which is on the way home." That was a little chicken and biscuits to-go restaurant.

Channie whined, "I don't like Miz Winner's."

I said, "I don't care. You have been awful driving home and you know it is upsetting to me." They were so shocked! They never thought I would do that and they talked about it forever.

The grandchildren loved the cemetery. On Thurman's grave

I wanted something different, so I ordered a custom monument. It isn't exactly as I envisioned, but it turned out very different from other monuments and gave the effect I wanted. The monument is to the left of the gravesite, with an urn on the top. There's a bench on the right for contemplation, and on that bench there perches a little bronze bird. While birds symbolize the spirit in flight, this bird is for our granddaughter Maclellan. Thurman adored that child and they had fed the birds together many times in our backyard under the big oak tree. Inscribed on Thurman's tombstone are these words by William Shakespeare:

His life was gentle, the elements so mixed in him,
That nature might stand up and say to the world,
"This was a man."

Marilyn's Wedding

There's nobody who loves a wedding more than I do, and I got to do my own sweet child's in 1974. When Sam was nine and Doree six, we held Marilyn's wedding to Ken Switzer from Paducah, Kentucky, in West End United Methodist Church. Afterwards they moved to Louisville, Kentucky where Ken would attend law school.

At this time, I was between the jobs where I was gainfully employed during our marriage. I was on a pretty tight budget, so I designed a plan. Edna and Henry Schofield were the photographers. It was great fun working with them, having known and loved them earlier. They had become like family.

While I was working on television commercials I'd met Monica Joy of Joy's Florist. I approached her about the flowers. The capable floral designer understood where I was coming from when I suggested using magnolia branches in large rented urns. Monica quickly said, "Don't worry about renting urns. You can use ours!" We arranged to deliver the magnolia tree branches to her the afternoon before. The morning of the wedding, the mother of the bride (Yours Truly) would rush the lovely blossoms to the florist's shop, where Monica would condition them to hold up during the ceremony.

Mike, along with Marilyn, cut the branches off the neighbor's tree. When I saw it later the tree looked terribly deformed and I was mortified. I apologized, however, my neighbor simply laughed, saying "That magnolia tree had spread too far and needed pruning. Don't worry! I'll enjoy seeing my contribution to the wedding, which I know will be beautiful."

On the morning of the wedding we had an electrical storm with high winds and pelting rain, both shattering the delicate magnolia blossoms. I panicked but Monica called me and said, "Relax, Mary. I anticipated the fact this could happen, and I have lilies and gardenias ready." She offered these to us at the wholesale prices, what a lady! The bridesmaids carried Woburn Abbey Roses, complementing the coral color of their long, raw silk dresses. Monica scattered the full blooms of the roses in the urn arrangements. Marilyn's wedding was beautiful and she made everything so easy. She kept saying, "Mother, whatever you do, I will love it!" So I went full steam ahead.

Returning home after all the festivities, it hit me. How empty the house felt! How much we would miss her and her friends coming and going! Especially Sam and Doree. Older brothers Charlie and Mike were both married and had homes of their own. Marilyn would have been gone before marrying had she not changed her plans.

Marilyn and her best friend, Becky Leech, were roommates at Middle Tennessee State University during their freshman year. My daughter intended to graduate at the conclusion of four years there. But she came to me with a change of mind. She was concerned about the fact that if she moved, and was gone for four years from our home, she would not know Sam and Doree as closely. She predicted that she would probably marry someone she met in college, and be forever gone from living in our home. How level-headed she was, when she sat there and explained it to me! I asked her where she would want to go to school in Nashville. I was shocked when Marilyn said, "David Lipscomb." She had always said "Don't talk to me about David Lipscomb." But there she went, getting a good education from David Lipscomb College. Thurman bought her a car and she commuted. What a blessing to have her at home during those years. Sam and Doree adored her, and to this day they still do.

Marilyn did meet the man she would marry at David Lipscomb College, Kenneth Marshall Switzer. Thurman and I agreed, the greatest joy of our lives had always been gathering our children around the dinner table. For a while that table setting included Ken. He spent many hours at our home, mostly around the dinner table, where I marveled at the food this six-foot-four man could consume, almost a whole fried chicken! I actually miss seeing him enjoy food to that extent these days, now that healthy food governs his lifestyle. The man ran fifty miles on his fiftieth birthday, if this tells you anything!

On a particular day, our little family and Ken were happy and content, seated at our dinner table, when Marilyn announced their engagement. An explosion erupted. I was horrified when Doree darted from the table saying, "I hate him, I hate him!" She threw herself across the bed sobbing where Sam joined her saying the very same thing, "I hate him!" I was absolutely mortified. Those two couldn't bear to think of losing their adored big sister!

Thurman excused himself, as did Marilyn, to hopefully quieten these two. I didn't know whether to shake them or console them, I was so concerned about Ken's reaction. Not to worry: Ken didn't miss a bite and never changed his expression.

Doree was junior bridesmaid. When I first glanced at the picture of her with Sam, among the many made on the day of Marilyn and Ken's wedding, I took another, closer look. I knew immediately by her expression that something was not right. Sam's hand, squeezing her shoulder tightly and forcibly, was inflicting pain! The poor child bore it, rather than make a scene while the pictures were being taken. I have a feeling Sam was probably bored and looking for a way to liven things up, as most of the time he and his sister were buddies, and still are. Those two I refer to as my "bonuses." What a joy they are today, at my age of ninety-four. Doree and Sam are in their fifties—where did the years go?

The greatest thing you'll ever learn is
just to love and be loved in return.

—Eden Ahbez

Mary Williams Guide Service

In the early seventies, life was moving on in our typical fashion, when I realized Thurman was bordering on a state of depression. This clinical depression was not by any means a constant in our lives. However, when it raised its ugly head, it could be terribly difficult to deal with. I found myself in a state of anxiety, believing I needed to make a plan to increase our family income. I knew full well I could get back at any time into the television world. I reasoned: I've been there, done that. Loved it! But all is changed now.

I was aware of how tourism was making great strides in the city. Now among the leading industries: printing and publishing, banking, insurance and health care. Along with that bit of news, I began to see charter motor coaches all over this town. With the now extremely popular music-themed Opryland opening its gates to the United States, Canada, and yes, Europe as well. A visit to the park, along with admission to view the oldest radio show, the Grand Old Opry, were the two greatest enticements for the travel companies offering a trip to Nashville. Their clients were buying it in droves. I had a brainstorm: I believe I'd really enjoy being a guide in this city I love!

I was open to anything other than a 9 to 5 job, knowing I'd never last, knowing my two young children needed my presence more than having a regular job would allow, anyway. My friend, Agnes Pennington, ran the first little guide service in the city from the parking lot on the side of the Grand Old Opry house downtown on 5th Avenue. It was just expected that she would be asked to run the new Gaylord company, Grand Ole Opry Tours. My mind was racing. I'll call my friend to see if I can ride on one of the tours. Also, to ask about any historic tours they surely were offering.

Agnes was more than excited that I showed an interest in her business, placing me on the next charter group. The guide, Evelyn Mayhew, was very knowledgeable concerning the country music part of Nashville. She had a charming personality and the people loved the tour, as did I. The one thought I couldn't dismiss, however, was that there was no information on the city as a whole, no speaking of the large range of music, from symphony to bluegrass, nor revealing the exciting stories of the history of Nashville. The only historic property, the Hermitage, home of our seventh president, Andrew Jackson, was offered in any of the brochures from the companies in the city. I very soon rounded these brochures up to study!

As the days wore on, I became more excited, signing up for classes on the history of Nashville and Tennessee. I complied a notebook on all I wanted to share. I needed to also delve into the country music and the lives of the entertainers, so I visited the library and the archives, took a walk, through Music Row, stopping at the studios to get information. Was I ever going to be ready to face a group of visitors, to be employed as their guide? And even if I felt confident to start out on my own, how was I going to get companies to commit to using "Mary Williams Guide Service"?

Of course, join the Chamber of Commerce! They had the names of all the travel companies coming into the city. I took my long list and settled in, at my antique plantation desk in the corner of my bedroom. I picked up the phone and proceeded to sell Nashville—and myself! Law of averages was working! I'll never, ever forget the very first time I stood in front of all those smiling faces and their escort, having to prove what I'd promised by phone and on the brochure I had mailed out. "Mary Williams Guide Service: the best in Nashville. All guides are native Nashvillians."

Thurman was more than a little skeptical, when he reasoned, "Now, do I understand correctly? You will be giving directions to the out of town drivers around the city and trips out of Nashville as well? Oh, hon, I can't see that happening when you have zero sense of direction!"

My comeback was always, "Oh ye of little faith." I won't pretend. That was the most difficult thing to master about my undertaking. Down through the years I have found this to be true of many of the guides. But just as I figured it out on my own, so did they. Except for the driver, the people warmed up to me when on occasion I messed up. And most of the time, the driver too ended up smiling.

Word of mouth, feedback from the drivers and escorts to myself and to my guides, critique by the escorts to the travel companies, and the Chamber of Commerce recommendation all proved to be of great help advertising my company's excellence and diversity. The very best source of presenting Mary Williams Guide Service would have been the trade shows and motor coach conventions held out of state. Except for the few times they were held in Nashville, this was impossible for me. With my children Sam and Doree and my husband needing me at home, I had to give up that idea forever. So, back to the telephone, and to training new guides. I knew I would be in need of more of them soon!

I was not only shocked but overwhelmed by the response, but very quickly I knew what I had to do. Find those perfect people to train and get ready for the overflow. College students who were the ones most seen employed by other companies? No, I was looking for young wives, homemakers who needed a part time job. Young women who would commit for years to come. Therefore, there would not be much turnover in my fleet of guides. Marilyn, my daughter, who was that age and lifestyle, was helpful in spreading the word among her friends. At first, Marilyn was not interested at all in being a guide. She finally agreed to join her mother's guide service, and she was excellent! These young women—and some men—had to be interested in this endeavor to take the two thick notebooks I handed them. One was the history of Nashville, the other contained Nashville's current events. There was also the expectation that they would read the newspaper daily to keep abreast of the news. This was quite a lot to expect of them, at their rate of pay. Fortunately, these guides received gratuities from both individuals on tour and the tour companies, and this pay often exceeded that which they collected from my guide service.

Would you believe, from time to time one of the guides would say, "I love this job so much, I would do it for simply the ego boost!" I knew what they were feeling. The entire experience was such fun for all of us. When a potential guide would think she was ready, having learned all the information and ridden with seasoned guides several times, she was then ready to hop in my car. I played the part of motor coach driver, and she was on her own. There was never a question as to their physical attractiveness, knowledge, charm or knowing they would be a good ambassador for their city.

The guides learned to continue narration while the alert driver noted their directions. It worked beautifully, most of the time. At the peak, I had eighteen guides listed. There were no freelance guides back then. After the city became aware of Mary Williams' guides, they were sought out by other tour companies, offering them more money. All remained loyal to me. Several who started out with me all those years ago are still my close friends, and among the freelance guides today who are in great demand.

The industry today has become more lucrative. Melanie Lokey, one of my "girls" and good friend, mentioned she would be able to retire from teaching and live off the income as a freelance guide. Carmen McNabb, the other of the two top guides in Nashville, who was with me from the beginning, shared over dinner how excited she is over her ever-increasing guide business. I am so happy for these two! When the three of us get together for dinner, I become excited hearing their stories about what's happening in the world of tourism in Music City today.

The decision to open Mary Williams Guide Service turned out to be a wise one. The children's school holidays didn't pose a problem. "Come on, kids, ride with me!" If my child woke with a fever, I didn't panic; I got on the phone and called one of the guides to take over. When Thurman became so ill with cancer, I was then able to rely on the guides who had been with me the longest to take over, allowing me to stay at home those last several months.

This time is a precious memory, one I have thought about so many times, feeling thankful for the little company I'd founded, all the friends I had made from all over the world, through my experience of first, being their guide, which of all things resulted many times in fast friendships. So many beautiful people I was privileged to meet and correspond with later! There was hardly a day I didn't find in the mailbox a lovely note from the escort with a travel company, even notes from the owners of the companies, after having read the feedback notes from their clients, and many times from the visitors themselves. They had fallen in love with Nashville: its history, its beauty, its hospitality, and diversity.

When I think about it today, I feel a bit selfish. Thinking of the fact I was in a position to choose and pick the tours I myself would take. At times I didn't choose. When the Chamber would call with a VIP group needing a guide, they would ask for me to lead it.

On one occasion I was asked to be the guide for a group of outstanding business people in the city. I had read about these people, seen them on television, so was a bit intimidated. I decided to forget that feeling and do my best. I must have pulled it off, as later, I was asked again to do tours for business groups in Nashville. There were special tours which I elected to do: the docents from the Governor's Mansion in South Carolina. I was happy beyond words they were so impressed with our governor's home and the city in general. I was with these ladies for five days, so of course there were a few side trips.

A retiree and his wife from Hershey, Pennsylvania. This gentleman was with the candy company for, if I recall correctly, as many as fifty years! This company appreciated and loved this man evidently, because when they contacted me I was told, "Find a week of fun activities, day and night!" They implied money was no object and expected a high-end tour. Of course, I chose Opryland Hotel for their stay, with all I could choose for their entertainment there, and Opryland Park. That was only the beginning. If you're wondering what on earth I did for a whole week of fun and entertainment, here are a few:

Dinner and tour at the Historic Hermitage Hotel (rave review), Belmont Mansion where they fell in love with the story of its mistress, Adelicia, who was known to be our Scarlet O'Hara from *Gone with the Wind*. Belle Meade Mansion where we had a delicious lunch and tour of the old horse farm, home of Secretariat, with its delightful stories of the Harding family. They were very interested in Vanderbilt University and the story of its founder, Commodore Cornelius Vanderbilt, who was a fellow Northerner. I could go on and on about our days and nights in Nashville, where the three of us became good friends while living it up. Our trip to Lynchburg, Tennessee, home of Jack Daniels Distillery, which they toured and found fascinating. However, I do think our midday dinner at Miss Mary Bobo's, the old boarding house on the square, where they were served the very best Southern country cooking anywhere to be found, was the highlight of their experience. I showed them the gardens where those fresh vegetables were gathered that they were raving about.

I still tend to love remembering more than I could possibly include in my memoir. Hope you get the idea what the tours were all about and how much fun they were, not only for our visitors but for those of us lucky enough to share in the experience.

Even after I closed Mary Williams Guide Service, when I was

eighty years old, I remained in the employ of Sweet Magnolia Tours. It was the only Nashville company allowed to employ my guides. My responsibility was to place the guides with the charter motor coaches, which kept my hand in. At eighty-six I realized that I would never, ever be computer-savvy, which now was a must. My time had come to bow out entirely. I cannot tell you how difficult I found this decision to make. However, as I have indicated, I kept up with some of the former Mary Williams guides as close friends, and find myself still included occasionally in a few activities where I meet a younger generation who have taken over where I left off. Such is life.

You have brains in your head, you have feet in your shoes
You can steer yourself any direction you choose
You're on your own and you know what you know
And you are the guy who'll decide where to go.

—Dr. Seuss

Mary's Tours
The Ryman Auditorium

The Ryman Auditorium is an historic landmark I grew to love! My first introduction to the Ryman Auditorium was through my mother. She told me of famous people she had seen in this building when it was a church, built in the late 1800s by a riverboat captain, Tom Ryman, who owned the largest fleet of riverboats on the Cumberland River. He became well known in this city after having come off the Cumberland River one Saturday more or less to heckle the fiery Sam Jones from Cartersville, Georgia. Jones was preaching under the tent during a revival, a familiar scene here on Saturday nights. My understanding is that the subject dealt with "Mothers and their Wayward Sons" and Captain Tom Ryman knew full well, as well as the people of Nashville knew, what a real scoundrel Jones was! Probably even Tom was shocked when he found himself at the conclusion of the sermon marching to the front, confessing his sins and being restored! His vow was to build a church, "The Union Gospel Tabernacle", for all the preachers coming to Nashville to hold revivals. They would find more to host them here than a big tent. Mother saw Caruso, Jeanette McDonald, Nelson Eddy, Helen Hayes and other big stars of her day at the building.

The Union Gospel Tabernacle architecture in no way resembles our other churches built before the turn of the century. Gothic, Greek Revival...Who would have guessed how beautiful it would be with its style and stained-glass windows? The most remarkable outcome would have to be the natural acoustics, becoming known as the most outstanding building in the South appealing to the theatrical world. Later, the same acoustics would appeal to country music fans, who from 1943 to 1974 held their Opry shows in the "Grand Ole Opry House" building, broadcasting from there over radio station WSM across much of North America. When I speak of this building, I can easily get carried away! Later, I was in a position to speak from its stage many, many times. The people were completely fascinated with its history. My audience might be country music fans or dignitaries from far and wide.

The diversity of the people interested made it exciting and fun to be involved. Actually, I chose the Ryman Auditorium to share in my memoir because I feel such a part of it. During the days of live commercials, the Bob Barker show *The Price is Right* was aired from its stage, and I played a part in the commercials for the sponsors of the show. A network show was big business. So I'll have to say I knocked myself out to make it memorable for Nashville!

One arrangement I made was for an antique table prop. My copy read: *To create in every shot as much of the Southern atmosphere as possible.* A small wholesale florist I used was the business that created the Southern Magnolia blossoms and branches from silk that looked for all the world "real!" The antique tureen I used was lent to me, and even Bob Barker was impressed! That was a fun night, with a party after the show.

There was also a time on the Ryman "boards" for me when I was a teen. I was sixteen, attending East High School. My drama teacher encouraged me to try out for a city-wide production to be held on the stage of the Ryman Auditorium. *On Our Way* was held in conjunction with the convention of the Tennessee Education Association and sponsored by the Nashville Council of Parents and Teachers. A musical revue, it depicted the close relationship of education and the democratic way of life. I was selected, joining the cast, with the Auditorium filled for both evenings of the show. I played "Sally" the Granddaughter who was going to be a teacher, and that was the lead role! The other principal, "Grandfather" was played by Joe Kraft, who became a well-known figure in Nashville. The production called for 12 elaborate sets of scenery, made by the local schools, a 27-piece orchestra, a singing chorus of 300, a large speaking chorus, and a ballet group.

So as a child, a teen, and an adult the Ryman Auditorium has held a special place in my memory, and in my heart. How happy I was to share these stories and more with strangers who admired the building and its history when I was a tour guide!

There is nothing that cannot happen today.

—Mark Twain

Doree's Graduation Dress

In 1985, I found myself looking for Doree's graduation dress when I heard about Jeanne's Fantasia. It was owned by Nashville designer Jeanne Dudley Smith, who not only restored vintage clothing, but designed originals as well. I never even stopped to consider if those dresses might be out of my price range. Really, I was more than anything, curious to see the shop in her home and see her line of dresses which I had heard so much about.

When Doree and I arrived, the owner was on the phone, stopping a moment to welcome us inside. The two of us began to browse. All the dresses were lovely. However, one caught my eye that I knew immediately was "Doree's dress." She tried it on, unfortunately. She was truly wearing the perfect dress. When the owner walked into the room she raised her hand, saying, "No further, she is a vision of loveliness." It finally dawned on me to check the price! Oh my! Quickly I began to help remove the dress from Doree's body, when the owner spoke up again. "I'm aware this particular dress of fine batiste fabric with French handmade lace is more expensive than others. However, watching the two of you it came to mind that I just found my "Mother-Daughter Team" to model for my company here in Nashville. I do hope you're interested. The dress you both really want will be yours after only a few shows, at which time I would hope you would continue modeling for me."

I knew I would enjoy the job, plus be able to look no further for her dress, but Doree had to decide. She thought for a brief moment, and I really thought she was positive with her answer of "Yes!".

Our very first job was at the Governor's Residence, where in the audience I saw several friends. I was having fun and thinking that Doree was as well. As soon as we stepped out of earshot, she half-whispered, "This is not for me!" Within the next few days, our next assignment was at the opening of an exclusive art gallery. Unfortunately, there was an open bar with a noticeable amount of social drinking taking place. She said she heard she was considered a real beauty, and added, "I was hit on, by I think more than one man!" That surely wasn't the first time this ever happened, but this was her opportunity to bow out of our unwritten contract. Even though we had agreed to a third show at Belle Meade Mansion, I surely didn't expect her to continue doing something she hated.

I spoke with the owner of Fantasia and offered to pay for Doree's dress, of course. This lovely lady understood completely, refusing to even talk about paying for her dress. However, she asked if I would model the vintage "Morning Dress" at the show coming up at the Autumn Fest held at Belle Meade Mansion. I didn't expect it to be as much fun anyway without Doree, but when I understood Jeanne to say "*Mourning* Dress" I was on the verge of begging off. Only to find it was a really beautiful "*Morning* Dress." There too, I saw several friends, enjoyed the young models, and all in all had a really great day.

The graduation dress was worn by Doree with great style. Her daddy was pleased that she looked so beautiful. However, if she had worn a burlap tow sack he would've thought the same. And really, so would I! A few years later Mike and Vickie's daughter, my darling granddaughter Amy, wore the same dress to her high school graduation. She, too, looked beautiful in it.

This little stint of modeling came well after my days of modeling clothes for Cain Sloan Department Store "live" during my years at Channel 4, WSM television and four seasons of enjoying the New York designers' clothing at Tinsley's on Church Street in downtown Nashville. Truly I have found myself completely enjoying each thing I've chosen to do throughout my life to be gainfully employed.

I guess five years ago, at eighty-six, it was okay to have hung it all up and enjoy the memories and laughter! Along with finding new and different friends and activities, while hanging on for dear life to my precious "old friends", some of whom can remember Doree's graduation dress.

Life likes to be taken by the lapel and told,
"I'm with you kid, let's go!'

Maya Angelou

Bernie

What a wonderful little private beach I have found here at my friend's on the bay in Fairhope, Alabama! Another friend and I drove down to spend a few days—a perfect place to write more stories for my memoir. We're heading back to Nashville in the morning, and I hate that we have to leave as I only found this spot late yesterday evening. It was designed just for me: just beyond the pier, below the road, a little strip of wide sandy beach, looking for all the world as if it were waiting for me to show up with my chair and hat, dragging my large beach bag. Not a soul in sight; just the birds watching me as if they might be wondering what I'm doing invading their space. A lovely breeze with a little cold nip, bright sun above, and the sound of the waves breaking as they rush to shore—just heaven to me.

One of my greatest blessings are my friends—young, middle-aged, older—and a few like me, where if I'm honest, I have to say "old." Honestly, I won't dwell on age today, but I do remember the beautiful age called "young" when I'd be wearing the latest style swimsuit, feeling good about my bronze skin and listening to music, living life to its fullest. Today I'll write about a friend who is, believe it or not, almost as old as I am. Now this isn't a friend of many, many years, but priceless nevertheless. Her name is Bernie, and she's as cute as her name.

In 1976, I first met Bernie in my home. She arrived with the newspaper photographer to do a spread on food for the newspaper article she writes. This was fun for both Doree and me, as my daughter was included in the article and photograph.

When all the pictures were taken and the interview was over, Bernie left and I really never dreamed that one day in the future our paths would cross again.

This time she would become one of my newfound friends. She was an Otter Creeker, the name we call ourselves at Otter Creek Church. From time to time I would see her across the sanctuary, sitting on the far side from where my pew was located. Little did I know in a short while she would become one of my Ya-Ya sisters, as well as my Secret Sister, a church activity. What a hoot that turned out to be!

Just in case you're not familiar with this group of sisterhood, we draw a name out of a hat, and throughout the year we remember this sister at holidays, birthdays, or just anytime we wish with a gift or card, all of this done very secretively. At the end of the year a party was held, and your Secret Sister is then revealed. Sounds like fun, right? Listen to this story when it all backfired, and it was even more fun. Well, at least I thought it was.

I can't remember the occasion, but late one evening after Bernie's lights were off, I dropped off a gift, quite a cute, whimsical, little tin frog I thought would be nice on her patio, close to a flower pot, or in her garden. Sometime later, Bernie and I were out shopping in the quaint little historic town of Franklin, Tennessee. We were casually moseying down Main Street when out of the blue, Bernie began to confide in me.

"Mary, my Secret Sister gave me this frog and frankly, I don't know why. I guess I could recycle and give it to one of the grandchildren. I don't know what to do with it. I don't even like frogs." It's a million wonders I didn't laugh out loud, but I kept my composure, assuring her that I thought recycling was a great idea and the obvious answer to her dilemma.

Bernie offered to have the party for the unveiling at her home. On the day of the party, she called and asked if I knew where she could find lime green candles for her table. I did know and told her I'd bring them by in just a little while. When reaching her back door, I saw the little frog sitting on the corner of her stoop. When Bernie came to the door, she pointed it out saying, "I had to put this little frog out. My secret sister will be here, and she might be looking to see if I'm using it some place."

I stepped inside with the candles, which were a perfect shade of green, placed them on the table, telling her I needed to get home, but would be back shortly for the party and unveiling. I couldn't stop laughing as I drove home and couldn't wait until Bernie found out I was her Secret Sister.

It was now my turn to reveal myself at the party, and I kept my eye on Bernie to see her expression as I very animatedly told my story, waiting for the point where Bernie would guess me to be her Secret Sister. I was beginning to think maybe I should not have done this to her, but it was too late now, and the story was just too funny not to share. I did later apologize for exposing her, and we got a great laugh together. I wonder if that story could be the reason we no longer include Secret Sister in our many church activities. I was questioned by one of the ladies in the group, "Weren't your feelings hurt when Bernie didn't like your gift?" That was followed with another, "Weren't you afraid Bernie would be embarrassed when you told the story?" My answer was, "Heavens, no! Bernie and I are good friends and we both found the humor."

Bernie and I are together, enjoying a couple of Bible classes, along with our Friday night group where we do a lot of socializing and find a new place for dinner, or just perhaps, sitting around enjoying munchies and a drink. She's a blessing in my life, as well as being a blessing to many hundreds of others. The truth is I would love Bernie if for no other reason than she is such an admirer of Marilyn, my daughter. Marilyn has a hard time saying *no* to friends who ask her to have a home party to sell whatever: jewelry, handmade baskets, makeup, something much superior to Tupperware, and on and on. I'm sure her friends and mine as well attend sometimes just to eat the goodies she's prepared, which are always delicious. I quote

Bernie, "Marilyn could serve dried cow pies and I'd be there." Can't get better support than that!

Beloved Bernie left us in 2015 to be with Buddy, her adored husband. She had requested that we, her Ya-Ya Sisters, would all dress in red and sit in our reserved pew at the church for her memorial service. Our Ya-Ya Sisterhood will never be the same without Bernie at our table. I'll always remember her through tears and laughter.

True wisdom lies in gathering the precious things
out of each day as it goes by.

—E. S. Bouton

Joseph P. Binkley, Sr.
"Brother Joe"
1923-2001

The flame of the inn is dim tonight
Too many vacant chairs
The sun has lost too much of its light
Too many songs have taken flight
Too many ghosts on the stairs
Charon—here's to you—as man to man
I wish I could pick 'em the way you can.

by Grantland Rice, from the Nashville Bar Association
Memorial Resolution for Joseph P. Binkley, 2002

The Patience of Dorcas

Without the help of this cherished friend, the idea for writing a memoir would never in a million years have been completed. There were days I'm sure she was sorry she had offered her time to this endeavor! As we strove to set aside Wednesdays to work, always at their Brentwood Baptist Church, we found ourselves laughing, talking, eating and just generally having a fun time. My friend is blessed with patience, great beauty, and the heart of Dorcas in the New Testament.

Dorcas was always doing good and helping the poor.

Acts 9:36

With her daughter, Renee, quite as beautiful as her mother, and Ronnie, her handsome artist husband, Dorcas came into our lives as a second-door neighbor when Renee and my youngest child, Doree Ann, were little girls. The two became special playmates. I felt a great loss when this family moved in 1976 to Franklin. However, Doree was invited many times to spend week-ends with them and even though the miles separated us, our hearts remained closely connected.

There is a reason I say that Dorcas is blessed with patience. When we met at the church, I handed her a bunch of papers in my pitiful, not-too-legible handwriting, which she struggled to decipher, type and print out on her computer! All of this in the face of my complete state of disorganization. However, Dorcas kept prodding me onward. How could I give up when I would so terribly miss our "meeting at the church"? One might have thought that by now, I'd haul my laptop out of the closet and learn to do all this myself. So logical, but I don't feel friendly toward that idea at all. Instead, I'll just keep rocking along and enjoying my time spent with my friend, and continue to jot down little stories. That is, if Dorcas doesn't throw in the towel!

Afterword: As it turned out, it was not Dorcas who quit, rather, I quit writing for a very long time, wondering if I'd ever write again.

True friends are those who really know you
but love you anyway.

—Edna Buchanan

Ronnie, Dorcas, and Renee Hester

Unexpected Tragedy

A great man and a great trial lawyer died on April 27, the day before his 62nd birthday.

Charlie Williams was a true believer in "the cause." He used his passion for the law to help people in need. He cared about his community and served on many boards and commissions to improve the world around him.

—from "Death of Charlie Williams"
by the Law Offices of John Day, P.C., April 28, 2006

It's 2013, and I've not had the heart in a little over six years to even begin to continue jotting down little stories about my life as they come to mind from time to time. I found the words too painful to write. Could it be because Charlie was the one who first took an interest in my attempt to write this book of memories, and now he is gone?

After completing a portion of what I hoped one day to be *My Memoir*, Charlie called. "Mama, exactly where are you in your writing?"

"What do you mean 'exactly where am I'?"

"Are you one-third finished, or maybe one-half?"

"Well, I have no idea. I'll continue writing, I suppose, until I feel there's no more to write, and I've no idea at what point that will be."

"How are you writing it?"

With some embarrassment, "I'm writing longhand since I've not yet mastered the computer."

"Mama, if I were doing what you've undertaken, this is exactly how I would do it. Do you know I have to ask for help when I use the law library, even though the computer is right there and available? Let me help you with what you've finished. I have a court reporter who can type as fast as you can read, so gather all you've done together. I'll set up a time with him, and together you will soon have this portion typed and ready to edit."

Within a few days I found myself in the office of this nice man whose typing speed was amazing. After our session, I walked out with forty pages typed and bound, thinking I had launched into my endeavor full steam ahead! It's shocking how little time I actually had to pick up pen and paper when the mood might strike. I continued plodding along in anticipation of returning with an armful of stories one day and accepting this nice person's invitation, "Come back as soon as you're ready and we'll do session two." He's probably retired by now, but I'm still grateful for his help.

I continue to battle the heart-wrenching sadness in the aftermath of the tragedy that struck this family over five years ago on April 27, 2006. Charlie took his life. Now I've finally written it, tearing my heart out with the words. I ask myself, "If I could write the words *Charlie died,* would it be easier?" I'll never know. Charlie chose to drive to Shelby Park on that fateful morning, the park where I had lived so many happy hours as a child and teenager, then later when he was a child. His ashes are scattered in this park I've loved for so many years. I don't know the exact location. It was a very long time later, until I could drive the beautiful roads winding through the park. However, thankfully today I find a sense of peace and closure in my heart while there.

❦

Charlie was our firstborn, adored by his Mama and Daddy; he was my mother and daddy's first grandchild. Mother was absolutely overjoyed and couldn't wait to get to Hampton, Virginia when he was born in 1944 at Langley Field during World War II. On our first trip home, Mother had all her best friends over to the house to see him, full of her "beautiful baby boy." She didn't feel inclined to be even a little bit modest about her feelings concerning him. My mother loved babies and children beyond any person I've ever known.

Being a wife and mother brought me great happiness. I look back and wonder that I panicked as a new wife, because I knew zero about cooking or housekeeping, but felt no panic over the fact I was having a baby. I had no experience in this field beyond the times I would sit on our porch with our neighbor's baby girl, Kitty Sue. What a pleasure it was, rocking her and singing for hours on end, to help her mother. I did read a number of books on new mothers and baby care. I would push "Bugsie" in his stroller to the library, watching his face beam when strangers spoke to him. It became evident early on: *He will be a people person for sure*. And that he was.

I'll bet you're wondering, "Why the nickname Bugsie?" When he cut his first two upper teeth, he reminded us of Bugs Bunny—a name we called him and shortened later to "Bugsie." Now you know.

Everybody was drawn to Bugsie's personality and good looks. Admiration wasn't confined to family and family friends. Even when he was a little boy, his playmates loved him and followed whatever he did. When Bugsie started to school, his first grade teacher, Bonnie Byers, called just to chat about him. She saw immediately that he was a very bright student, but she was "somewhat concerned as to whether he was a good well-rounded student." She took the time to watch him on the playground where she observed, "He's quite as at home there as he is in the classroom, being a leader in each environment."

She questioned me about where he had already learned so well, so early, his reading, writing, and math. This was an easy question to answer, as I explained that both his grandmother and granddaddy were teachers who spent many hours enjoying their first grandchild's quick mind as he responded to whatever they chose to teach. I can see my daddy sitting in his big, comfortable chair reading to him. Charlie never seemed to tire of listening and learning. This picture is etched on my heart forever—my beloved child with my daddy sitting in the same comfortable chair listening to the same stories I had heard when his age.

This child of ours was surrounded with love on all sides. Our lifelong neighbors, the Davises and the Mosbys, adored him along with all of Mother's friends. Mother's best friend, Annie Gary, who had no children of her own, adopted Mother's children and quickly claimed Charlie as her first grandchild. "The Draper Girls" were Mother's neighbors when she was a child and all the years after. Ollie and Bess, the oldest of the Draper Girls, never married. They doted on Mother and Daddy's children, and their love extended down to their grandchildren. Bugsie, of course, was the first grandchild to be blessed with the gift that I had known and loved all of my life.

Bugsie was big brother to little brother Mike and to their sister, Marilyn (Mell). What happy memories I have of these special years—Charlie at that time was everybody's hero, including his brother and sister. He was in the second or third grade when new neighbors moved in. The family had two boys who caught the school bus at the corner of our road with Bugsie. I shall never forget him agonizing over the fact that on cold mornings the boys didn't have warm clothing. "Mama, they're shivering. Please take them some warm sweaters!" At this age he couldn't understand their mother could very well be offended by this offer. His pleading continued in such earnest that I finally promised to pay them a visit and determine what we should do. It killed me to see his heart broken over this, but I knew I couldn't barge in with help if they didn't need nor want it. Even if they did, I didn't know what to expect, but I was a bit surprised when I noticed a Cadillac in the driveway.

Thurman's driving a much older Dodge, I casually thought to myself. The mother invited me into the kitchen where her children were getting ready to sit down to eat their supper which was already on the table. I noticed that it was not a nourishing meal for growing children, but then I thought there were some nights occasionally when I didn't cook my usual well-rounded "meat and three" so maybe this was one of those nights for her. But I had to wonder. This was also after passing through the living room where a large TV was on with voices blaring and my thinking, *Charlie has so often mentioned, "Mama, all the kids at school are getting a TV. When is Daddy going to get ours?"* I knew full well when I said to him, "Daddy will see to that, maybe pretty soon now," that it wouldn't be THAT soon! But then "Daddy" was seeing to it that he had warm clothes, good food, and vitamins prescribed by our pediatrician. In other words, "the most important issues first."

Try explaining that to a seven-year-old, and why, on finding the neighbors weren't lacking for money, but spending it differently than we did, I was sure that the mother would be offended if I offered to help. His answer was, "Mama, that doesn't change anything. The boys are still cold." The next morning it was freezing and he was bundled up for zero weather carrying two heavy sweaters! I ran to the window, curious and wondering what reaction the boys would have. I saw them shake their heads refusing Bugsie's offer, which is what I expected. Thankfully, he wasn't upset, but ran quickly to the door which I had now opened, handing the sweaters to me.

I share this one story which is absolutely indicative of Bugsie's kind, caring heart all of his life. While he never mentioned nor agonized over these two neighbors any longer, many stories could be told similarly involving other children and adults as he lived his life aware of the downtrodden.

Charlie was a born leader, serving as president of the Isaac Litton High School freshman, sophomore, and junior classes.

What fun Thurman and I had his senior year during his campaign running for student council president! He laid out his strategy on our kitchen table, where of course the two of us were eager to help with the parade he was planning and were thrilled that he included us. The fact is, Charlie for many years included his Daddy and me in his life. During his illness, Thurman began to reminiscence about those days and the other ages of our oldest child. The memories were happy ones.

❦

When Charlie was older, there was a terribly sad day to remember as well—the day he was diagnosed with having multiple sclerosis. The debility moved slowly. However, it began to manifest itself beyond his ability to appear "all was normal," the manner he chose to cope with it for many years. With clinical depression and debilitating disease, I do have to wonder what this wonderful, kind, successful man was thinking when he dressed that fateful morning, probably on his way downtown to his law office. On the morning of April 27, 2006, a tragedy struck in this family that has devastated us all.

Many hearts were broken the day he took his life: his wife, his children, his siblings, a host of friends who loved him, and a mother who only today, after much time has passed, brings to the surface the sorrow and sadness hidden in the depth of her heart. The words were spoken that a mother should not have to hear. A mother should not have to bury a child, to carry that weight. Even though he may be a grandfather, he is always your child.

Charlie had a wonderful mind and a wonderful disposition. He was experiencing the devastating damage inflicted by an incurable illness, multiple sclerosis. I've experienced great sorrow of losing people I loved deeply in my family and among my friends. The loss has taken its toll in a very different way. Each of us who loved him will deal with our loss in different ways as well. Those beautiful years of loving my precious first child are locked away in my heart forever. I may choose to spend a day going through pictures, reading the uplifting notes he wrote so beautifully, going through memorabilia. Cry a while, laugh a while, and again tuck it all away until the next time. I thank God for his life. Although my heart, mind, body and soul tell me that his death cannot be real, I know it is.

I'm reluctant to share this story because there's so much more to be told. Finally, how do I, as his mother, cope and continue finding joy in living? Our four children born after Charlie—Mike, Mell, Sam, and Doree—their spouses, their children, and their children's children, all bring to me their love and understanding. They bring a closeness which has even been strengthened since losing the head of the family of siblings who loved and respected their brother so much. Although he's no longer with us, Charlie's spirit remains. When asked, "How many children do you have?" my answer is, without hesitation: "I am blessed with five wonderful children."

A bird doesn't sing
because it has an answer.
It sings because it has a song.

Maya Angelou

A Mother's Survival

Life is not always as we imagine in our youth. Certainly there will be, for all of us, times of disappointments, indecisions, death of loved ones, questioning God and times of little faith. Reflecting on the picture, I know God walked with me through it all. All of those things never appeared tragic.

I'm sure I never thought or entertained the thought that terrible tragedy could occur in my life, when almost six years ago that awful word struck our family! My first born, beautiful, accomplished, loveable child—the son, as a mother, I dreamed of one day having, took his life. There's no point in going into factors that contributed to his decision—only, how, did I as a mother, survive?

This is my story as I remember it. I couldn't grasp the horror, blocking out completely the first hours on into several days. I was numb, which I suppose was a good thing, but when reality struck, there are no words to describe my grief. I longed for his daddy, my Thurman, to talk me through the long sleepless nights, but I was alone—so heartbreakingly alone! I didn't feel God was even in my presence, just a terrible ache in my heart that I could not share with anyone. I can't tell you how frightened I was finding myself night after night walking the parking lot at two and three o'clock in the morning. Sleep was not possible. My fear was not of the dark or any person, only the realization I was spinning down into the pit of depression.

On one of these nights I was so exhausted I sat down on a stone wall to rest. The night was giving way to dawn and the sun would be coming up soon! I felt a chill in the early morning air and wrapped my arms around my shoulders. Maybe at that moment God understood that along with much needed sleep, the words I longed to say were lost! My son died on April 27 and this was a month or so later. Ironically the world was blooming, while my thoughts were only dark. I walked up my back steps to the deck and fell in my chair which was surrounded by hanging baskets filled with beautiful flowers that someone else had hung. The birds were beginning to welcome this summer day.

I hope all of you believe in angels, otherwise, you'll think I'm a bit daft. As for myself, I am as sure of the fact I have a Guardian Angel as I am sure of God, ruler of the Universe! As I lowered myself into that chair, it was as though a hand touched me and I felt the tension begin to leave my mind and body—a feeling of peace that I can't explain, engulfed me!

My first impulse was to step inside, grab a pencil and paper and write my story of Charlie and all he meant to me and this family and to all the people of all walks of life he had touched and left with the memory of his wonderful smile and warmth. He was a people person, loved and admired by so many!

By the time I'd finished writing about Charlie, the sun was well overhead and the birds were singing joyfully in anticipation of a lovely day and the food they would find in their feeders. The rest of the morning I spent thanking God, who loved me enough to send His angel to save me, even though I hadn't even the strength to ask!

The stone of pain that had weighed heavier and heavier with unsaid words had lifted from my heart. This gift of writing has allowed me to return to life with joy in my heart and on this day I'm able to tell you my story and why I find meaningful these words of Psalm 33: 20-22...

We wait in hope for the Lord. He is our help and our shield—in Him our hearts rejoice for we trust in His holy name. May your unfailing love rest upon us, Oh Lord, even as we put our hope in you.

Snow Day
Sam & Doree

Shelby Park, the Dutch Windmill, from a cherished postcard

The Old Mushroom in Shelby Park, Photo by Marilyn Switzer

A Lifetime in Shelby Park

When I return to my earliest memories from my childhood, Shelby Park memories are unique, for I was a very little girl when the memories began, and they have accumulated over a lifetime. Those many years were filled mostly with fun, wonderment, and changing activities during the changing stages of my life. Today, there is an overpowering sense of sadness as I drive through the winding roads through the mass of old trees along the lakes and banks of the Cumberland River.

The park was dedicated on July 4, 1912. I'm sure Mother and Daddy had already enjoyed many walks in the Park before I, probably around 1929 as a four or five- year-old, began to form my memories. Daddy was principal at DuPont School during those years, so he was at home for the summer. How many times I, along with brother Joe, Jim Davis, and other neighborhood children piled in the car, lighting out for the rather short distance to the park. The playground was filled with swings, seesaws, the merry-go-round, monkey bars, "shooty-shoots" (as we called the slides), a big sandbox and a concession stand. Mother was always there seated either on a bench or swing keeping a watchful eye as we played.

Shelby Park Saturday night movies became the second attraction. Again, the invitation went out to all neighborhood children to join us. Joe and I had to curtail our afternoon playtime however to "Come inside now. It's time to learn your Bible verses for Sunday school." Not until after we mastered the verse would we be leaving. You can bet we learned quickly!

Most homes of this time didn't include a bonus room or a recreation room. We gathered at the Park's Sycamore Lodge, across from the lake. It was a large building literally built of logs from sycamore trees. More than likely the logs had been cut from the many stately shade trees that grew inside Shelby Park. The Lodge was a very spacious informal room with a huge stone fireplace used for casual entertaining. The Centennial Club downtown was offered for young people's more formal entertaining.

All parties were chaperoned. As middle school students, one of the games we always played was Spin the Bottle. It was a game I refused to play, for what if the spinning bottle stopped and pointed to me, spun by a boy whom I didn't want to kiss me on the cheek! The boys didn't care about my selectivity. They just pegged me as a "Prude" (which I probably was). There were plenty of cute girls though that weren't so picky.

Shelby Park was not only enjoyed by children. As a teenager I loved the baseball games played there during the summer and attended many. The summer night ball games were where I first began really noticing the boys! I was so naïve that I had to be told one of them was noticing me. What an ego boost! All innocent flirting and fun.

No air conditioning in summer in the South, so Mother planned many picnics at the park to entertain her Nashville friends, as well as out-of-town friends and relatives. The picnic tables, covered with cloths, flower arrangements in the center, were set up in the shade. What a feast: Daddy's fried chicken, fried corn, apple sauce made only from June apples, watermelon and cantaloupe, big red sliced tomatoes, yellow squash cooked to perfection, and yeast rolls… all meticulously transported by Daddy and Maggie, the family friend and help. Big wicker picnic baskets along with two large thermos jugs of iced tea with mint and lemon or lime.

Had I been Daddy, with all that work involved, I think I would have insisted: "Dora, let's have this in the dining room at home with the two, large rotating electric fans blowing on us." Perhaps it's best he didn't say that for I have the memories of sitting outside in the shade of those lovely trees and the little breeze blowing, making delightful memories for all guests.

When snow is on the ground, I am drawn back to the hills of Shelby Park where Joe and I as children, along with our neighborhood friends, spent hours on end sledding. Many times Daddy let us stay over well into the night, until we became completely exhausted. Then we were ready to pile into the warm car and head home, where Mother would have something hot to fill our tummies. Sometimes a bowl of soup, little sandwiches, a steaming cup of hot chocolate.

When Joe and I became teenagers, he was driving Daddy's car, filled to the brim with our friends, ready to take on the evening. On these summer evenings, as well as for trips to the pool and days of fun, Daddy would give Joe and me a handful of dimes. These dimes were only to be spent using the pay phone in Shelby Park if anything went wrong, and he or Mother needed to be contacted. I well remember using my dime on several occasions when the older teenagers were drinking, and I felt things were getting out of control, or if I was "just plain bored." Daddy was always a welcome sight when he came pulling up. I could crawl in next to him, feeling safe and sound. But I never snitched on Joe!

My love for Shelby Park is handed down to my five children. Each one of them, Charlie, Mike, Marilyn, Sam and Doree, surely remember feeding the ducks on the lake and fishing there, Mike's favorite pastime. They too played on the playground.

Marilyn has memories of her Granddaddy pushing her in a swing as she reached her toes toward the tree leaves, hoping to touch them. The boys played Little League baseball and football, with Doree a cheerleader for Sam's football team. Sam, even today at age fifty, bicycles over to the park to walk the trails at Shelby Bottoms, watch a game or simply sit and meditate in a quiet spot. Charlie and his dad played tennis on many summer evenings while I was their most enthusiastic spectator, cheering both sides. As Doree matured she could join in playing her favorite sport as well, coming away the winner almost always.

Shelby Park with its 361 acres is still as beautiful today as I remember it over ninety years ago. The Sycamore Lodge and the Dutch windmill I loved as a child unfortunately burned in the 1940s. The tennis courts and swimming pool that came later for my children to enjoy all are gone now. What continues to draw me there? Its natural beauty, walking trails, the Little League baseball fields, and the fact that my beloved son Charlie's ashes were strewn in the park he loved so much. I will drive those winding roads again, even though I am ninety-three as I write this. Whether a summer or winter day—when my thoughts will begin to run rampant and childhood memories begin to rumble in my brain.

Within you there is a stillness and sanctuary to which you can retreat at any time and be yourself.

—Herman Hesse

Marilyn, Charlie, Me holding Sam, Thurman, and Mike
The Williams Family, Riverwood Church of Christ

Vickie with her brother-in-law, Sam

Mike adored his little brother Sam.

Thurman and Me

Mrs. Marilyn Williams Switzer, above, and with her daddy, July 5, 1974 West End United Methodist Church

Doree and Sam

Sam and Doree take part in Marilyn's wedding. Notice the grip on Doree's shoulder.

Thurman and Sam, on the go!

Pepper and P.J. (Pepper Junior)

Mr. and Mrs. Stewart Hubbard, above, and the Williams Family, below, June 29, 1991, The Hermitage Hotel

Mother and Daddy, Dora (Anderson) and Samuel H. Binkley

Annie Gary Bentley

Our 50th Wedding Anniversary Celebration with children Mike, Marilyn, Charlie, Doree, and Sam

GETTING ON IN LIFE

Dwelling in the House of the Lord

One thing I ask of the Lord, that I may dwell in the house of the Lord all the days of my life to gaze upon the beauty of the Lord.

Psalm 27:4

There were seasons years ago, while I was in my pew on Sunday mornings, that my thoughts were focused more on worldly "comings and goings" than on the spiritual world. From childhood I've always felt in awe of God as Creator of the universe. But I didn't fully understand my need of him until disappointments, failure, wrongful accusations, death of loved ones—things over which I seemed to have no control—left me terribly vulnerable, with a cold empty feeling.

Contributing to this was my feeling of guilt that I couldn't shake. Guilt! Because I simply couldn't adhere to everything that the good men of our church taught my children and me. I wouldn't invite my friends to join me at church if they were Catholic, Methodist, Baptist, or anything other than the name our church wore. It had a monopoly on the house of the Lord. My friends might be blasted by the preacher and reminded that they all were lost! After some questioning, which resulted in being ignored, I felt like an imposter when I made the decision to make no waves. I wanted so badly to discuss this with Mother, my best friend. I didn't, for fear of hurting her, thinking she would never understand. I learned much later that not only would she have understood, but agreed with me on most of the issues. I loved all the wonderful people of our church, but felt like I was "on the outside looking in."

Thankfully, Daddy—being Methodist—convinced mother of these truths and so I was allowed more fun than Mother's church condoned, fun like dancing and swimming. Even then, I was worried! I prayed earnestly to God asking for guidance on this, hoping that I was not wrong. I began to feel good about myself and closer to God than I ever thought possible, with faith so strong that I knew somehow I would be stopped in my tracks, if indeed, it was needed. I began to bring all my fears to Him.

I told my little children, "Yes, you can dance to music with joy in your heart!" They had no sex in mind, though that is what I was taught, that dancing was sexually motivated and sinful. Naturally, I didn't use that word! Heaven forbid! Another issue was swimming. You can swim and not think of it as "mixed bathing." We didn't bring soap, you see! Rather, swimming is a wonderful exercise.

These were the years I found myself praying almost without end. Praying in the bathtub before retiring at the end of a long busy day. Seeking understanding of God's relationship with me, and the church's presentation of that relationship. This was a time I needed somebody a lot bigger than I was. Thank goodness, I, of little faith, had enough faith to seek God. I knew that I was His child and could lay every little thing at his feet, no matter how small! Thankfully, I turned to prayer. To my confusion came clarity. For years when I awoke at 6:00 AM, the same two prayers, Psalm 118:24 and Psalm 20:14 were said:

This is the day the Lord hath made, let us rejoice and be glad in it...
May the words of my mouth and the meditation of my heart
be pleasing in your sight, O Lord, my Rock and my Redeemer.

These were not merely words but became a way of life. Often, I feel the need to pray these words during the day as well.

Being the baby and only girl, I grew up in my world where it was "all about me." How quickly that role changed when my baby boy, first of our five children, arrived. Life was no longer all about me when my dreams and prayers became "all about him." Paul prayed for the faithful brothers in Christ at Colossi, who were all about the Lord's work. He prayed for their patience and endurance, just as I prayed for my own patience and endurance in the rearing of my child. There was no motive, other than a heart full of love. With each child my heart grew bigger and more prayerful, asking for guidance and wisdom. The prayers may have been shorter, but even more earnest as the children grew older, taking place in the strangest places.

During the daytime, I found myself conversing with God. I remember several times on my knees looking for *whatever* in the lower cabinet. I used this time, while in a kneeling position already, to stop and pray! I'm not 100% sure that praying while behind the steering wheel of a car was such a good idea. As I became more focused on prayer, my thoughts began to weigh and my foot became heavier on the gas: too many speeding tickets! (Or at least, being stopped and hoping the patrolman wouldn't issue the ticket.)

During those years of taking care of little ones, along with my cherished parents, who died natural deaths, seven hours apart, I never considered the fact that I was doing the Lord's work. But without planning or organization, I was growing in the knowledge of the Lord.

Our nest had been empty for a while after our last child's marriage. Thurman and I were no longer running in circles and were actually having time for each other. It was a very precious time in our lives, only to be cut short when he was diagnosed with cancer. This caring man, who always looked after all of us, was now needing our care. I think I never loved him more than when "My Rock" needed *me* as *his* rock! Thankfully, I could turn my guide business over to my guides and stay with Thurman constantly. He lost his battle, leaving me so desperately alone in my heart. Our children were amazing—giving love, understanding and support, but I sent them home to their families.

Gone were all the people who had needed me: children, parents, my Aunt Mary (who had lost her only child), and Annie Gary, my mother's best friend of seventy-five years who was childless, both claiming me as their "daughter" all my life. I had no clue then, but now I know that I was surely doing the Lord's work.

Circumstances in my life eventually brought me to Otter Creek Church. I know my awesome God is smiling with me today as I feel so at home in the House of the Lord, and not "on the outside looking in."

And we pray that you may live life worthy of the Lord and may please Him in every way: bearing fruit in every good work, growing in the knowledge of the Lord.

Colossians 1:10

Losing Your Life-Long Love: How To Cope

Delivered in Ladies Bible Class,
Otter Creek Church of Christ, 2004

Perhaps you knew my husband. If not, I wish you could have known him. My husband was tall, strong, dependable, handsome, dignified, athletic, and a great wit. You would have loved him; everybody did! His name was Thurman and it suited him. *Rather aristocratic,* I thought. Like many of our friends, we married during World War II. Thurman was not among my wonderful group of school friends, for he was almost five years older. Mother and Daddy, both educators, were not happy that we didn't wait until I finished school and the war was over.

We married on a Saturday, March 13, 1943 at Scales Chapel in the West End Methodist Church. I was all of eighteen years old, Thurman was twenty-three. This was the beginning of a marriage that lasted fifty-six years, a marriage of endless bliss.

I lie. We ran the gamut of tears and laughter, disappointments, disagreements, disillusionments, dreams unfulfilled. Thurman was a caring, loving and wonderful father to Marilyn, my oldest daughter, and her sister Doree, fifteen years younger, who are as close as sisters could possibly be. He was a caring, loving and wonderful father to our three sons, who are good men with tender hearts: Charlie, Mike and Sam. How they loved their Daddy and felt the warmth of his love and strong shoulders, as I had always felt. It is they who asked, "How do you cope with losing a loving husband?"

Twelve and a half years before Thurman died, he was diagnosed with cancer. This didn't mean the good years were ending. He continued to work while undergoing radiation. There were times we were both convinced that the long months of therapy had worked. We continued taking trips together with our friends and family. I continued to do what I had always done, having a well-balanced dinner with dessert ready by six o'clock each evening.

I'll never forget how I was preparing dinner as usual, standing at the stove, when Thurman came in, giving me a big hug, lingering for a moment. He said, "You know, if you never cook another meal, you're still way ahead of the game." And I was thinking it meant we would eat out more, a sacrifice for him because he loved my home cooking, often telling me, "Not a restaurant in town can compare to your dinners!" (After the beginning of my married life, when I was void of any cooking skills, I became a good cook in short order. I got great joy in cooking for both family and friends.) However, Thurman, like many people in our town, did have a favorite restaurant: the family-owned Belle Meade Buffet. This became our hang-out. Every Sunday after church and two or three times during the week, we would head across the river to enjoy the Buffet. Vegetables, fried chicken, fried and baked fish, or whatever they served was all good eating. Thank goodness, the desserts were an exception to the rule.

Gradually, Thurman became more and more unwell. The children wanted to spend more time with their daddy, and so we moved across the river. They visited just about every day, and memories associated with that time are precious to me. There were frequent calls from Sam in Green Bay. There were the fond conversations between Mike and his daddy, showing Mike's obvious concern and love for him. Vickie, who was Thurman's girl from the days even before she and Mike married, because of her unassuming way of showing love. From the very start Thurman and Vickie were good buddies! My compassionate granddaughter—their daughter Amy—was a nurse at St.

Thomas Hospital. She spent some of her hours off duty to help. On those days I could leave knowing Thurman was in good hands. Anderson's visits that were so unexpected and so appreciated. I'll never forget the pill container for "Gandy" that Mary Pullias made. All of you: Marshall, Michael, Charlie, Joe, Annie B, and of course the fact that Doree brought her two, Maclellan and Cole, almost daily. These gave him ties to young people that always brought a smile to his face.

Then came the departure of my life-long best friend and mate in the fall of 1998. Afterwards, on awakening each morning my prayer was for God to give me the will to find peace and joy for just this day, and I would deal with the tomorrows later. My children were there for me, keeping in touch, the girls sharing their memories of their daddy with me. Mike was very good at this, too. Charlie helped with business matters I didn't grasp. Sam called every morning from Green Bay, Wisconsin, while traveling to his place of work. The days were busy and I did feel at peace until around dusk.

I wanted Doree and Marilyn to feel free to turn all their attention on their families and homes now, so I never shared my despair at this particular time of day. Knowing all I had to do was make a phone call and be invited to this or that home for dinner, I was tempted. It wasn't that I didn't have food in the house, for there were still all the wonderful dishes friends had brought over at the time of the funeral and later. I was also determined to shop for groceries and eat properly. There were fresh vegetables and fruit in the refrigerator along with good cuts of meat and chicken. The only problem was that when I went in the kitchen to prepare a meal for one, I balked, put it all back, thinking: *I'll eat that tomorrow*.

I grabbed my keys and headed for the mall where there were people around. The sound of their voices helped to relieve my state of loneliness. I couldn't count the times I ate at Cheeseburger Charley's on the upper level sidewalk. There I could look down on the people below shopping or jogging. Often I would be joined by them at my table for a quick conversation. When the twilight hour faded, and it was now dark, I could go home. Even this felt strange, but for the rest of the evening until bedtime I wasn't restless. Just a short time later I was to meet my unbelievably good friends on this side of town, and I have not felt lonely since. I continue staying busy during the day and if I hit a slump, I know exactly what to do.

I visit old friends, some who need cheering up a bit, as their health might be fading, or maybe they too have lost their spouse and are feeling lonely. This visiting became a lifestyle. As a younger person I spent so much time with older people; I was the caregiver for my mother and daddy, for my Aunt Mary, and for Annie Gary. Aunt Mary had lost her only child; Annie Gary had no children. I loved them all so much, and when they voiced their concern that I was overdoing it, I would answer again and again, "Don't you know that you can't live long enough for me to do everything I'd love to do for you?" They are all still living now, in a special place in my heart reserved just for them.

I was thrilled that their faces would instantly light up; it was a joy to have an opportunity in my small way to create happiness. Visiting older friends is a win-win situation.

I was aware there were many resources available to cope with grief, such as counseling or group sessions. They all seemed to sadden me more somehow. We're all so different and when I found my way, visiting older friends brought us both joy. I have faith that when the time comes with God's help, you will find your own way to cope with grief.

Oh, my friend, it's not what they take away from you that counts.
It's what you do with what you have left.

—Hubert Humphrey

Dear Neighbors

When we moved into our second home after World War II, the first visitor was my neighbor from next door, Josephine Kornmeyer, bringing supper along with her famous silk chocolate pie. Delicious! I knew in a split second we would become the best of friends. Her husband, Dick, arrived later in the evening, offering to help. Thurman accepted his offer, and I do believe it was midnight before that gracious man left. What a neighbor!

From that first encounter, meeting their two boys as well, we all agreed this was going to be a great relationship. While Charlie and Mike were older than Carl and Dickie, Marilyn and Carl were the same age and were great friends then and now. Because Josephine and Dick had no daughter, they latched on to Marilyn as though she were their own. It was a special bond that grew with the years, as we watched our children grow to adulthood.

For forty-two years the Kornmeyer and the Williams families shared life in every way possible. There was love that flowed from one to the other—children and parents for a lifetime. Josephine and Dick were strong Baptists living their lives in a Godly way. Josephine was a frequent visitor, the two of us sitting in the rocking chairs on my front porch in the evening, talking for hours; at the patio table over coffee in the mornings. During the winter I could be found at her kitchen table either morning or evening. This happened often, however we were both busy people outside of home and sometimes our visits were interrupted for days on end. Those were the times, should we run into each other out somewhere, we exchanged big bear hugs and then laughed, saying we could have just stepped next door for that hug!

With every move, I have had the good fortune to have neighbors I enjoyed and loved. I did not expect anything less on Moran Drive. This time, I had forty-two years to continue our neighborly friendship. We shared plenty of tears and laughter, and thoughts on every subject, not agreeing on everything by a long shot! At the conclusion of our debates we came away with each of us knowing we hadn't made a dent in changing the minds of the other, never wavering in our mutual love and respect.

What a sad day for us when Dick died. He was buried in Spring Hill Cemetery, with his monument inscribed: "God is my Rock." He lived a beautiful life influencing so many, simply by living.

When the day came for Thurman and me to move across town, Josephine and I had already shared our tears, but refused to say "Goodbye." She called before the hour for the moving van to appear to say she was leaving for the day—she did not want to watch us go. It was a sad day, despite our happiness at moving closer to Marilyn and Doree, one of those days when I could be found laughing out of one eye and crying out of the other. We remained close until the day she died.

We continued being a big part of each other's lives. When Josephine's health failed to the point she moved into McKendree Manor, assisted living in Donelson, Tennessee, I was able to visit and take her out to lunch. After surgery on my shoulder for a tear of the rotator cuff, I was no longer able to lift her in and out of the car and get her walker out of the trunk, so our mutual friend and former neighbor, Dorcas, joined me for the day. The three of us continued our day out for several years until Josephine could no longer go. Then it was a visit at McKendree Manor! Just before her last Christmas, I gave Josephine a luncheon, inviting several of her friends from her

Dick and Josephine Kornmeyer, our forever next door neighbors

Our monument is directly behind Dick and Josephine's in the historic Spring Hill Cemetery, Nashville.

Sunday School Class at Dalewood Baptist Church, where she taught the Ladies Bible Class for years.

Thurman, as I've written, was not well when we made the move across town, so I wasn't surprised when he called Charlie, asking him to ride along to Spring Hill Cemetery to select a plot for us. He had mentioned he hoped he could find one close to Josephine and Dick's. Could you believe there was one available, as close as possible? Thurman knew that some years back I found a watercolor by a good artist at Christmas Village that I was thrilled to gift Josephine for Christmas. The painting was of two houses side by side—on a street in a neighborhood that looked much like ours on Moran Drive. Flowers bloomed in pots on the porches and bluebirds flew randomly, a dog trotted down the middle of the street, so like our dog, a black Scottie-Poo! The artist had painted his collar red just like the collar of our dog, Pepper. I thought the painting was adorable and so did Josephine. Most meaningful was the verse painted in Old English Script:

In my Father's house are many mansions. John 14:2
I hope mine is next door to yours.

And so, these three are buried as close as the houses where we lived as earthly neighbors for all those years, waiting for me! I can only imagine the glorious day that will be when we unite as neighbors in Heaven.

"A single conversation with a wise man
is worth two month's study of books."

—Chinese Proverb

Paulette and Irene: Servant's Hearts

I never, in a million years, imagined finding such a friend as Paulette in my later life. Young enough to be my daughter, she stepped in out of a clear blue sky to fill so many roles: sister, daughter, confidant, activity planner, chauffer—and amazing friend. The work "lucky" comes to mind—however, Paulette would be quick to say, "God's hand placed us together on this earth."

When I first met Paulette at Otter Creek Church, it was at a time I felt blue and a little lonely. Service was over, and it was time to head home. For sure, I could let my feelings be known, and any one of my children would have taken me home with them. They all had already gone far beyond what I would ever expect during this difficult time of trying to set up a new lifestyle. I had left my old friends on the other side of town and had not yet had time to meet new people, although I felt confident that would come. I loved being a part of the Otter Creek congregation for many reasons, one being that Marilyn and her family attended and loved this church.

I shall never forget the moment. Sunday services had ended; the last hymn had been sung. I thought, "Time to leave...wish I could hang around a while longer." I looked up and watched Paulette and her good friend Irene coming my way. A fleeting thought sprang up, "Maybe I'll ask them to join me for lunch." I really wanted to plead, "I'm so lonely! Do you go to lunch after church? I'm looking for friends on this side of town..."

Before I could actually bare my heart, which would have been a supreme effort, I heard two voices, speaking at the same time.

"Why don't you join us, along with a few others, for lunch? We do this every Sunday and would love to have you join us." The bells were ringing, the birds were singing, and my Guardian Angel was laughing at my pure delight. It was the beginning of a cherished friendship with these two that grows sweeter as time passes. So many stories to tell could fill another book with memories.

We are three of the Ya-Ya Sisterhood—Maxine and Bernie are the other two. We are three of the Friday Night Group, meeting at each other's homes for wine and cheese and then either together at the hostess' dining table or out on the town for supper.

Irene is the creative one who is our floral designer for special occasions, the friend who shapes up a birthday gift like no other, so unusual. She has a "heart of gold." Friends are one of life's greatest blessings.

Today, June 18, 2018, I was sitting by my window, winding up my stories, when the phone rang. It was the voice of Paulette.

"I'll pick you up at 5:40 to go to Irene's house for dinner," she announced.

How many similar calls are made, now that I don't drive at night! I'm never stranded for lack of a chauffeur while Paulette is in town.

She and Irene have servant's hearts.

For what we proclaim is not ourselves,
but Jesus Christ as Lord,
with ourselves as your servants for Jesus' sake.

2 Corinthians 4:5

Boots and Shoes

Today is Sunday, February 19, 2006. It is a wonderfully cold morning. As I look out on my car covered in ice and snow, I long to bundle up, grab my broom and ice scraper, clean it, and get ready to drive to church. This I've done on several occasions since Thurman died. Eighty is not old, and as I love cold weather, this has not been a difficult task until today.

Now I'm eighty-one and what a difference a year can make. Since February of last year, I've had four surgeries on my right shoulder, all rotator cuff tears, none of which were successful. I've had very little mobility in my right arm, not to mention the pain in the meantime. The left shoulder also has a rotator cuff tear, and because of overuse, it is almost as painful as the right, and its mobility diminishing.

After calling my friend Paulette to come get me, I put my boots on with great difficulty, and off to church we went. Afterward Paulette, Irene, Bernie, Donna, Maxine and I went to the Soup Kitchen as Maxine's guests. As I was leaving and attempting to hug my friend goodbye, both arms were useless. What frustration!

When Paulette drove me home, I knew there would be no way I could get my boots off, so again I had to ask for help. While she was on her knees performing that task in a split second, I thought of how many boots or shoes I had dislodged from people's feet—babies, old people, sick people, people I loved—feeling privileged for the opportunity that came so easily for me.

I recall Thurman asking me "Please get off your knees," when I was putting on his shoes during the last months of his life. However, his suggestion that he lie down so I could put them on more easily didn't work at all! I asked if he wanted me to get his house shoes. This he simply didn't want to do, so I explained that he would have to accept me on my knees. That was not a sad day, but we found the humor in the dilemma. How I miss him! He was the perfect nurse and caregiver always. I think of how he would take care of me now if he were here. As life unfolds, I'll have to say I'm just so glad Thurman wasn't left without me to take care of him.

The most ordinary little things can serve
an important purpose, and they have their stories, too.

—Deborah E. Wilbrink

Equal Rights

I always had strong sympathy for the underprivileged, particularly the African Americans. Unfortunately, this term was never used when I was growing up! Even as a child I was horrified at the heartlessness exhibited by the adults who expressed their dislike for an entire race of people.

I found one occasion in Shelby Park to be extremely stressful, and it probably formed my thinking about justice for African Americans. Several little girls around my age were enjoying the merry-go-round when I jumped off along with my little friend I had just met, seated beside me. We ran together hand-in-hand out the sidewalk to the water fountain, for we both were hot and thirsty. All was well and happy till my little friend remarked "I'll have to find the water fountain that says *Colored.*" She added, "They won't let me drink from this fountain."

That was my first act of defiance against the Powers-That-Be. It was not my last. I boldly told her, "You go right ahead and get your drink from this fountain and I'll tell my mother if anybody says anything to you!" I was so angry when I got back to the playground, almost screaming as I told Mother what had happened. She shushed me in her kind way, saying, "Go on and play with your friend and we will discuss this later at home." We did, but not to my satisfaction then, or ever!

My family employed African Americans as hired help in our home. A lack of prejudice in the treatment and attitude of my parents toward these friends of ours must have been what influenced me for a lifetime. Shep was the neighborhood handyman, and Daddy made sure he used the front door, not the back one. Our friend Maggie, the well-loved lady who helped my mother, had a daughter that was a year or two younger than I. She was a darling, and on many occasions Maggie would bring her with her to our home. Margaret became my favorite playmate. When Mother gathered my outgrown dresses together to give to Margaret, she never failed to add two or three new ones into the bundle. This was not the only child Mother found to shop for; there were others in Maggie's neighborhood who benefited from her kind heart. I remember Daddy buying Maggie a big turkey every Thanksgiving and a ham at Easter.

I'll never forget when my own housekeeper and friend Aline came to my home when she was older and had retired from her job with a printing company. Aline laughed and said, "Mary, I have help now in my home!" She has lived alone for many, many years in the same neighborhood since we began our acquaintance, now enabled with paid "help."

I'm eighty-five years old, and so thankful to have lived long enough to see a wonderful family in the White House who do not bear the same white skin color as I. However, even now I see prejudice on all sides against not only the African American, but against people of all races different from themselves. I cringe when people I consider of at least average intelligence put down or make fun of our President and the First Lady. I have to wonder: Are they jealous of their intellect, of their Harvard credentials? When I see these critics obtain something of significant value themselves, then perhaps I will lend an ear to what they have to say! Why not voice opinions on the actual running of the country, instead of about "them" who are so "different." I do hope that I never again hear, "They are just not like us!" in the silly tone of superiority which I came to recognize and detest.

I wish that I had been at the time in my life where I could have joined the 1961 Freedom Riders. I wish I could have been a champion like Rosa Parks! How fulfilling it would be to know that I played a part in every African-American child feeling free to enjoy a drink without a sign designating *Colored* or *White*. A part in African Americans being able to sit where they chose on a bus without being driven to the back by stupid laws put into effect by uneducated people.

It may be wise not to go back and reveal some of these times. I honestly try NOT to make waves and realize this was law—something I had no control over. On several occasions I lost my cool completely and found myself in the face of authority looking at me as though I was way out of line, even threatening arrest if I did not shut up! You know what? I didn't shut up this once and won the battle:

I stepped on the crowded street car and found a small section on the very end of a long seat in front. At the next stop a very pregnant young African-American woman boarded the street car, working her way back to the Colored Section in the back. I watched, hoping someone in the back would offer her their seat. To my dismay, no one did. Still watching, I saw her grab on to the leather belt above for security. No force at that moment could have stopped me when I jumped up and headed to where she stood. Passengers on the streetcar had both shock and anger on their faces when I insisted she come with me. I escorted her back to my seat and told her to sit there. That poor girl was trying to tell me she couldn't and at the same time the driver, seeing what was happening, stopped the streetcar immediately. He was going to take care of this fifteen-year-old troublemaker! It never occurred to me to be afraid. I looked him in the eye and firmly explained, "Please listen to me. If this woman were to fall, she could have her baby on this street car. Then what would you do? I'll take full responsibility for insisting she take my seat." I gave him Daddy's name and phone number, letting him know that my father was a well-known educator in Nashville, laying it on thick. At the same time, I was privately worrying as to how Daddy would react to my impulsiveness. By then I had determined to stand by this mother-to-be until she got off, would then ride to the end of the line, step off, and find a phone to call Daddy to come and get me…

Daddy didn't realize I detected a twinkle in his eye as he proceeded to reprimand me. He cautioned that I could get into some real trouble, real danger if I didn't learn to squelch my emotions better. I'm afraid I've never mastered this feat even to this day! It isn't always confined to African Americans who are being abused. On several occasions I saw the abuse of little children by their mother or father, who had skin the color of mine. Witnessing emotional or physical abuse of a child enraged me before I could stop myself. I'm not sorry, because I know I did the right thing and proved to be of some help in pointing out their actions as abusive.

Everyone is necessarily the hero of his own life story.

—John Barth

Doris, My Playmate

I sit here wishing the phone would ring, as it would every Monday morning when my darling friend Doris Kilzer called, or when I called her, to share the goings-on of the weekend. Midweek I could expect a call in the evening, when she liked to talk, often till after bedtime. And I admit that after a full, busy day, there have been times I was nodding when I hung up. But now, how I miss those times.

This last week my friend's health was in a fragile state, but how she longed to live, and be the active person she had always been. So she pushed on gallantly, day after day, with hope that she would indeed reach her goal. Today, November 2, 2011, she was stopped in her tracks, and God saw fit in His mercy to take her home. Her great loving heart refused to mend this time, leaving me devastated. I will keep her in my heart as long as I live and remember not her dying, but rather remember her for living—as my beautiful, vivacious, fun-loving friend.

We were first church buddies, and soon began to seek each other out during the week. This was twenty-five years ago. Our husbands, Thurman and Hugh, began to join us on weekends, either eating out or in each other's homes. This was great fun as we all enjoyed each other's company. Our foursome was cut short, as Hugh became unwell.

Doris and Hugh were planning their fiftieth wedding anniversary when he passed away. The Sunday of their anniversary, my thoughtful husband suggested I take Doris to the Opryland Hotel for dinner. We talked, and I lent my ear to her reminiscing and it was a good experience for us both. Thurman also encouraged me to invite her to dinner on birthdays and holidays. I well remember on one such occasion she was inclined to refuse because she said, "You're including me so often! This time you might really just want your family."

Sam was listening to my side of the conversation. He took the phone and said, "What do you mean you're not coming here? We'll all be disappointed and I'm coming to get you, so be ready."

Is there any question why Doris loved my family? Because both her sons lived out of state, we were afforded the opportunity to develop an even closer relationship. Memories were shared, and we found such fun relating those to others as we deemed it suitable. Here are three we always loved to share:

Where in the Heck Is My Car?

Doris and I drove to Cool Springs Mall to shop and have lunch. I'm sure we were talking and laughing heartily with absolutely no thought of where I was parking. We spent the day enjoying everything around us, then it was time to return across the river back home to our husbands. Walking out of the mall I stopped, not knowing whether to turn right or left. Go forward, or where? Doris, I found, didn't have a clue either. So we just stood there laughing till we found a place to sit down and regain our composure. We decided to walk up and down each lane, and surely our car would show itself. Having done that, and still no car, our laughter was becoming a bit restrained. Finally, it dawned on me and I revealed, "Doris, this is not the entrance we came in!" That brought on a fresh shriek of laughter and we decided, "Well, heck! Let's just have supper and we'll deal with Hugh and Thurman's reaction to that idea later."

Dare We Be This Late Again?

We both loved the movie *Dr. Zhivago*. When we learned it was playing off the beaten path at the Belmont Theater across town, Doris and I told our husbands we were going, and would grab a bite after. We failed to remind them of the length of the movie (three and a half hours). And that we never successfully "grabbed a bite."

Hugh was not quite as upset as Thurman when we returned much later than either had anticipated. Thurman had called Hugh and his reaction was, "Thurman, who knows when those two will show up? I feel sure they're okay." Now remember, Thurman was my worrywart, and didn't exactly accept that explanation. So by the time I had dropped Doris off and walked into my house, I found a very disgruntled husband. In these situations, he always said, "You might have called me!" and he would make it very clear that I was to find a telephone and call him at night when I was running late. No cell phones then. Inconvenient at times. But most of the time afterward, *I made that call!*

Where Did That Ball Go?

Doris and I both felt we were in need of some body firming. We decided to walk the track around the football field at the high school in my neighborhood. We walked very early in the morning before school started. My gait was somewhat quicker than that of Doris, well, a whole lot quicker, perhaps due to my long legs.

One morning we took off and I was done before Doris was even half way around the track. I suggested, "Tomorrow, why don't we mosey over to the tennis court after our walk and play a little tennis?" Please understand I've never been an athlete, though secretly I longed to be. I did have a tennis racket and knew how to keep score, while Doris had never picked up a tennis racket.

Getting the ball over the net was an accomplishment that warranted high fives and created laughter for the event. I can't tell you how many balls went crazy, off the court and into a sort of wooded area. Our best exercise was remembering to bend over from the waist when retrieving the ball and jogging back to the court! Quite a workout and much laughter to boot; it can't get much better than that.

Then I found Doris telling a friend at church, "Oh yes, Mary and I play tennis every morning." I became a little worried, hoping she hadn't revealed where we played. I did not want any spectators watching this game!

These are just a very few of my memories I'll tuck away in my heart. And hopefully I'll read this verse again and again:

A happy heart is good medicine and a cheerful mind works healing.

Proverbs 17:22

This is how Doris chose to live and so do I:

Weeping may endure for a night, but joy comes in the morning.

Psalms 30:5

Goodbye, my sweet friend, you'll remain in my heart forever.

Diana, A Free Spirit

Among young and not so young friends I have loved and admired during my lifetime, this one has to be way at the top. We bonded soon after joining a Bible class held in her home several years ago. Earlier I thought: *Who exactly is this young woman with the big, I do mean BIG, smile, with a twinkle in her eyes, who seems to be a free spirit with seemingly few forces to weigh her down in life?* This was the image she kept while struggling with more than a normal person could handle with even an occasional weak smile.

I got to know Diana sitting in on the sessions studying God's word, sharing sometimes hilariously funny stories and some not so happy, when we would gather together and shed tears for one another. She experienced everything with intense passion: excitement, anger, joy, music, dance, friends, funny jokes, new events, and, above all, her love for God and for her beloved husband and children.

Diana and I enjoyed the same movies, actually a bit weird to others, we learned. On September 18, 2012, she, along with two other friends, made plans to view a movie we both expressed a desire to see. Sometime earlier on this day, I received a call from Diana, "Mary, it occurred to me that I have an appointment at the hospital for an epidural injection, after which I am not sure I'll be up for a movie."

"Not to worry," I said, "you and I can see it later together." Something we did on several occasions, always stopping for a bite to eat afterwards. Bless her heart, forever anxious about

Wayne, wanting not to be late getting back to be there for him. How I loved her caring heart.

As fate would have it, we did not make that last movie together. I, along with over a thousand others, are left to mourn, sort things out, knowing in honoring her we must dwell on our days and years spent in loving, enjoying, and in admiring her, remembering her family and Wayne Reed Christian Childcare Center, so close to her heart. Our earthly age difference was a whopping thirty-two years, yet in our souls and spirit we were both young together. I'll greatly miss you, Diana, we will be dance partners for ever on any occasion I find a good band playing.

Diana Reed died October 3, 2012, at age fifty-six. Her death was the result of what should have been a routine epidural injection. Diana and Wayne led Otter Creek Church in the 1998 creation of the Wayne Reed Christian Childcare Center, a Three-Star-Quality preschool for at-risk children.

You turned my wailing into dancing, you removed my sackcloth and clothed me with joy that my heart may sing to you and not be silent. Oh Lord my God, I will give you thanks forever.

Psalm 30: 11-12.

The Patrolman

Well, of all things! Never in a million years would I have dreamed a Highway Patrolman was following me! I was on my way to Bible class at my church. Now, I'll have to admit I was in a big hurry! I've gotten more accustomed down through the years to being stopped by a man of the law, when my foot got heavy on the accelerator. It no longer causes me great panic. At least, for that, I'm grateful.

My friend Dorcas and I met this morning, March 17, 2010, at 9:30, which we're attempting every Wednesday. This is the time we spend a few delightful hours together at Brentwood Baptist Church, where she's a member, working on my memoir. We've picked out the perfect place in this huge, magnificent building to spread out our paraphernalia and get to work. It won't be too far up in the morning till the aroma of food, being prepared in the grill just below us, becomes a distraction. We may manage to put it off a little while, before moseying down to enjoy splitting a delicious sandwich, topping it off with a Snickers Bar. The Grill is a large, glassed-in space with a very pleasant atmosphere and I love being there.

This Wednesday is no different—it's a dark, gloomy day, but we've been enjoying ourselves too much to take full notice. I am determined to leave on time today to drive the short distance to my church for Bible Class. I warned Dorcas, "Keep track of the time. I don't want to make my fourth 'grand entrance' in a row!" Even so, the time got away and I found myself having to rush. After pitching my stuff into the car, I lit out of the parking lot to the traffic light at its entrance. Of course, the light was red! After waiting several minutes before pulling out on this busy road, I looked both ways, no cars coming; I made it! Turning left on down a block or two I reached the main highway, Franklin Road. I had no thought of my speed, though I was traveling far, far beyond the limit. I turned in the parking lot at my church, thinking: *How lucky for me, there's one spot left right in front of the big glass doors! I'm only a few feet away from the Gathering Room inside, where class is about to begin. I MADE IT.*

As I swiftly swung the car door open, a car pulled in just behind me. *For Heaven's sakes, it's a patrol car! He must have seen me turn left on a light as red as red could be, and for that I could be put under the jail.*

I had made my fourth Grand Entrance. Several of the Bible class members were watching from inside the glass doors while I was fumbling around, trying to get my license unstuck and out of my billfold. When I opened the glove compartment, everything inside flew out the door on to the ground. Wouldn't you know, I had only last year's insurance verification! The patrolman, who looked all of twelve years old, was smiling. I was so grateful when he left laughing, without writing that dreaded traffic ticket to the tune of one hundred dollars. While I thought I was lucky, a friend suggested that I confused the poor man so much that he simply forgot to issue the ticket.

Who knows? Maybe next Wednesday I'll walk into my class unnoticed. It's something to dream about.

A Conversation between my friends, Ronnie and Dorcas Hester

Dorcas to Ronnie: Do you think Mary's secret to longevity is maybe the fact she eats an orange every day?

Ronnie to Dorcas: Heck no! The death angel can't find her, and if he does, he can't catch her. And if he does catch her, she'll talk him out of it!"

Never A Dull Moment

by Doree Williams Hubbard

When I think of my mom, Mary Williams, my brain immediately goes to the hilarious. Although I could write my own book on this subject, alas, that's for another day. Just one example of what I'm talking about:

Mom, Marilyn, and I used to meet very often for shopping and lunch. On this particular day, time was running thin, so a "lunch on the go" was our necessary evil. Picture—Mom is driving, I am in the passenger seat, and Mellie is in the back. We agree that Wendy's has pretty tasty burgers, and we can eat quickly, as not to waste our precious time. Mom pulls up and we hear, "Welcome to Wendy's, may I help you?"

Mom proceeds to give her order, "Yes, I would like a 'quarta-poundah' with cheese." (What?!)

The voice replies, "Ma'am, we don't have quarter pounders with cheese."

Mom quickly replies, "What do you mean you don't have 'quarta-poundahs' with cheese?"

Surely, you can understand at this point why my sister and I were in the floor laughing hysterically. We were finally able to get Mom's attention to explain that she was horribly mistaken on her choice of burger—she would need to visit the Golden Arches (McDonald's) to get her 'quarta-poundah' with cheese! After making complete fools of ourselves, we finally get our order out of our mouths at the drive-thru. I can only imagine how utterly disgusted the poor girl was who was desperately trying to take our order. But, we succeeded; the Williams girls accomplished ordering our burgers at Wendy's! The girl on the intercom asks us to drive around to the window to pay. Whew, I'm so glad that is over!

Only, it wasn't... Mom puts her car in gear and starts off promptly towards the window—wait, no! She has her car in reverse! I completely remember wetting my pants and my body aching from such intense laughter. She has always loved a hearty laugh, even if it's at her own expense.

I love you, Mama. More than you will ever know. Thank you for all the good times, the silly times, and the hysterical times that you provided us all through the years. Cheers to many more!

Hermitage Hotel Memories Since 1929

Living a lifetime in Nashville has been a "storybook" experience in many ways. Memories of the magnificent Hermitage Hotel certainly play their part in creating my desire to write my own story book for my children, grandchildren and great-grandchildren.

As a young child, my first visits to the Hotel were by invitation when my uncle, who was an attorney in Louisville, KY, came here frequently to visit my family. He most often stayed at the Hermitage and my brother and I were always included in his invitation for dinner at the Hotel. What a splendid occasion it was!

In those days of early childhood, I had a vivid imagination, so on those evenings I became the beautiful princess who lived in this wonderful castle right out of the storybooks my parents had read so often to me. It was much more than a Hotel!

Some years later, my mother was going to the beauty salon at the Hermitage which was located on the mezzanine. Daddy would drive us there and while waiting, he would sometimes get a shoeshine off the lobby, somewhere in the vicinity of the men's restroom as I recall, while I could be found nestled in one of the big comfortable chairs in the lobby, reading a book. Even at that young age, I can remember pausing to enjoy my surroundings and observing the beautiful carvings in the architectural design.

Following those years, as a teenager, I was enjoying the Hotel in a different fashion—sorority meetings on Saturday mornings when I felt so sophisticated following the movie stars like Bette Davis, Joan Crawford, and Loretta Young, all who smoked along with the older sorority girls. My mother and daddy would have killed me! But, so they wouldn't know, I hid my cigarettes with the potted plants in the beautiful urns, ready for my next party at the Hermitage.

Sorority and fraternity dances were held in the Grand Ballroom with its exquisite rich wood paneling. All brass features throughout the Hotel shone with a mirror finish. I remember being a little reluctant to use the handrails as I was fearful of leaving fingerprints.

On one particular evening, I was escorted by my handsome date who was driving me to the Hotel for his fraternity dance. I was sort of in a panic as I, before leaving the house, decided to find Daddy's tool chest, using any tool that I could find to pry the high heels off my new evening sandals dyed to match my evening dress. Of course, to my horror, the heels came off, but the nails were left intact. I had no choice except take them to my daddy and say sweetly, "Please do something." He actually laughed when I explained that my date was probably about my height and those heels would make me look taller than he was. I knew my daddy was laughing when I walked very awkwardly out the front door.

When we arrived at the Hotel, the doorman, dressed in his beautifully tailored clothes and top hat, was even more elegantly dressed than my date who probably was wearing a rented tuxedo. Bellboys, doormen, every person, male or female, employed by the Hotel were sharply dressed all with excellent posture and manners. The band was playing—I'm wondering was it Frances Craig? Everybody's favorite! The huge vases were filled with fresh flowers and I danced away the night, never giving my shoes another thought. Beautiful evenings like this came to an abrupt end when World War II was declared.

The next memorable event would be after my handsome Army-Air Force Lieutenant and I were married at West End Methodist Church located just a few blocks out of downtown.

Our wedding dinner was held at the Hermitage Hotel and the beautiful wedding suite with a large arrangement of fresh flowers and chocolate on the pillows was ours for the night. Just as when I was a small child, I felt like a princess in my castle, which was of course, my beloved Hermitage Hotel.

After my husband and I returned to live out our lives in Nashville, the Hermitage Hotel memories would continue. My mother was still going to the Hotel beauty salon, when one morning having my baby boy in tow, I found myself back in that familiar area. Wanting all of the hairdressers to see my beautiful little boy, we stepped inside where I would burst with pride! While we were walking to the lobby, my child tugged on my coat sleeve, asking "What were those women doing with those big buckets on their heads?" Well, those old hairdryers did look like big buckets!

On that day, sitting in the big comfortable chair with a book in my hand reading to my child while waiting for my mother, a wave of nostalgia came over me and I shared with him the story of when I was a little girl sitting in the same beautiful Hotel lobby waiting for his grandmother all those years before.

Except for an occasional lunch with friends or a very special dinner, I was not spending a great deal of time at the Hermitage while we were raising our family of five children. Our youngest child, a daughter, would be the one to bring the Hotel back in my life when her wedding reception was held there in June 1991. The wedding was held just a few blocks down the street at Fifth and Church in the historic Downtown Presbyterian Church. Many guests walked the short distance while others rode the trolley, which was not difficult to spot, as on the front was a large wedding wreath with white ribbons flowing lightly in the breeze. All the wonderful people employed by the Hotel seemed to get into the spirit of the evening as we had all become good friends during the weeks of planning. Also, they loved my having loving memories of the Hotel which I was eager to share.

Walking out of the ballroom at midnight, we watched the

bride and groom being whisked away in their limousine and I cried. I turned to walk back, glanced around the lobby, took a quick look at the veranda where two young couples were still partying, told them "good-night," then walked down the steps out those handsome doors with a tinge of sadness as an era in my life was now closed.

Just a few years ago, this same daughter's children, my grandchildren, were old enough to appreciate a tour of downtown. I took them to the old church where their parents married and the Hermitage Hotel where they celebrated afterwards. Of all they saw and loved, they were most impressed by the Hotel.

I could see their excitement when we first walked through the doors and they didn't know which direction they wanted to go first. We covered it all – every nook and cranny! They kept saying, "Nunny, I've never seen anything this beautiful." Those children could understand how at an even younger age than they were, I viewed it as my castle! I'm sure the Hermitage Hotel has never been host to more appreciative young visitors.

Just recently, a group of younger friends asked where they could take me for lunch to celebrate my eighty-fifth birthday and my choice was the Hermitage Hotel. What a treat! As I stepped out of my car once again, that rush of nostalgia engulfed me and I had to contain myself to not dominate the conversation as I yearned to share every memory.

Just this morning, one of those young women said she hadn't gotten to see it all on that day, so she and I will return in the near future.

I can hardly wait. I'll, one more time, have a captive audience to share the grandeur and my memories of the Hermitage Hotel.

(This story was written in November 2009 and first published in *Reflections from the Past: The Hermitage Hotel – Historical Quarterly*, Vol. 1, 2012, Tom Vickstrom, Editor. Reprinted by permission.)

Heaven and Earth
The Devastating Tornado of 1933

Sometime in the middle of this past summer, I came in rather late in the afternoon. My cell phone was ringing in my purse and as I entered, my home phone was also ringing off the wall. I grabbed the cell first, hearing, "Mom, where are you? Are you in the car? IF YOU ARE, GO HOME RIGHT NOW! The weather report looks really bad with the possibility of a tornado!"

"Don't worry, Doree, I'm home," I replied, taking up the other phone.

My grandson Cole was speaking quickly and decisively, "Nunny, I'm in Green Hills and the weather calls for heavy storms and the possibility of a tornado. I'll pick you up in about five minutes and you can eat supper with us and spend the night."

"Let me call you right back," I said, picking up the cell phone again. This time it was granddaughter Maclellan.

After assuring my family, "I'm really fine," and thanking them profusely, I donned my PJs. I picked up the delicious sandwich I'd made and settled in my comfortable living room chair to listen to the weather news blaring on all three local channels. Gazing out the picture window it was evident we were in for a stormy night. I watched the lightning streaks light up the sky and listened to the deafening thunder claps. The lights went out. That meant the end of listening to the repetition of the weathercast, which was honestly, a relief.

I was alone and quiet except for the noises of nature. The thought came, "I'm so glad I'm not afraid of this storm, nor unduly afraid of the many intermittent storms of life. Thank you, Lord." I had an urge to stand in front of the window and sing church hymns in my loudest voice, when I was suddenly whisked back in time to the year 1933, and I was nine years old.

It was the 14th of March and an unusually gloomy, humid day. The temperature had climbed above freezing a couple of days before. Today by three o'clock it had skyrocketed to an amazing 80° mark. After an early supper my brother Joe and I lit out to meet our next door neighbors at the fence dividing our yards. This had been a ritual since we were little children planning our activities for the evening. It was the perfect place to congregate because this fence had a ledge wide enough to use as a bench. At this hour the weather was becoming unusual—there was a heaviness, an eerie sense of foreboding hanging in the air. Extremely dark, heavy clouds, the like of which we had never seen, seemed to envelop us. Darkness was moving in earlier than usual, and a bat was circling the lamp post. Bats were never out until well into the night; what was going on? We knew a storm was brewing.

The rain came, our neighbors Martha and Jim ran home, and Joe and I ran and took cover on our big front porch. We joined Mother and Daddy sitting in the swing, but not for long. A huge gust of wind blew the rain over the entire porch, causing us to rush indoors where we either read or listened to the radio until bedtime. It seemed the storm had passed, so I went upstairs, fell into bed, and went to sleep. Sometime in the middle of the night the deafening thunder and howling winds woke me. As always when frightened for any reason, I scampered down the steps and crawled in the daybed in Mother and Daddy's big bedroom. There I felt safe.

The next morning, I awoke believing we just had a thunderstorm in the middle of the night. Daddy had heard the news: Five tornadoes tore through Nashville! East Nashville, where we lived, was hit the hardest, leaving 11 DEAD and 4000 homes, 16 churches, 36 stores, and schools in shambles. Devastation beyond comprehension had struck. Not until Daddy took us in the car into these stricken areas bordering our own—all my old stomping grounds where many of my close friends lived—did I begin to understand the extent of the damage left in the wake of last night's tornadoes. I was horrified. I've not forgotten the grotesque sight of the giant trees uprooted, their roots exposed, some as large as twenty feet in width! I simply couldn't get my mind around the fact it had skipped our little neighborhood altogether. It would be sixty-five years before Nashville, again mainly east Nashville, would be hit by tornados of similar magnitude: April 16, 1998. The date was Maxine's birthday and we were together. Another story, another time...

The following Sunday night after the tornado I was still shaken by all I had seen. Oh, dear Lord, I felt another storm brewing and began to cry. I became hysterical when, from the back of the house, I heard a loud, tremendous noise. It was the roof on our back porch being blown off! I must have been a pitiful sight, wringing my hands and sobbing, by now burying my face in Mother's lap, when I heard Daddy singing at the top of his lungs. He stood in front of the very large windows in our dining room, motioning to the three of us to join him in a contest of "Who Can Sing the Loudest" church hymns. We gathered around him, holding hands and singing our very loudest, off key, gazing at the dark sky, singing. "Jesus Loves Me" and "On Jordan's Stormy Banks" were first, then a song I had never heard. Surely it was not in our hymnal at Chapel Avenue Church of Christ, but from Daddy's hymnal at East End Methodist Church. Daddy began singing, "His Eye is On the Sparrow" but only remembered the chorus.

I sing because I'm happy
I sing because I'm free
His eye is on the sparrow
And I know he watches me

I loved this new song and so we sang it over and over, louder and louder! Louder still, until we drowned out the thunder.

As it always does, the storm subsided. We were ready for bed when Daddy thought it appropriate that I read aloud from our Bible.

My own footnote to this story, written many years before publication, read:

"Thank you, my sweet parents, for the legacy you've left your children."

Are not the sparrows sold for a penny? Yet not one of them will fall to the ground apart from the will of your Father. And even the hairs of your head are all numbered, so don't be afraid. You are worth more than many sparrows.

Matthew 10: 29-31

Cure the World

Snow, deep, soft, beautiful snow, blanketing the ground, getting close to eight inches here in my neighborhood! It's January 22, 2016, and it has been many years since snow this deep has happened here in the South. When I opened the blinds in my bedroom at around six o'clock this morning, I fell back on my pillows, pulled up my warm down comforter, and switched on the music channel. So many thoughts running through my head–the sort that kept me from waking up fully: *Are all the homeless people inside enjoying the same from a warm place? Their stomachs full or at least waiting for a hot breakfast? Were all the little children being cared for, none shivering from the cold, none without warm clothing to don in anticipation of sledding safely…if not on a sled, perhaps in a plastic laundry basket, if available?*

My tears I feel trickling down my face as I pray for the world, including all the precious animals that feel the same loss as we humans. No person to love and comfort them. No place to go for warmth and food. I read only this week in our local newspapers about the dog chained in its owner's yard freezing to death. Whoever you are, I have to ask of you, "Where is your heart?" I pause to reflect on the fact that perhaps you and others like you may have never had the opportunity to learn the beauty of receiving love, as well as learning how to give the greatest gift of all, that of love.

While I was thinking, my phone rang, jerking me out of that hopeless feeling of depression of not being able to "cure the world." I heard the voice of my youngest son, Sam, a voice

I look forward to hearing often just as I always loved picking up the phone hearing the voices of Charlie and Mike, his older brothers. There is never a day I don't think of my sons.

My Sam is an outdoorsman and he called me while he was still outside in the cold, after a long walk in the clean untouched snow. It seems he stopped to rest on the patio. He reluctantly faced having to go back inside, even though his thoughtul wife Lisa brought him a steaming cup of coffee to warm his bones. As we were talking, the ice which had formed on the chair he was sitting on began to thaw, causing moisture to seep through his heavy clothing and then began to freeze his skin. We both laughed at the absurdity of his ninety-one-year-old mama saying, "Sam, go take off those wet clothes before you catch your death of cold!" That took him back to those snowy days when he was a little boy.

I put a chicken in the oven to cook and eat later in the day. There is no possibility of getting off my hill and even down my steps for that matter, at any time today. These are the rare times I stop abruptly and jot down a story to add to my memoir. Today I find myself longing for the days of long ago. Then, on a day like this my house was full of young people come to sled down the hill outside our picture window. The dryer was going constantly, when my children along with their friends dropped in and threw their wet clothes in to dry. A pot of hot chocolate was simmering on the stove to warm their tummies. My warm hand, rubbing ears almost frozen! And like a darling Picture Postcard scene, our little black "Scotty-poo" sporting his red dog collar, running up and down the hill chasing the sled, barking over the top of the children's squeals.

I stop and thank God for this lovely day of snow and for past snows spent with my children—memories vivid in my mind even today. I close with a prayer for this entire, beautiful world.

If we will listen, O God, you speak to us in ways we miss,
Such as the ways you speak to us through the snow...

from "Pastoral Prayer, 1/24/16" by Chris Caldwell

Girls at the Beach
(Not Age but Attitude)

It is October 7, 2004, and in seven days I will be eighty years old. It seems ridiculous to say I'm eighty but I can't deny it, with a son who is sixty. What exactly is wrong with being eighty? The world frowns at being old and clamors for youth. Well, I've experienced it all and loved it as I lived it, and still love it!

Waiting on the beach for the setting sun with my two daughters, who are fifteen years apart in age and as close as sisters can ever be, proves again there's no problem with age. Can I think I'm too old to enjoy a week sunning and drinking in the beauty of God's handiwork, listening to the sounds of the waves, the squawking of the seagulls, and talking to some bird who wouldn't shut up with its loud and strange sounds? The crow hovering around, even alighting on the foot of my chair and chatting in his obnoxious voice. Too old? I think not.

It's been a week of sheer contentment and other joys. My girls could not confine the celebration of this spectacular year with the birthday get-together lunch they hosted of my old and new friends. Another reason for my happiness then and today are my close friends of all ages and different personalities. Thurman used to say, "Mary, please don't make any more friends!" But I just love people! *It is not age that brings us into friendship, but attitude.*

After the birthday lunch, there was another event. That evening the girls gathered me with my family, five children and ten grandchildren and six great-grandchildren. Why would they plan, along with all mentioned, a trip to the beach where we would be beach bums for a week? What fun could it be for them, fooling with an eighty-year-old?

It's not the age but the attitude one holds towards it. Once again we can laugh hysterically at everything and anything that may not be comical to a soul but us. We can sit on the beach for hours reading, or like myself, writing my memoir, and never say a word. Moving out of the room while the TV is on, climb in bed one by one, never feeling the need to say a word. Do you think for a moment they feel I've slowed them down? Well, maybe when they had to pass through the sand dunes? which I find difficult, but even then without a lot of grumbling...okay, they grumbled, but I hope in fun, most always.

Today's the last day of our trip. I would hope to put the last thought on paper as I bask in the sun for the last time for at least a while. Soon I'll enjoy my sack lunch: fresh pineapple, cheese and crackers. Diet Coke with lime is just the thing to tide me over till sunset, after which we'll maybe take our last walk on the beach and drag up to the condo where we will shower, don our pajamas and eat our last supper. Mell boiled shrimp one night. For our last meal here, Doree made a lemon-chicken casserole this morning, and we'll add steamed broccoli. We agreed as beach bums not to dress, so we've lived in our swimsuits and PJs the entire time with one exception, when we walked across the street and had seafood.

There have been several trips to the beach with Marilyn and Doree, and sometimes taking the children along. I've loved every trip and the special bonding. The beach is also a wonderful place to heal. On one occasion I had a terrible hacking cough, and the girls set me up under an umbrella to bask in the shade in the fresh sea air, with cooling crushed ice to sip, readily at my side. For one who never suffered from allergies, it helped me to realize how Thurman must have endured for years on end without complaint.

My girls even took me to the beach when I was wearing a sling after shoulder surgery. That was a tough year, beginning on a Saturday in December. I was well into the festivities of the holidays, shopping, cooking, and entertaining, when I drove to the store to buy flowers for the table and to pick up a few last-minute items I needed to provide for my luncheon on Monday. Walking back to my car in the parking lot, I fell flat on my face with great force: breaking off a tooth, damaging my mouth, requiring twenty-seven stitches, breaking my wrist, and giving a shocking jolt to my left shoulder. That shoulder already had a rotator cuff tear, which I and my surgeon agreed did not require surgery. With the fall, I felt a change taking place. The pain became so intense that I gave in and surgery was performed on April 4. After that, I did not have the use of either hand! The pain in the right wrist had not cleared up and I had no use of the left arm and hand. Thankfully, I had a brainstorm a few days before and realized I wouldn't be able to care for myself so made arrangements to stay in rehab as long as possible. I only desired to put all this behind me now and move forward to the time I'd be back to normal. Without my beloved family and amazing friends, I would have lagged much farther behind in the healing process. Then my girls spirited me away to the beach, where I had time to relax, regain my attitude, and realize:

My cup runneth over!

Afterword: One reason for my happiness in yesteryear and today are my close friends of all ages and different personalities. We have a group called the Ya-Ya Sisters: Paulette, Irene, Maxine and Mary, that's me. Bernie was in this group before she left this world. I will be ninety-two years old this October, and I've lost so many friends that it's heartbreaking! If I had not made younger friends, I could be lonely at times. These are friends cultivated after I moved out of my home across the river. Every Friday night the Ya-Yas and other friends get together, one of us hostessing at home or arranging dinner out.

Friends also come by way of family! A few weeks ago I had over thirty guests for dinner. Last night I cooked supper for Doree's family. My grandson, Cole, and his friends went out to dinner. About 10:30 PM his girlfriend called me and soon they came over, visiting me with their friends, and the group stayed until midnight. I am so blessed!

It is not age that brings us into friendship, but attitude.

—Mary B. Williams

The Blessing of Friends

Several years ago, summer humidity penetrated to the inside of the house, where I should have been enjoying the cool of air conditioning. However, it had gone on the blink early that morning, which meant I was sweltering by lunchtime. The repairman would arrive, I was told, between two and four o'clock the following day—not the news I wanted to hear.

Before I could make a plan to leave the house, the phone rang. Dorcas, my friend, was calling to let me know she was in the Green Hills area, having lunch with her Birthday Group of friends and would be here afterward to bring me something. I suggested she leave it inside the storm door, because I was leaving to find a cool place.

Dorcas sounded excited. "Oh, Mary! Come join us. We just arrived and it's good and cold inside here."

What a lovely group of Dorcas' friends I met, enjoying every minute of the conversation, good food, and cool temperature. From that unexpected time spent with them I was invited to join their Birthday Group. I've enjoyed these years of getting together and adding to my circle of friends.

Which sparks a memory: When my husband suggested, "Mary, you have enough friends. Please don't make any more!" I'm sure he was kidding me—or maybe not. Thurman enjoyed our friends, however, he loved our evenings spent with just the two of us. The ultimate joy for both was when our children and grandchildren were gathered around our table for a home-cooked meal, all from scratch.

My much younger friends call me Nunny. I want you to meet them all, impossible in a book this size. However, Pat Ward has influenced me during my time of tragedy and losses. When I find a card in my mailbox with her handwriting on the envelope, it immediately brings a smile. It will be an ego booster, and I just might be in need of it on that particular day.

Pat is full of love, understanding and a gift of words for literally hundreds of other people who will be thrilled to find her card in their mailbox. She is a heart-to-heart sister and friend from my church family.

Now I know for a fact that one cannot have too many friends. They have enriched my life during every stage of living, and today I must conclude that my friends are priceless.

Just as lotions and fragrance give sensual delight,
a sweet friendship refreshes the soul.

Proverbs 27:9

Lucky and Blessed

It is now well over twenty years ago, when I chose to begin to jot down a few stories to leave for my children, grandchildren and great-grandchildren. Since then I seem to have moved into what society terms "old." I am ninety-four. Looking back, I'm fully aware of why these years have been, and are still, an important enjoyable and lively time: Family and Friends. If I may leave a thought to those of you who are younger: Don't give up what you enjoy now. It may take a little more effort or maybe even a lot more effort to plan a day spent with friends, a vist with a shut-in, or enjoy an evening out. The rewards are so worth the effort.

When Maclellan, Cole and Channie, the children of my youngest child, Doree, came along, my life was freer than it had ever been. There was time to enjoy the young ones. The older grandchildren were now grandparents themselves and their little ones bring the greatest joy to our family get-togethers today. How could I have ever known when at forty-two and Doree was born that her children would keep my life fun and exciting when I was ninety-four? I see these children having inherited the best of both parents—Doree and Stewart. All they choose to do for me is beyond and over the top.

Just yesterday in conversation with a friend of eighty-one years, it was suggested I might be interested in using the grocery store's policy of delivering my food as she was doing. All of a sudden, I thought: I am the luckiest and most blessed older person. Why, these children shop for me constantly! As for groceries, they take my list—not only bringing those items to my house, but before putting them away, make sure the items are opened to where I don't have to struggle with some overly tight seals.

Trips to the doctors are becoming more frequent, much to my dismay. I'm always happy when I feel comfortable to drive myself. Occasionally, there are times I have to make other arrangements. Mell and Doree try to make sure one of them is available. This usually works. However, I never panic because I know Maclellan will always make it possible because the lovely woman she works for has a policy of "family first," and I consider her family. Even Cole, who is in college in town, has on several occasions been the one to bound in the door, all smiles, ready to help me get to my destination. These trips always turn out to be fun for me. In the fall both Channie and Cole plan to go out of Nashville to college. Both have good scholarships—I am so proud and happy for them to get on with their lives, even though "I'm gonna miss 'em like crazy!" Not simply because of all they choose to make life easier, but because of their many ways of filling this time in my life with laughter and fun.

"A burden of these years is to allow time to hang heavy on your hands, to simply sit and wait for life to be over—as the Irish say, 'Knocking another day out of it till the Great Day comes.'

A blessing of these years is to realize what an important and lively time this period is—I can, if I will bring it all together into the final and the very best of me."

—Joan Chittister

Epilogue

These have to be my waning years, so every day counts. These are still beautiful years. Although I find I decline in power and importance, it has been pointed out that my life, in some small way, can still have an influence on those around me. Each day is a gift from God. I pray not to squander it. I pray for knowledge and wisdom. I pray to live each day embracing the beauty, joy and countless blessings it holds, as I grow closer to my Lord.

Thou preparest a table before me in the presence of mine enemies:
thou anointest my head with oil; my cup runneth over.
Surely goodness and mercy shall follow me all the days of my life:
and I will dwell in the house of the Lord for ever.

Psalm 23: 5-6

Mary Pullias, Marilyn and me are all dressed up for Halloween. We go all out!

Enjoying a cruise to Hawaii with Betty Yates, 2008

Celebrating Ann Garrett's 75th birthday. Ann's husband, Johnny, and Thurman were best friends. Ann and I became good friends too!

The Ya-Ya Sisterhood gathered this time in Sarasota, Florida. Maxine Bivins, Irene Acuff, Me, Paulette Fewell, Bernie Arnold

My 78th Birthday

My 87th Birthday, 2011, Hermitage Hotel

90th Birthday, with Dorcas Hester, The Hermitage Hotel, 2014

Celebrating with Friends at the Parthenon

"Now I know for a fact that one cannot have too many friends." *Thte Birthday Group. Back: Peggy Smith, Emily Binkley, Patsy Burnette, Mary, June Goodwin, Josephine Smartt. Front: Joni Holt, Dorcas Hester, Anne Smith.*

One of my guides who became a great friend, the "intimidating" and lovely Carolyn Winney, and me celebrate at an Atlanta wedding on New Year's Eve.

With Doris Kilzer
Sarasota, Florida

With special friends Betty Plummer, Helen Newson, Josephine Kornmeyer, and Josephine Smartt

What a difference a few years can make! Cole and me at family weddings: above, 2003, below, 2017

Maclellan, Cole, and Channie

With My Girls, Marilyn and Doree

With great-grandchildren Maggie, Sam, and Anna Todd, grandchildren of Mike and Vickie, while holding my first great-great-grandchild, Jackson.

Sam and his wife, Lisa

Our family gathered for a Williams Wedding. Back: Stewart Hubbard, Olney, Maggie and Amy Todd, Vickie Williams, Doree Hubbard, Sheri, Marshall and Ken Switzer, Cole Hubbard, Josh Henderson, Maclellan and Channie Hubbard. Front: Anna and Sam Todd, Lisa McGuire (bride), Sam Williams (groom), Mary, Marilyn Switzer, Mary P. Henderson.
The Cannery Ballroom, Nashville, 2017

Simeon, Violet, and Max, three of my great-grandchildren, are the grandchildren of Marilyn and Ken.

Hallelujah! I have lived to celebrate my 94th birthday at the Milky Way Farm with children, grandchildren, great-grandchildren and great-great-grandchild Jackson.

Annie (black) and Phantom (white) helped me celebrate, too.

A Word of Thanks

...is due to those who prodded me on when I would reach periods of disenchantment with what I had undertaken.

First of all, my son Charlie who planted the thought, encouraging me along the way early on—his confidence meant everything in my "keeping on keeping on." Dorcas Hester, my friend of many years, who kept the joy going by our meeting weekly, turning my handwritten pages into typed ones with comments, until I took an extended break. Perhaps the greatest source of encouragement has been Tom Vickstrom, Historian and Director of Finance at the Hermitage Hotel, whom I met in 2006 by chance, there in the lobby. Tom, a writer, expressed interest that made me feel there may be some charm in my style of writing about old Nashville and my lifetime spent in the city I love. Wanda Vickstrom, Tom's wife, is a researcher and helped me get the stories of my family recorded in newspapers. From this connection came a special friendship. Lynn Golden and my grandaughter, Maclellan Hubbard, provided extra support in the final stages, helping me cross the finish line.

Lastly, Deborah Wilbrink, whom Tom sought out as the person to help me untangle it all. It has been, I'm sure, the most hectic memoir she has dealt with in her business, Perfect Memoirs! Our relationship passed beyond that of business and client. While I'll truly be relieved and joyful to finally hold my published book, I'll miss our meetings: the sharing of coffee and English muffin with apricot marmalade while she tried to keep me focused. We have decided to keep our friendship going as long we are able.

CPSIA information can be obtained
at www.ICGtesting.com
Printed in the USA
LVHW020005230419
615150LV00002B/2